What Do Points Make?

The inside story of Nottinghamshire's LV= County Championship success

Dave Bracegirdle

Published by Nottinghamshire CCC in association with Reid Publishing, Loughborough

© Dave Bracegirdle 2010

This book is copyright under the Berne convention

All rights reserved. Apart from any use permitted under UK copyright law no part of this publication may be reproduced, stored in a retrieval system, or transmitted, in any form or by any means, without the prior written permission of the publisher, nor be otherwise circulated in any form of binding or cover other than that in which it is published and without a similar condition being imposed on the subsequent purchaser

The right of Dave Bracegirdle to be identified as the author of this work has been asserted by him in accordance with sections 77 and 78 of the Copyright, Designs and Patents Act, 1988.

Published by Nottinghamshire County Cricket Club
in association with Reid Publishing

A CIP catalogue record for this title is available
from the British Library

ISBN: 978-0-9558807-5-9

Designed by Andrew Searle

Printed and bound in the UK by MPG Biddles

Contents

Acknowledgements	4
Introduction	5
Match 1 – Kent (h)	7
Match 2 – Somerset (h)	14
Match 3 – Hampshire (a)	21
Match 4 – Durham (h)	30
Interview – Hashim Amla	39
Match 5 – Hampshire (h)	40
Match 6 – Essex (h)	48
Interview – Ryan Sidebottom	54
Match 7 – Kent (a)	56
Match 8 – Essex (a)	67
Match 9 – Warwickshire (a)	75
Match 10 – Somerset (a)	82
Match 11 – Yorkshire (a)	90
David Hussey – 13th Best	98
Match 12 – Warwickshire (h)	99
Match 13 – Lancashire (h)	105
Match 14 – Durham (a)	113
Match 15 – Yorkshire (h)	123
Match 16 – Lancashire (a)	131
LV= County Championship Final Table	141
LV= County Championship Averages	142
LV= County Championship Statistics	143
Reflections:	
Mick Newell	144
Chris Read	148
Peter Wynne-Thomas	150
Friends Provident twenty20 Cup	152
Clydesdale Bank 40	156

Acknowledgements

It was very early in the season when I made the bold pronouncement that if Nottinghamshire were successful in their quest to lift the LV= County Championship then I would be more than honoured to commemorate the achievement in print.

Results from the first four matches went better than almost anyone could have expected and I spent a few late nights typing up those games. By the halfway point of the fixture calendar I'd decided that perhaps I'd tempted fate and prepared to put those notes into mothballs, but as we all now know, after the most dramatic finale ever witnessed to a championship season, the title was secured on the last afternoon.

That brought about a time for reflection and a time to adjourn once again to the keyboard to bring you this tribute to a wonderful group of men who collectively realised one of their sporting dreams.

At no point in the season – no matter how low any of them may have felt after a poor session – did any of the Nottinghamshire staff or players shy away from giving their thoughts or expressing their feelings on the day. Many of those comments have been included and, hopefully, add something to the description of each day's play.

So, first and foremost, many thanks to Mick Newell, Chris Read and the rest of the staff and players for making themselves available and for the time they've given in assisting this project. Your success has brought pleasure to many and it has been a privilege to witness it from close quarters.

Additional thanks must also go to Derek Brewer and Lisa Pursehouse for their support throughout the season; to Michael Temple – a 'Prince amongst Press Officers'; to Peter Wynne-Thomas for his contribution, and to everyone else at Trent Bridge who helped to make each and every visit so memorable.

The old saying 'A photograph is worth a thousand words' prevented this book from being twice the size it is, so grateful thanks for all the pictures supplied by the Nottingham Post and by Portrait Collective. Ady Kerry provided most of the Tunbridge Wells content and the author's old 'Box Browning' came in handy on a number of other occasions.

Thanks also to Andrew Searle and David McVay at Reid Publishing for their expertise and patience in putting it all together and to all at Radio Nottingham, particularly Mike Bettison, Colin Fray, Robin Chipperfield, David Jackson and Chris Ellis for their help and guidance throughout the summer.

Finally, a huge thanks to Karen, who never lets me forget that "Watching cricket isn't proper work!"

Dave Bracegirdle
October 2010

Introduction

Just after ten minutes to five on the afternoon of Thursday 16th September 2010, Lancashire's Shivnarine Chanderpaul edged a delivery from Andre Adams into the waiting hands of Samit Patel at third slip.

In isolation it was just another wicket, coming at the end of a drawn four day County Championship match. The deeper meaning to that dismissal was that it brought Nottinghamshire a sixth bonus point of the day and, with it, confirmation that they would become the new LV= County Champions.

Amidst scenes of great celebration and joy, and with a general outpouring of emotion, it was nationally acclaimed as being the most dramatic conclusion to a cricket season of all time.

Much of Nottinghamshire's success was due to the meticulous plotting and preparation of their Director of Cricket, Mick Newell. Since leading the county to their previous domestic crown in 2005 the aim had been to strongly challenge for it once again.

In both 2008 (narrowly) and 2009 (by a distance) they had finished as runners-up to Durham, but in order to go one better in 2010 some fresh faces were deliberately introduced to bolster the existing squad. Neil Edwards, a left-handed opening bat, was recruited from Somerset, Steven Mullaney, an exciting, yet unproven all-rounder, joined from Lancashire and Graeme White, a promising slow left arm spin bowler and outstanding one-day fielder, was drafted in from Northants.

All would play a part, to some degree or other, as would Hashim Amla, the South African Test batsman who was signed for the first four Championship matches of the season.

So, having assembled a stronger squad, Newell guided them through a pre-season campaign which featured workouts against Kent and Leicestershire, plus a three day first class match away against Durham University Centre of Cricketing Excellence.

Dress rehearsals out of the way, Nottinghamshire's County Championship programme began in earnest on Thursday 15th April. Over the next five months there were more twists and turns than an Alton Towers rollercoaster before finally, as dusk began to set over Old Trafford, champagne corks were popped and the players hugged each other and sang raucously.

'What Do Points Make?' tells the inside story of a more than eventful campaign.

Match 1

NOTTINGHAMSHIRE v KENT

April 15th, 16th, 17th 2010
(match scheduled for 4 days but completed in 3)
Venue: Trent Bridge, Nottingham
Toss: won by Kent who elected to field
Umpires: RK Illingworth & P Willey
Result: Nottinghamshire won by an innings and 32 runs
Points: Nottinghamshire 24 (Batting 5, Bowling 3) Kent 4 (Batting 1, Bowling 3)

15th April – Day One

What a splendid way to start the new season. On a cloudy, chilly day – which eventually revealed some blue sky and some watery spring sunshine, Nottinghamshire – put in to bat by Kent skipper Rob Key – rattled along at a high tempo all day and reached 396-8 by the close.

Neil Edwards – on his Championship debut for Notts – was the stand-out performer during the morning session. The tall left hander bears an uncanny resemblance to Marcus Trescothick at the wicket and it was very evident that some of the former England opener's best habits have rubbed off on Neil during his time at Taunton.

Neil Edwards impressed with a fine 85

Driving superbly, especially straight down the wicket, he gave the innings early impetus against some wasteful new ball bowling.

Bilal Shafayat, fresh from a big hundred in the first class warm-up against Durham UCCE, was first to fall – edging to slip – and was soon followed by Mark Wagh, who perished in the same way.

At 43-2 Hashim Amla arrived at the crease in possession of the second ranked position in the ICC World Test rankings. As befits someone of that standing, a certain aura seemed to arrive in the middle with him and there was an air of inevitability about the way he began his innings.

Early season batting at Trent Bridge has proved to be notoriously difficult over the years and it's assumed that Hashim would have had one or two nerves as he set about making a contribution on his home debut.

Like all high quality batsmen, he appears to have plenty of time in which to play his strokes and he was certainly selective during the early stages of his innings. Treating every ball on its merits and punishing anything loose, he reached 36 in just nine scoring strokes – all boundaries, caressed with placement and timing.

Edwards reached his half century from just 55 balls and in 66 minutes but eventually perished for 85 – a disappointment for him to miss out on a deserved century but a reassuring beginning to his Trent Bridge career.

Amla pressed on meanwhile and brought up a chanceless century from just 152 deliveries (224 minutes, 17 x 4s).

Chris Read added a breezy 62, which included two maximums over mid-wicket from the bowling of Matt Coles, before squandering his wicket with a wasteful run out. Pushing to Key at mid on, the Notts skipper had advanced halfway down the track before being sent back by Amla, but the accurate throw into Geraint Jones's gloves did for him.

Jones also played his part in ending the major contribution of the day. With Amla on 129, Darren Stevens – Kent's seventh different bowler to try and stem his flow of runs – set up a seven/two off side field. In what must either rank as the biggest double bluff of the summer – or a rank bad piece of bowling – he speared it down the leg side. The South African pushed forward, missed and was stumped by a smart piece of work from the Kent 'keeper.

Paul Franks remained unbeaten at the close, although he lost his partner to the final ball of the day. With four needed for maximum batting points Andre Adams had a huge mow at Phil Edwards and produced another victim for Jones, who had a long wait before claiming the catch.

Adams trudged off to a less than enthusiastic reception – he would enjoy better days later in the campaign.

Close of Day One – Notts 396-8 (Franks 35*, 96 overs)

16th April – Day Two

Notts began the second day by quickly gathering the four they needed for maximum batting bonus points. 400 runs in the first innings of the season was no mean effort from the home side, and they looked set to inflict even greater harm on a wilting Kent attack as Franks brought up his half century before losing partner Luke Fletcher, who was caught at slip by

Martin van Jaarsveld for 13. Ryan Sidebottom gave valuable support for the final wicket before Franks was last to go, bowled for an excellent 73.

Kent's reply was soon in tatters as Sidebottom, gaining useful match practice before heading out to the Caribbean for England's WorldT20 bid, nipped out both openers in quick time.

Ryan's first bowl of the season with Rob Key looking on

It became 33-3 with the final ball before lunch when Adams picked up his first wicket of the season, clean bowling Jones, who looked aghast at having left one that nipped back and re-arranged his stumps.

Having made a far from ideal start the visitors struggled to build any sort of partnership as Notts' four seamers applied constant pressure. All of them claimed wickets and each had cause to thank Neil Edwards. Apart from his impressive efforts with the bat, he proved himself to be a high quality close catcher. Standing at second slip, he held on to sharp nicks from Stevens, Northeast, Tredwell, Coles and Khan to become the first outfielder since Derek Randall in 1987 (v Yorks at Trent Bridge) to take five catches in an innings.

Azhar Mahmood's 52 and a 32-run partnership for the last wicket brought the visitors one batting point, but with his bowlers having taken just 62 overs to skittle Kent out, it was no surprise when Read decided to enforce the follow-on.

Luke Fletcher nipped one back to uproot Rob Key's off stick and Andre Adams collected the 400th first class wicket of his career when he bowled James Tredwell, who had been elevated to open the innings after going in at number seven first time around.

Close of Day Two – Kent (2nd inns) 51-2
(Edwards 5*, Jones 5*, 14 overs)

What Do Points Make?

17th April – Day Three

Nottinghamshire's march to a 24 point opening match victory rarely looked in doubt as Kent wickets once again tumbled cheaply.

The prospect of them acquiring the 205 runs needed to make their hosts bat again seemed remote once Fletcher had sent back Jones and van Jaarsveld in quick succession, although there was a little concern for the bowler's welfare when he then had to leave the action midway through an over.

Kent were six wickets down by the lunch interval, having also lost Edwards and Northeast in the session – the latter just before the break to a fine stumping off the bowling of Samit Patel.

It had been a quiet game for Samit up to that point, but he had the satisfaction of polishing off the tail midway through the afternoon, bowling both Coles and Khan to wrap up a convincing innings victory with more than four sessions in hand.

The season couldn't really have got off to a better start. Not only was it a maximum points win from the first match but there were significant contributions from all areas of the team. Neil Edwards and Hashim Amla both enjoyed exceptional Championship debuts for their new county, with the former looking assured at the top of the order as well as demonstrating that he had a safe pair of hands.

Amla had come into the match (the Durham UCCE warm-up apart) having played just one game since hitting 253 not out in Nagpur and then 114 and 123 not out in Kolkata in South Africa's two-Test tour of India in February.

Hashim Amla

Understandably, he was delighted when he spoke to me afterwards:

Q – That couldn't have gone much better, could it?
"No – thank you. I think the team played excellently and I think it was a fantastic team performance. Obviously we managed to get a big total on the board on a wicket that was bowler friendly for most of the time."

Q – When you went to the wicket on the first day at 43-2 there was a re-building job that needed to be done.
"I think it was a tough time to bat – Neil (Edwards) was batting really solidly at the other end, which made it quite easy for me to settle in. I took a long time to get going, but that's how it is in testing conditions. Fortunately we got a good 100 partnership going and then began to score quite quickly and gained some momentum for the other batters to follow."

Q – The only disappointment must have been the manner of your dismissal – stumped down the leg side.
"Yes – it's very rare that you get out in that fashion, but fortunately the team was in a good position by then."

Q – What have you made of Notts' seam attack over the last few days?
"The guys have bowled really well. The conditions favoured the seam bowlers, but you've still got to put the ball in the right areas and they did that for as long as we were on the field. They made it really difficult for the opposition batsmen to score and built up sufficient pressure to get the wickets."

Q – And the catching has been special in this game also.
"Yes, especially behind the wicket. It's been excellent. I couldn't have asked for a better first Championship game – for us to finish it off inside three days gives the bowlers a day off and then it's back to hard work as we start again on Wednesday."

Luke Fletcher looked fit and bowled with plenty of pace, control and aggression. *"We won pretty much every session and to get 450 in the first innings was a big score, especially at this time of year. From then on we seemed to be always on top and bowled well as a unit.*

"On the final morning the key was patience. We knew that there was still a bit left in the pitch and it was nipping around and there was a bit of swing as well, so we knew we had to stick to our lines and be patient and the wickets would come."

On having to leave the field midway through an over: *"I had a bit of soreness in the hip flexion. I had it last year and carried on bowling then and it put me out for two weeks – so I knew it wasn't worth carrying on this time. I spoke to the skipper, nipped off, had a bit of a stretch with the physio and was able to come back on.*

"All four seamers have done their jobs in this match and I think we've bowled well in partnerships and Samit came on to give us big fast bowlers a rest and he helped himself to some wickets as well, so fair play to him – he put the ball in the right area and got his rewards.

"It's been a great start for all of us – the batters have got runs, the bowlers have got wickets and hopefully we can take this form with us into the next game and throughout the season."

SCORECARD

Notts first innings		Runs	Balls	Mins	4s	6s
NJ Edwards	lbw b Tredwell	85	127	147	15	-
BM Shafayat	c Tredwell b Khan	4	18	35	-	-
MA Wagh	c Tredwell b Khan	0	2	3	-	-
HM Amla	st Jones b Stevens	129	203	304	19	-
SR Patel	c Jones b Azhar Mahmood	15	14	11	3	-
AD Brown	lbw b Khan	18	35	34	-	2
*+CMW Read	run out	62	111	102	8	2
PJ Franks	b Coles	73	104	122	14	-
AR Adams	c Jones b Edwards	19	12	19	2	1
LJ Fletcher	c van Jaarsveld b Coles	13	25	31	2	-
RJ Sidebottom	not out	8	25	29	2	-
Extras	(9 b, 7 lb, 10 nb, 4 w)	30				
Total	(all out, 111.4 overs)	456				

Fall of wickets:

1-41 (Shafayat, 8.4 ov), 2-43 (Wagh, 8.5 ov), 3-146 (Edwards, 36.5 ov), 4-165 (Patel, 40 ov), 5-203 (Brown, 49.4 ov), 6-328 (Read, 81.2 ov), 7-367 (Amla, 90.3 ov), 8-396 (Adams, 96 ov), 9-429 (Fletcher, 103.4 ov), 10-456 (Franks, 111.4 ov)

Kent bowling	Ovs	Mdns	Runs	Wkts	Wides	No-Balls
Khan	25	5	108	3	2	3
Azhar Mahmood	26	5	75	1	-	-
Edwards	14	3	77	1	-	2
Coles	15.4	2	65	2	2	-
Tredwell	18	2	68	1	-	-
Denly	1	0	4	0	-	-
Stevens	12	1	43	1	-	-

Kent first innings		Runs	Balls	Mins	4s	6s
JL Denly	b Sidebottom	0	13	16	-	-
*RWT Key	lbw b Sidebottom	4	15	26	1	-
+GO Jones	b Adams	28	27	31	6	-
M van Jaarsveld	c Read b Adams	7	41	51	-	-
SA Northeast	c Edwards b Fletcher	38	65	92	6	-
DI Stevens	c Edwards b Adams	7	13	12	1	-
JC Tredwell	c Edwards b Adams	19	66	82	3	-
Azhar Mahmood	c Brown b Franks	52	56	71	9	-
MT Coles	c Edwards b Sidebottom	6	12	13	1	-
A Khan	c Edwards b Franks	24	34	49	4	-
PD Edwards	not out	6	31	33	1	-
Extras	(1 b, 6 lb, 2 nb)	9				
Total	(all out, 62 overs)	200				

Fall of wickets:

1-4 (Denly, 4.1 ov), 2-13 (Key, 6.1 ov), 3-33 (Jones, 11.5 ov), 4-44 (van Jaarsveld, 19.4 ov), 5-58 (Stevens, 23.2 ov), 6-100 (Northeast, 35 ov), 7-140 (Tredwell, 45.1 ov), 8-151 (Coles, 48.3 ov), 9-168 (Azhar Mahmood, 52.3 ov), 10-200 (Khan, 62 ov)

The inside story of Nottinghamshire's LV= County Championship success

Notts bowling	Ovs	Mdns	Runs	Wkts	Wides	No-Balls
Sidebottom	16	6	31	3	-	-
Fletcher	13	2	47	1	-	-
Adams	18	3	63	4	-	-
Franks	11	2	35	2	-	-
Patel	4	1	17	0	-	1

Kent second innings		Runs	Balls	Mins	4s	6s
JC Tredwell	b Adams	20	36	48	4	-
*RWT Key	b Fletcher	15	27	40	2	-
PD Edwards	c Wagh b Sidebottom	13	35	54	2	-
+GO Jones	c Adams b Fletcher	11	23	26	2	-
M van Jaarsveld	lbw b Fletcher	1	6	7	-	-
SA Northeast	st Read b Patel	18	63	87	3	-
JL Denly	lbw b Adams	37	75	77	6	-
DI Stevens	not out	42	59	80	5	1
Azhar Mahmood	c Read b Adams	19	29	41	3	-
MT Coles	b Patel	28	28	23	4	1
A Khan	b Patel	9	13	14	2	-
Extras	(2 b, 9 lb)	11				
Total	(all out, 65.4 overs)	224				

Fall of wickets:
1-41 (Key, 10.1 ov), 2-45 (Tredwell, 11.2 ov), 3-66 (Jones, 19 ov), 4-70 (van Jaarsveld, 20.4 ov), 5-72 (Edwards, 21.5 ov), 6-125 (Northeast, 44 ov), 7-125 (Denly, 44.1 ov), 8-163 (Azhar Mahmood, 54.5 ov), 9-194 (Coles, 61.1 ov), 10-224 (Khan, 65.4 ov)

Notts bowling	Ovs	Mdns	Runs	Wkts	Wides	No-Balls
Sidebottom	14	6	35	1	-	-
Fletcher	15.2	8	43	3	-	-
Adams	18	1	78	3	-	-
Franks	11.4	4	33	0	-	-
Patel	6.4	1	24	3	-	-

Match 2

NOTTINGHAMSHIRE v SOMERSET

April 21st, 22nd, 23rd 2010
(match scheduled for 4 days but completed in 3)
Venue: Trent Bridge, Nottingham
Toss: won by Nottinghamshire who elected to field
Umpires: TE Jesty & G Sharp
Result: Nottinghamshire won by 2 wickets
Points: Nottinghamshire 21 (Batting 2, Bowling 3)
Somerset 5 (Batting 2, Bowling 3)

21st April – Day One

Buoyed by their convincing start to the campaign, Nottinghamshire were handed a pre-match boost when the ECB allowed them to give Stuart Broad a rare county run-out. His inclusion was designed to give him some match practice ahead of the World twenty20 tournament – but at the expense of Ryan Sidebottom, who had already had his run-out having featured against Kent.

Having picked up a maximum points haul batting first against Rob Key's side, it might have been easy to be tempted to go down the same route again, but Chris Read thought otherwise by inviting Somerset to bat first.

As in the first match, this contest was played slightly towards the Fox Road side of the square and the dangerous Marcus Trescothick showed his intent by clipping a couple of delightful fours to the shorter boundary.

Andre Adams maintained his fine start to the campaign by dismissing Arul Suppiah with just his third delivery and then Broad got the key scalp – Trescothick mistimed a pull and the ball looped up to midwicket where Amla, initially appearing to misjudge the flight, toppled backwards but hung on.

James Hildreth fell to Luke Fletcher and Paul Franks struck either side of the lunch break to leave the Cidermen reeling at 78-5, but 66 from Peter Trego and 40s from Compton, Wright and Thomas steered the total to a workable 272 all out.

Last man Charl Willoughby produced a highly-entertaining impersonation of a mad woodcutter flailing away with his axe as he tried to garner some late runs. Two boundaries flew away off thickish outside edges before he inevitably holed out – to Mark Wagh – at long-stop!

When the home side batted, Neil Edwards, so impressive a week earlier and determined to succeed against his former employers, and his opening partner, Bilal Shafayat, both fell cheaply before the close to leave the game evenly balanced, a viewpoint that Paul Franks shared:

"I think it's probably quite even after the first day. It was important to win the toss on a pitch that we felt would have a little bit of pace and bounce and to try, and exploit that and to bowl a side out is important.

"I feel whenever you put a side in, the minimum you are looking for is to be batting by the end of the first day. To have lost a couple of wickets ourselves is not ideal, but a little bit more of what we've already produced this season would be fantastic."

On coming on as the fourth seamer: *"We are all part of an attack and we get asked to do a job as and when required. When it's my turn, you go through your processes and work out the best ways of getting guys out and it was nice for me to get a wicket either side of the interval – it gave us a bit of momentum – and to get two decent players out was important (De Bruyn and Keiswetter).*

"I thought their tail-enders played quite nicely and got them up to a respectable total – I think it showed what can happen when the ball gets a little bit softer on this pitch.

"It was a boost getting rid of Trescothick early on because he looked in good touch. This should pan out to be an excellent game.

"I'm not taking anything for granted when it comes to my own form – I've got this opportunity to try and fill a void and hopefully I'm going to make a decent fist of it. It's important to keep contributing to the team effort."

Paul Franks continued his fine start to the season

Close of Day One – Notts 26-2 (Wagh 12*, Amla 4*, 17 overs)

22nd April – Day Two

Day Two of this match will forever be recalled as the one in which Stuart Broad produced his most hostile spell for Nottinghamshire at their county headquarters. He tore the heart out of Somerset's top order with a burst of five wickets in just 27 deliveries – but more on that later.

The day had begun with Mark Wagh and Hashim Amla in occupation of the crease, but the South African lost his companion, plus Samit Patel and Ali Brown, before he himself went for 58.

Paul Franks manufactured his second half century in a row before the last pair, Adams and Fletcher, brought up a second batting point. At 250 all out Notts faced a first innings deficit of 22.

What Do Points Make?

Umpire Trevor Jesty looks on as Stuart Broad begins his 'spell of terror' with the wicket of Arul Suppiah

Somerset's second innings began calmly enough. For the first four and half overs there was no indication of the mayhem that would soon follow. Broad then got Suppiah, fending a short-pitched ball to third slip. Adams took the catch and then invited Compton to feather one through to Read.

Broad, haring in from the Radcliffe Road End, looked like he was up for a bit of a battle and his appreciative fans were with him.

Midweek crowds at early season County Championship matches generally tend to incorporate the 'less rowdy' end of the spectator market. Senior members, the cricket connoisseur sampling a rare day off, young couples enjoying some together-time and the 'working-from-home' business types all appreciate and enthuse their hours in the fresh air, but seldom do they generate the kind of atmosphere heard on this Thursday afternoon..

Long jumpers and triple jumpers like to whip up the crowds as they set off down the runway at major athletics events. The 20 minute session that Stuart Broad then turned in was remarkably similar and extracted maximum audience participation.

They roared their approval as he tore into the Somerset batters. Notwithstanding the fragile state of the game (Notts were already 50 behind), this was an outstanding spell. Bowling with searing pace and unplayable bounce, he ended James Hildreth's brief stay by trapping him plumb in front for a duck and then sent Zander de Bruyn on his way first ball, steering a throat-ball to Adams.

Craig Keiswetter, about to depart for the Caribbean as England's opening batsman, then showed an obvious dislike for the 'chin music' as he survived the hat-trick ball before getting smacked around the helmet from another terrific Broad bouncer.

After lengthy treatment he wisely got his head out of the firing line from the next delivery – but not his bat – and his brief stay in the middle was at an end.

This was gladiatorial combat – and Stuart Broad was Caligula.

33-5 became 43-6 when Peter Trego, attempting to be positive against the snarling quickie, fell to an astonishing catch. Clipping firmly to leg he was pouched by Samit Patel just a few feet from the bat under the helmet at short leg. With barely a split second to react he held on to give Broad his fifth wicket.

There was a sense of fulfilment when that wicket went down. It was clear that the bowler was nearing the end of his spell. He had given his all – and the crowd had played their part also. If ever there was a five-for that had been shared around several hundred people, this was it.

Somerset's lead was only 65 with four wickets left, but they still had Trescothick, although he should have gone on 18. Edging Adams to the hitherto reliable Edwards, he had a life when his former team-mate spilled the offering moving sharply to his left.

The Victorian all-rounder Damien Wright gave solid support to his captain and saw it through to stumps without any further alarms

Close of Day Two – Somerset 120-6
(Trescothick 63*, Wright 37*, 24 overs)

23rd April – Day Three

Depending on whether you view life as a glass half-full or half-empty person, the match entered its third morning intriguingly balanced. With a lead of 147 already, Somerset were well set to post a challenging fourth innings run chase – or would it be four quick wickets and a comfortable stroll to a second successive home victory for Nottinghamshire?

As it turned out the outcome remained in doubt until late in the day.

Fresh from his heroic performance a day earlier Stuart Broad may have been hoping to end the innings with a really special analysis but - both before and after his five wicket burst - he had been picked off with great regularity by the Somerset batsmen. Damien Wright began the day by counter-attacking impressively and he hit three successive boundaries off Broad to bring up the century partnership, shared alongside his captain.

With 15 boundaries in his 78, Wright had suddenly overtaken Trescothick as the man that Notts needed to dismiss in a hurry, and it was Luke Fletcher who answered Chris Read's clarion call by sending him on his way with a ball that may have kept a touch low.

In both Championship matches against Notts in 2009 Trescothick had been dismissed in the 90s – and he failed to make it into three figures yet again, falling for 98 when he opened the face and steered Franks straight to Ali Brown, the solitary slip fielder.

The last two wickets only added eleven more, meaning that Notts had just over five sessions in which to score 250 runs – exactly the total they managed in their first innings!

Amidst the euphoria of knocking over the Somerset tail was the slight disappointment that they hadn't quite timed it as they'd have wished because the Nottinghamshire openers were now to be subjected to a tricky ten minute spell before lunch.

Sadly for Neil Edwards, he was able to tuck into a second helping of crumble and custard because he fell in that brief passage of play, edging Charl Willoughby to slip where Trescothick hung on to a sharp chance, clearly not feeling that he owed his old team-mate a favour for spilling him a day earlier.

What Do Points Make?

When play resumed, a serene passage to victory seemed assured as Bilal Shafayat and Mark Wagh added a century stand during the afternoon session to reach tea on 104-1.

They then moved their side halfway towards the victory target before Shafayat fell one short of his half century, trapped lbw by Wright. As so often happens after a lengthy stand, one wicket was quickly followed by another. Mark Wagh's annoyance at getting out for 70 was clear for all to see.

It was obvious from the body language of the fielders that they sensed there had been a shift in the balance of power. Nottinghamshire still had a lengthy list of reliable batsmen to guide them to the finishing line, but someone had to do the guiding.

On or off the field Hashim Amla gives off the impression that there's not too much that fazes him. With bat in hand, he's a premier performer – one of the classiest around – and during the two hours he was at the crease it seemed inevitable that his side would win, even though he saw Samit Patel, Ali Brown, Chris Read, Paul Franks and Stuart Broad all arrive and depart at the other end.

Amla took 18 from one Damien Wright over as he wrested the match back in Notts' favour, until, at 239-7, the home side asked for the extra half hour to be played. There were those in the crowd that admitted to being equally as anxious during the day as they'd been excitable 24 hours earlier.

Broad, hero with the ball, fell for just 6 with only four runs needed. Only two wickets remained as Andre Adams marched out to the middle, but he wasn't required and there were no more calamities as Amla pulled Alfonso Thomas away for the winning boundary. His 64 not out was cheered to the rafters amidst a general outpouring of nervous emotion.

Notts had completed back-to-back wins against a tenacious Somerset side. It had been quite a battle, as Samit Patel confirmed:

"It went right down to the wire – we were looking pretty comfortable at one stage, but you can lose wickets at crucial stages and we did that today. But finally we got home and it's good to get two wins under our belt.

"Chasing 250 we felt pretty comfortable in the dressing room. But every team does it, you lose some wickets and then things change, but I felt the guys batted well. Hashim was excellent at the end and got us over the line, but Waggy and Billy set it all up with their partnership during the afternoon session.

"I got starts in both innings but didn't go on, so that was frustrating on my behalf. Getting caught at cover in the first innings was a bad execution of a shot, and in the second innings I thought it was maybe going down the leg side, but that's cricket and you've got to live with it and move on in the next game.

"Broady's spell was excellent in this game. I can't imagine too many batsmen would want to come in and face him when he's bowling like that. Fielding at short leg I felt involved in the game every ball and I was pleased with the catch I got there. I don't field there too often but it was nice to hang on to one.

"I think we've got a great squad and we've got to keep winning – two wins at this stage of the season is hugely important and I think, right now, we're a good tip for honours this season."

The inside story of Nottinghamshire's LV= County Championship success

SCORECARD

Somerset first innings		Runs	Balls	Mins	4s	6s
*ME Trescothick	c Amla b Broad	22	38	53	4	-
AV Suppiah	c Brown b Adams	10	29	33	2	-
NRD Compton	c Wagh b Fletcher	42	112	158	6	-
JC Hildreth	lbw b Fletcher	14	31	39	3	-
Z de Bruyn	c Edwards b Franks	1	8	5	-	-
+C Kieswetter	c Read b Franks	1	12	12	-	-
PD Trego	c Read b Franks	66	95	115	11	-
DG Wright	c Edwards b Broad	43	58	59	6	1
AC Thomas	not out	40	54	55	8	-
DA Stiff	c Fletcher b Broad	14	15	25	2	-
CM Willoughby	c Wagh b Adams	8	8	10	2	-
Extras	(7 lb, 4 nb)	11				
Total	(all out, 76.1 overs)	272				

Fall of wickets: 1-23 (Suppiah 8.3ov), 2-35 (Trescothick 13.2ov), 3-65 (Hildreth 25.1ov), 4-66 (de Bruyn 26.4ov), 5-78 (Kieswetter 30.3ov), 6-142 (Compton 49.2), 7-199 (Trego 60ov), 8-220 (Wright 66ov), 9-254 (Stiff 73.3ov), 10-272 (Willoughby, 76.1 ov)

Notts bowling	Overs	Mdns	Runs	Wkts	Wides	No-Balls
Broad	19	1	79	3	-	1
Fletcher	16	5	48	2	-	-
Adams	19.1	4	68	2	-	1
Franks	16	6	45	3	-	-
Patel	6	0	25	0	-	-

Nottinghamshire first innings		Runs	Balls	Mins	4s	6s
NJ Edwards	lbw b Willoughby	2	3	1	-	-
BM Shafayat	c Trescothick b Thomas	1	28	30	-	-
MA Wagh	b Stiff	16	87	116	3	-
HM Amla	c Kieswetter b Wright	58	131	176	11	-
SR Patel	c Wright b Willoughby	33	46	54	6	-
AD Brown	lbw b Thomas	2	6	5	-	-
*+CMW Read	lbw b Trego	29	101	123	4	-
PJ Franks	lbw b Willoughby	61	97	127	11	-
SCJ Broad	c Hildreth b Willoughby	1	12	15	-	-
AR Adams	b Wright	10	13	14		1
LJ Fletcher	not out	5	4	6	1	-
Extras	(4 b, 14 lb, 12 nb, 2 w)	32				
Total	(all out, 87 overs)	250				

Fall of wickets: 1-2 (Edwards 0.3ov), 2-4 (Shafayat 7.5ov), 3-56 (Wagh 30.2ov), 4-121 (Patel 45.2ov), 5-124 (Brown 46.3ov), 6-129 (Amla 53ov), 7-231 (Read 78.4ov), 8-235 (Broad 83.3ov), 9-236 (Franks 85.3), 10-250 (Adams, 87 ov)

Somerset bowling	Overs	Mdns	Runs	Wkts	Wides	No-Balls
Willoughby	23	8	40	4	1	-
Wright	19	10	41	2	-	-
Thomas	17	7	34	2	-	3
Stiff	12	1	52	1	1	2
Trego	7	2	22	1	-	-
de Bruyn	6	1	31	0	-	1
Suppiah	3	0	12	0	-	-

What Do Points Make?

Somerset second innings		Runs	Balls	Mins	4s	6s
*ME Trescothick	c Brown b Franks	98	130	189	17	-
AV Suppiah	c Adams b Broad	11	17	23	1	-
NRD Compton	c Read b Adams	1	7	6	-	-
JC Hildreth	lbw b Broad	0	4	15	-	-
Z de Bruyn	c Adams b Broad	0	1	1	-	-
+C Kieswetter	c Read b Broad	0	5	1	-	-
PD Trego	c Patel b Broad	3	11	11	-	-
DG Wright	b Fletcher	78	71	80	15	-
AC Thomas	c Edwards b Franks	12	44	52	-	-
DA Stiff	not out	5	5	14	1	-
CM Willoughby	b Franks	4	3	3	1	-
Extras	(5 lb, 10 nb)	15				
Total	(all out, 48.5 overs)	227				

Fall of wickets: 1-23 Suppiah (6.1ov), 2-26 Compton (7.4ov), 3-33 Hildreth (8.5), 4-33 De Bruyn (9ov), 5-33 Keiswetter (10.5ov), 6-43 Trego (14.3ov) 7-179 (Wright 34.5), 8-216 (Trescothick 46.1), 9-223 (Thomas 48.2), 10-227 (Willoughby, 48.5 ov)

Notts bowling	Overs	Mdns	Runs	Wkts	Wides	No-Balls
Broad	15	2	89	5	-	5
Fletcher	10	1	49	1	-	-
Adams	14	5	59	1	-	-
Franks	6.5	0	22	3	-	-
Patel	3	1	3	0	-	-

Nottinghamshire second innings		Runs	Balls	Mins	4s	6s
NJ Edwards	c Trescothick b Willoughby	1	5	3	-	-
BM Shafayat	lbw b Wright	49	125	172	6	-
MA Wagh	c Wright b Trego	70	146	173	11	-
HM Amla	not out	64	73	123	9	1
SR Patel	lbw b Thomas	10	20	30	2	-
AD Brown	lbw b de Bruyn	16	27	34	3	-
*+CMW Read	c Trescothick b Willoughby	0	4	1	-	-
PJ Franks	c Kieswetter b Thomas	12	19	24	2	-
SCJ Broad	c Suppiah b Willoughby	6	18	15	1	-
AR Adams	not out	0	0	3	-	-
LJ Fletcher						
Extras	(6 lb, 12 nb, 4 w)	22				
Total	(8 wickets, 71.5 overs)	250				

Fall of wickets: (1-2 (Edwards 1ov), 2-127 (Shafayat, 44.5 ov), 3-127 (Wagh, 45.4 ov), 4-171 (Patel, 53.2 ov), 5-195 (Brown, 61.4 ov), 6-198 (Read, 62.2 ov), 7-233 (Franks, 67.2 ov), 8-246 (Broad, 71 ov)

Somerset bowling	Overs	Mdns	Runs	Wkts	Wides	No-Balls
Willoughby	22	5	83	3	1	-
Thomas	15.5	3	54	2	1	4
Wright	10	1	30	1	-	-
Stiff	5	0	36	0	-	-
Trego	13	4	30	1	-	-
Suppiah	4	2	3	0	-	-
de Bruyn	2	0	8	1	2	2

Match 3

HAMPSHIRE v NOTTINGHAMSHIRE

May 4th, 5th, 6th, 7th 2010 (4 day match)
Venue: The Rose Bowl, Southampton
Toss: won by Hampshire who elected to bat
Umpires: RJ Bailey & JW Lloyds
Result: Nottinghamshire won by 5 wickets
Points: Hampshire 6 (Batting 3, Bowling 3)
Nottinghamshire 22 (Batting 3, Bowling 3)

4th May – Day One

Having won both of their Trent Bridge fixtures inside three days, Nottinghamshire's away programme began on the south coast against a Hampshire side that had lost all of their first five matches in both the four day and one day formats.

One of those losses had come just 48 hours earlier, with Notts winning a rain-reduced Clydesdale Bank 40 over clash on the same ground, played over a typically damp May Bank Holiday weekend. The win, though, had come at a price, with both Andre Adams and Luke Fletcher picking up knocks. With Stuart Broad in the West Indies on England duty, it meant that Mick Newell had to make three changes from the side that had beaten Somerset.

Darren Pattinson had recovered from an ankle injury and would share the new ball with Charlie Shreck, who was also returning to the side after undergoing knee surgery during the winter. The third addition was Steven Mullaney, a 23-year-old all-rounder who had moved from Lancashire during the close-season. Having begun the season with a century for the second team and then picked up three valuable wickets in that CB40 win over Hants, he was in the right place at the right time to step in and make his Championship debut for his new county.

On a blustery morning Nic Pothas won the toss for his Hampshire side and elected to have a bat. Paul Franks made the initial breakthrough, Jimmy Adams edging to Read after three quarters of an hour, and then Shreck struck twice to reduce the home side to 77-3.

Michael Carberry, meanwhile, emphasised what a class act he had become at the other end. Buoyed by his England debut in Bangladesh just a few weeks earlier, he drove and cut the ball with precision timing and placement to bring up his fifty from just 69 deliveries.

The afternoon session followed a similar path – Carberry batted on towards his century, whilst Notts nipped out three wickets at the other end. James Vince had looked the most likely of the home batters to keep the opener company. Racing to a run-a-ball 39 with exquisite straight drives off Mullaney, Shreck and Franks, he then perished tamely, chipping Pattinson to Mark Wagh at midwicket.

216-6 at tea soon became 229-7. Carberry pushed Samit Patel for a single to reach his ton, but the bowler responded by trapping Dominic Cork lbw with his next delivery.

— 21 —

Steven Mullaney (bowling) enjoyed a fine Championship debut for Notts

Franks came back at the Pavilion End to end the openers long vigil. Mullaney then got rid of Kabeer Ali to pick up his first wicket and ensure the third bowling point was safely gathered, before Pattinson ended the innings by firing one through Griffiths' defences.

To dismiss the home side for exactly 300 on a good track represented a decent day at the office for the Notts attack, according to vice-captain Paul Franks:

"To have lost the toss on what looked an excellent pitch and to have then bowled a side out on the first day is always a good effort. All five bowlers contributed well to what was a strong effort, bowling into a really stiff breeze at times. I think we made a good fist of it so we are quite happy at the moment.

"We've picked up a few niggles over the last few days but that's part and parcel of the job. To miss Andre and Luke, who've bowled so well in the last two games, is disappointing but it shows the depth we've got with Charlie coming back from injury. He was excellent and just needs a few miles in his legs to be back to his best, and Darren showed what a good strike bowler he is.

"I think we all did a good job and don't underestimate the job Steven Mullaney and Samit did into that breeze.

"I thought Michael Carberry played fantastically well and he applied himself really well and I hope our guys have studied that and watched what he did. He didn't try anything flash or anything fancy and to pick him up towards the end of the day was obviously good for us because had he hung around we might have been coming back to bowl at him again tomorrow morning. As a group we're happy with how the day went and when we get out there tomorrow we need to cash in and make a substantial score."

Close of Day One – Nottinghamshire 3-0
(Edwards 3*, Shafayat 0*, 1 over)

5th May – Day Two

Hopes of the top order building a really solid platform were wiped out at the start of the day as Kabeer Ali took three wickets with his first 18 deliveries. Shafayat edged behind, Edwards was given out caught in the gully, although the bowler appeared to be already up appealing for leg before wicket, and then Mark Wagh lost his off stump.

To compound a dreadful morning, the ever-reliable Amla feathered Sean Ervine's first delivery down the leg side and Pothas pulled off a stunning catch.

At 33-4 Hampshire's total of 300 suddenly didn't look so bad after all!

Samit Patel – aggressively – and Ali Brown – more circumspectly – repaired some of the early damage by hoisting the score to 102 before the former drove the Sri Lankan slow left-arm spinner Rangan Herath to Cork at mid off.

When Cork then knocked Chris Read's off stump back the visitors were 122-6, teetering on the brink of a sizeable first innings deficit. Hampshire's hold on the game was soon loosened though. Either side of the tea interval Brown, and his new partner Steven Mullaney, added 111 in 31 overs for the 7th wicket.

The senior man appeared to be steering the Notts ship to calmer waters when he unexpectedly fell for 81. Despite batting for three and a half hours Brown had resisted the temptation to try and hit Herath over the top, but when he did come at him aggressively he dragged his shot straight to Cork, who took another important catch at mid-wicket.

Nottinghamshire's Chief Executive, Derek Brewer, was on the ground to see Mullaney bring up his first half century in Notts colours, and the youngster moved on to an unbeaten 72 by stumps, with Paul Franks on 26.

Ali Brown gave his assessment of the first couple of days play: *"I think it's a good wicket we're playing on and we felt we'd done well to restrict them to 300. Michael Carberry batted well yesterday but we felt we were ahead in the game. We didn't have a good start today but we've come back pretty well and still have everything to play for over the next couple of days.*

"It was nice to be able to get a few runs myself. Hashim has done that for us in most of the games he's played in this season so far, so it's quite nice of him to let some of the rest of us have a chance to score a few runs ourselves!

"From the position we were in I had to be very patient. Although I would have liked to have been a bit more aggressive the situation just didn't demand it, but I felt in good touch and was frustrated not to kick on from there ten overs from the new ball.

"I felt it was time to try and go after him – it would be the last thing he would expect – unfortunately I didn't expect to mis-time the ball as I did.

"Steven Mullaney has played very well – he's a very competitive cricketer and he's good for the dressing room and today he's proved that he's a good player and he's got us back in the game."

Close of Day Two – Nottinghamshire 273-7 (Mullaney 72*, Franks 26*, 86.4 overs)

6th May – Day Three

The third morning of this match produced one of those ever-to-be-cherished moments as a young cricketer celebrated an important milestone. Steven Mullaney had reached three figures before, for Lancashire against Durham University in a first class friendly, but this was significantly more important. He'd moved from Old Trafford to Trent Bridge during the close season and had already deeply impressed his new employers with his skill and his enthusiasm.

Probably not expecting to break into the four day game during the early part of the season, Steven had been the fortunate recipient of a call-up when Adams and Fletcher had picked up knocks prior to the start. He'd bowled well enough, picking up 1-30 from 12 overs, and his fielding had been sharp.

Coming in at number eight, he'd been helped by having Ali Brown as his first partner and on a good track he'd helped himself whenever the opportunity came to add runs.

The enormity of what confronted him didn't appear to weigh too heavily on his shoulders as he helped add 39 runs in the first half hour before his partner fell – lbw to Cork – just a couple of runs away from what would have been his third half century in as many matches.

Steven moved on to 96 before losing Darren Pattinson, caught to a juggling catch at slip, meaning that he only had Charlie Shreck for company if he was to reach his hundred.

The big fast bowler saw out the remainder of Cork's over, leaving 'Mull' to face Herath. This was to be the batsman's lucky day.

Charging – a touch recklessly – at the first delivery of the over, he was beaten by the flight and turn and should have been stumped by a country mile. The ball, though, had also bounced quite viciously and Nic Pothas' desperate attempt to stretch far to his right and gather the ball enabled the fortunate Mullaney to scramble home.

Reprieved, he defended the next three balls before sweetly lofting the ball over the inner ring to the mid-wicket fence for his 12th boundary – his century coming in just under four hours from 184 balls.

With understandable joy, he took off his helmet, raised his bat and accepted the congratulations from Shreck, an appreciative crowd and a noisy Notts balcony.

It became an unbeaten hundred when Shreck fell in the next over with the visitors having established a 28 run first innings lead.

Second time around Carberry fell cheaply during an impressive opening burst from 'Patto'. Jimmy Adams batted beautifully to reach a half century, but he became the second wicket to fall to Samit Patel, aided by a fine diving catch at short leg by Bilal Shafayat.

The statisticians on the ground enjoyed the rare novelty of five penalty runs being awarded when Chris Read misjudged some late movement from a delivery by Paul Franks and turned to see the loose ball trickle behind him onto a helmet, which had been stationed behind him.

Neil McKenzie's poor start to the season (it would get better during the return fixture!) continued when he edged Shreck to Read, before Vince and Pothas shut up shop during a quiet closing session.

Although the bulk of his runs had come a day earlier, Day 3 is one that Steven Mullaney will never forget, thanks to his debut century.

"I'm over the moon – delighted – I can't really explain it – it's not really sunk in yet." he said afterwards.

"We are in a strong position – only 150 behind and they're four wickets down already. We need to go again in the morning and get the remaining six wickets and hopefully push for a win tomorrow afternoon."

Steven had gone to the crease with Notts at 122-6, yet the number eight wasn't too concerned about the overall match situation at that stage.

"I didn't think we were in that much trouble – Ali Brown was still there and Paul Franks was still to come, and he's having a phenomenal season with bat and ball."

His biggest moment of concern came as he approached three figures.

"I thought I'd been playing the spinner quite well and had used my feet quite well against him, so I thought I'd take a bit of a calculated risk, but I missed it – luckily it bounced too much for the wicketkeeper. I then thought they'll bring the field up for the last two balls so I'll wait for that and then take another risk and luckily it came off for me with the boundary.

"I think the rest of the lads were pretty pleased for me. Coming to Nottinghamshire was a big move and a big decision for me in the winter, but it was 100% the right thing to do – and it's now pleasing that I've put in a performance which will hopefully go towards another win for us tomorrow."

Cold but sunny – day 3 at The Rose Bowl

Close of Day Three – Hampshire – 177-4
(Vince 29*, Pothas 29*, 79 overs)

7ᵗʰ May – Day Four

In a full and eventful day Nottinghamshire made it three wins out of three thanks to a spirited and successful run chase, although the bowlers also deserved a huge stack of credit for their part in the morning's proceedings.

The new ball was taken as soon as it became due and even though there was an initial flurry of boundaries, Pattinson and Franks combined to each send back one of the overnight batsmen.

Hampshire seemed stuck between trying to show enough positive instinct to set Notts a run chase or to block for as long as they could to try and ensure a draw.

Either way, Sean Ervine and Dominic Cork frustrated the bowlers for much of the first session until Patel dismissed the latter. Shreck took wickets with successive deliveries to remove Ali, bowled without playing a shot, and then Herath, who edged behind.

Shortly after lunch it was all over when Ervine gave Patel a fourth wicket, once again taken by Shafayat at bat/pad.

Notts' target was 246 from a minimum of 63 overs. Kabeer Ali had wreaked havoc during the first innings, but it was quickly apparent that he was struggling with a knee injury and he had to leave the field. David Griffiths took over the bowling duties from the Northern End and picked up a bonus straight away. A short, wide delivery to Edwards was slashed powerfully, but Carberry at backward point dived and clung on to a 'once a season effort'.

Mark Wagh showed his intent from the off, driving and cutting with outstanding certainty. 'Billy' was twice put down in the slips but – as they'd done in the win over Somerset – the pair set about building a platform from which the victory assault would be launched.

At tea Notts were on 83-1, still requiring 163 from the remaining 40 overs, with Wagh having raced to a 42-ball half century which had contained ten boundaries.

Shafayat went shortly afterwards, but by the time Hampshire broke through again – 25 overs later – victory was looking increasingly likely for the East Midlands side.

With Kabeer Ali off the field, there was further cause for home anxiety. Skipper Pothas injured a hand and also had to leave the action, replaced initially behind the stumps by new acting captain Dominic Cork.

Former Hants gloveman, and now assistant coach, Iain Brunnschweiler was summoned from a teaching session on the academy ground to keep wicket as Cork tried to stem the flow of runs.

Wagh and Hashim Amla had added 118 in typically stylish fashion, with Amla reaching 54 before he fell pulling Griffiths to deep square leg, where he was caught by Benny Howells fielding as substitute for Ali.

By now 'Waggy' had become the third centurion of the game, hoisting Ervine down the ground in emphatic fashion shortly after majestically lifting Herath over long on for two huge maximums.

Although the light was closing in – during a bitterly chilly final session – Notts were so far ahead of the run-rate they could cope with the loss of Samit Patel, caught at third man for 1, and then Ali Brown, who whacked 14 from eight deliveries before top-edging Herath.

Chris Read had the satisfaction of hitting the winning runs, although it was Mark Wagh's 131 not out that had paved the way for this completed run chase.

To make it three wins out of three in the Championship clearly delighted Mick Newell. *"It was a really satisfying victory – you know, to chase a score down in a limited period of time like that and to win with seven overs to spare is very impressive and Mark Wagh and Hashim Amla deserve an awful lot of credit for that partnership.*

"Mark is a fantastically talented player and we know he's always disappointed when he doesn't make a major contribution, so I'm sure he'll be very pleased to have done that today. He's a lovely timer of the ball and to be not out at the end is always very important as well."

Leaving the south coast at around 8pm on the Friday evening, the Notts camp faced a quick turnaround before they hosted Kent in the CB40 competition the following day – nevertheless, there was plenty to reflect on during the journey home after extending their perfect start to the Championship season to three wins out of three.

SCORECARD

Hampshire first innings		Runs	Balls	Mins	4s	6s
MA Carberry	c Wagh b Franks	132	236	338	14	1
JHK Adams	c Read b Franks	15	39	45	1	-
CC Benham	c Brown b Shreck	9	31	28	-	-
ND McKenzie	lbw b Shreck	2	11	16	-	-
JM Vince	c Wagh b Pattinson	39	39	51	8	-
*+N Pothas	c Read b Pattinson	6	10	10	1	-
SM Ervine	c Brown b Patel	25	36	46	3	-
DG Cork	lbw b Patel	21	74	65	2	-
K Ali	c Shreck b Mullaney	10	53	69	-	-
HMRKB Herath	not out	16	17	28	2	-
DA Griffiths	b Pattinson	3	11	8	-	-
Extras	(4 b, 9 lb, 8 nb, 1 w)	22				
Total	(all out, 92.1 overs)	300				

Fall of wickets: 1-40 (Adams, 11.4 ov), 2-59 (Benham, 18.3 ov), 3-77 (McKenzie, 22.4 ov), 4-133 (Vince, 36.1 ov), 5-139 (Pothas, 38.5 ov), 6-177 (Ervine, 51.3 ov), 7-229 (Cork, 71.3 ov), 8-276 (Carberry, 85.5 ov), 9-289 (Ali, 89.2 ov), 10-300 (Griffiths, 92.1 ov)

Notts bowling	Overs	Mdns	Runs	Wkts	Wides	No-Balls
Pattinson	20.1	1	85	3	-	4
Shreck	24	4	74	2	-	-
Franks	21	4	58	2	-	-
Mullaney	12	1	30	1	1	-
Patel	15	3	40	2	-	-

Nottinghamshire first innings		Runs	Balls	Mins	4s	6s
NJ Edwards	c Vince b Ali	3	17	29	-	-
BM Shafayat	c Pothas b Ali	2	9	11	-	-
MA Wagh	b Ali	11	19	25	2	-
HM Amla	c Pothas b Ervine	5	24	33	-	-
SR Patel	c Cork b Herath	41	79	89	4	-
AD Brown	c Cork b Herath	81	144	210	7	-
*+CMW Read	b Cork	9	32	30	-	-
SJ Mullaney	not out	100	185	238	12	-
PJ Franks	lbw b Cork	48	82	90	7	-
DJ Pattinson	c Adams b Cork	1	23	19	-	-
CE Shreck	c McKenzie b Cork	0	6	8	-	-
Extras	(6 b, 10 lb, 9 nb, 2 w)	27				
Total	(all out, 102.3 overs)	328				

— 27 —

What Do Points Make?

Fall of wickets: 1-5 (Shafayat, 3 ov), 2-16 (Edwards, 6.2 ov), 3-17 (Wagh, 8.5 ov), 4-33 (Amla, 15.1 ov), 5-102 (Patel, 31.2 ov), 6-122 (Read, 40.4 ov), 7-233 (Brown, 71.4 ov), 8-312 (Franks, 94.5 ov), 9-324 (Pattinson, 100.4 ov), 10-328 (Shreck, 102.3 ov)

Hampshire bowling	Overs	Mdns	Runs	Wkts	Wides	No-Balls
Ali	24	2	92	3	-	-
Cork	16.3	7	34	4	-	1
Ervine	13	0	48	1	1	3
Griffiths	14	1	70	0	-	-
Herath	34	7	68	2	1	-
Carberry	1	1	0	0	-	-

Hampshire second innings		Runs	Balls	Mins	4s	6s
MA Carberry	c Read b Pattinson	14	30	34	2	-
JHK Adams	c Shafayat b Patel	60	153	174	7	-
CC Benham	lbw b Patel	18	44	51	-	-
ND McKenzie	c Read b Shreck	12	55	63	-	-
JM Vince	lbw b Franks	46	120	161	6	-
*+N Pothas	lbw b Pattinson	30	109	120	4	-
SM Ervine	c Shafayat b Patel	45	88	109	6	-
DG Cork	lbw b Patel	28	30	42	5	-
K Ali	b Shreck	0	5	2	-	-
HMRKB Herath	c Read b Shreck	0	1	1	-	-
DA Griffiths	not out	5	25	43	-	-
Extras	(2 lb, 8 nb, 5 pen)	15				
Total	(all out, 109.2 overs)	273				

Fall of wickets: 1-34 (Carberry, 8.2 ov), 2-73 (Benham, 23.3 ov), 3-109 (McKenzie, 42.5 ov), 4-121 (Adams, 49.3 ov), 5-190 (Pothas, 82.2 ov), 6-200 (Vince, 86 ov), 7-248 (Cork, 95.3 ov), 8-249 (Ali, 96.3 ov), 9-249 (Herath, 96.4 ov), 10-273 (Ervine, 109.2 ov)

Notts bowling	Overs	Mdns	Runs	Wkts	Wides	No-Balls
Pattinson	21	5	66	2	-	3
Shreck	23	6	70	3	-	-
Patel	36.2	14	55	4	-	-
Franks	22	4	63	1	-	1
Mullaney	7	1	12	0	-	-

Nottinghamshire second innings		Runs	Balls	Mins	4s	6s
NJ Edwards	c Carberry b Griffiths	8	15	18	1	-
BM Shafayat	c Benham b Herath	12	66	97	1	-
MA Wagh	not out	131	158	214	17	2
HM Amla	c sub b Griffiths	54	76	103	6	-
SR Patel	c Benham b Griffiths	1	8	7	-	-
AD Brown	c Griffiths b Herath	14	8	9	1	1
*+CMW Read	not out	7	8	9	1	-
SJ Mullaney						
PJ Franks						
DJ Pattinson						
CE Shreck						
Extras	(5 b, 3 lb, 6 nb, 5 w)	19				
Total	(5 wickets, 56 overs)	246				

The inside story of Nottinghamshire's LV= County Championship success

Fall of wickets: 1-12 (Edwards, 4.1 ov), 2-86 (Shafayat, 23.2 ov), 3-204 (Amla, 48.4 ov), 4-209 (Patel, 50.5 ov), 5-229 (Brown, 53.2 ov)

Hampshire bowling	Overs	Mdns	Runs	Wkts	Wides	No-Balls
Ali	2	0	11	0	-	-
Cork	7	2	16	0	-	-
Griffiths	16	4	59	3	-	-
Herath	23	2	111	2	2	-
Ervine	8	1	41	0	-	3

Match 4

NOTTINGHAMSHIRE v DURHAM

May 10th, 11th, 12th, 13th 2010 (4 day match)
Venue: Trent Bridge, Nottingham
Toss: won by Nottinghamshire who elected to field
Umpires: JH Evans & G Sharp
Result: Nottinghamshire won by an innings and 62 runs
Points: Nottinghamshire 24 (Batting 5, Bowling 3)
Durham 3 (Batting 1, Bowling 2)

10th May – Day One

Just 27.2 overs were bowled on a damp, murky Tuesday in Nottingham. The groundstaff performed heroics to ensure that play could start at 1.35pm, but the joy was short-lived as steady rain returned with only five overs having been bowled.

A lengthier session after tea brought Notts three wickets against the reigning two-time champions before bad light curtailed the session.

After announcing the same side that triumphed at The Rose Bowl, Chris Read won the toss and elected to insert Durham. With a greenish tint on the wicket and heavy cloud cover overhead, it looked a good toss to win.

Kyle Coetzer fell to the first delivery after a two hour stoppage, lifting Charlie Shreck to widish mid off, where Paul Franks took an excellent diving catch. Darren Pattinson sent Michael Di Venuto on his way with the help of a catch in the gully, and then former Notts player Will Smith edged behind to give 'Big Charlie' his second scalp.

Dale Benkenstein and Ian Blackwell ensured that there was no further damage as the visitors closed on 79-3.

Close of Day One – Durham 79-3
(Benkenstein 20*, Blackwell 24*, 27.2 overs)

11th May – Day Two

Having finished the last two seasons in the runners-up berth, behind Durham, Nottinghamshire looked as if they had something to prove as they gained the initiative on a day which was thankfully devoid of the wintry conditions of the opening day.

Tight, penetrative bowling, backed up by some solid batting, had swung the encounter towards the home side.

Benkenstein and Blackwell batted with positive intent during the opening half hour before the latter drove Pattinson to Shafayat in the gully. The pair had added 81 for the 4th wicket, but the breakthrough seemed to inspire Notts, who then soon had another success to celebrate – Charlie Shreck flattening two of Benks' stumps.

18-year-old Ben Stokes came dancing down the track to Samit Patel's first delivery and was comprehensively stumped – and then Phil Mustard fell to Paul Franks in the next over.

Lunch was taken at 191-8 on the fall of Liam Plunkett's wicket and Franks finished the innings off by getting rid of Ben Harmison and Chris Rushworth. Harmison had edged to Chris Read, giving the 'keeper his 700th first class victim.

Ben's brother, Steve Harmison, had ended on 4 not out, but it was how he would bowl that created most of the speculation between innings. 'Harmy' had taken a 6-fer at Trent Bridge a year earlier in his side's huge win.

Although initial stiffness gave way – it was his first outing of the summer – the former England quickie accelerated through the gears as the day wore on, but Notts batted soundly to move within 27 by the close.

Liam Plunkett had removed both of the openers – 'Billy' lbw and Neil Edwards chopping on – and then Hashim Amla had fallen for 67 to a catch at the wicket off Ben Harmison.

After the day's play Chris Read acknowledged that Notts had enjoyed the better of the first half of the match.

"It's been a good two days for us – obviously we didn't play a great deal yesterday but picking up those three wickets by the end of the first day was a good achievement for us. And the boys have bowled fantastically well today to get them out for around two hundred.

"I thought we batted really well. Neil Edwards set the tone and then Hashim and Mark Wagh built a really good partnership – it was just a shame to lose Hashim right at the end there because he was starting to look quite imperious."

The sight of the day was undoubtedly Benkenstein's stumps being flattened by Charlie Shreck.

"Charlie had two ops during the winter and that's never easy to come back from, and if I'm being honest I don't think any of us thought he'd be back so soon, but the work he's done and the rehabilitation he's done in the winter is a real credit to him and it was a fantastic spell he put in. He bowled 20 overs unchanged from one end and he was swinging the ball nicely and he can bowl all day – it's actually quite hard to get the ball out of his hand at times and this was a case in point."

Bilal 'Billy' Shafayat

On reaching 700 dismissals, the Notts captain admitted he wasn't aware of the impending milestone. *"I had absolutely no idea – I suppose you average about 40 dismissals a year in first class cricket, so I'm really happy with that. I'm not one for stats so I couldn't have told you within the nearest 100 where I was, but it's always nice for these things to tick over."*

Mark Wagh had ended the day unbeaten on 44 and he admitted to having enjoyed his lengthy stand with Amla.

"Hashim is such a fine player – he's played beautifully every knock pretty much that he's played for us. It's just a pleasure to be at the other end and watch him. He's very relaxed at the crease and doesn't get worked up at all."

On the overall match situation 'Waggy' agreed that the bowlers deserved a lot of credit. *"Durham are a fine side and they bat a long way down, so to get them out for just over 200 was really good – so now it's up to us to put a bit of a score together. Beating them would be a fantastic achievement for us.*

"It was nice batting out there today. It's quite a sporty wicket, you get some good balls but the bad balls hold up a little bit for you to hit."

Close of Day Two – Nottinghamshire 191-3 (Wagh 44*, Mullaney 4*, 54 overs)

12th May – Day Three

The statistics would back up the sentiment that this was one of the best days of County Championship cricket that anyone could wish to see, with 456 runs being scored for the loss of 9 wickets.

Even more importantly, from a Nottinghamshire perspective, the prospect of a fourth consecutive win was still very much alive thanks to some outstanding strokeplay from the lower middle order.

Without a wicket from his only other first class appearance for Durham, Chris Rushworth had toiled away equally unsuccessfully on the second day of this match, but the new day delivered better news as Wagh nicked his first ball of the morning loosener to Di Venuto at second slip.

He followed this up by getting the verdict on an lbw appeal against Samit Patel (which did look a little high!) and when Mullaney followed Wagh in chasing one to slip, the Sunderland-born seamer had reduced Notts to 226-6, an overall lead of just 8.

That wicket brought Chris Read out to partner Alistair Brown – two old hands together who seemed from the very outset to want to put their opponents firmly on the back foot. The importance of their stand cannot be overestimated.

In 41.3 overs they added 237 runs with positive, attacking cricket. Both batsmen hit Ben Harmison for leg side maximums early on and it was Brown who reached his half century first – from just 50 deliveries. Read followed suit having faced just 72 balls.

Lunch was taken at 333-6, but it was only a brief respite for the Durham attack as they came under a brutal assault during the afternoon.

Brown's 46th first class century of his career included another pulled six, this time off Rushworth, and was brought up by a push into the off side from the bowling of Ben Stokes. He had faced only 103 deliveries for his ton and then pressed the accelerator once more, hitting Liam Plunkett over the ropes before the same bowler gained a modicum of revenge when an intended upper-cut down towards third man flew sharply through to Mustard.

The partnership was the highest for the seventh wicket in English domestic cricket during 2010.

Read, meanwhile, was closing in on his own century and had a bit of lifeline when he was caught in the deep on 87 from a Stokes no-ball. His ton came shortly after Brown's departure when he lofted Ian Blackwell straight down the ground for four. The Notts skipper had emulated the unusual achievement of Mullaney in the previous match by scoring a century batting at number 8 in the order.

If Durham thought they were now in a position to wrap up the innings, they had severely miscalculated. In one of the knocks of the summer Paul Franks bludgeoned his way to 64 off 45 deliveries during a stand worth 116 in just 13 overs.

His half century was brought up with a switch-hit boundary off Blackwell – just his 38th delivery faced – and then he blasted Steve Harmison over the ropes at long on.

The elder 'Harmy' ended the stand – thanks to a fine diving catch from Mustard – to finish with figures of 1-123.

Ali Brown accepts the applause after his splendid innings

Read declared at the fall of Franks' wicket – with the score on 559-8 – and was taken with Nottinghamshire having established a first innings lead of 341.

Durham had four sessions in which to save the game and preserve a 23-match unbeaten run in the Championship. Two hours later those hopes seemed to rest solely on the weather coming to their rescue.

Di Venuto fell to a slip catch from the bowling of Pattinson, Mullaney ended Smith's hopes of a happy return to Trent Bridge and Franks and Shreck also struck before the close to leave the champions in disarray.

Ali Brown agreed that it had been an extraordinary day's cricket – and a good one for the County Championship in general.

"I think the new format seems to be producing more aggressive and positive cricket and we proved it again today.

"I just had a feeling that we would lose a couple of early wickets today – we had a great day yesterday and then Hashim got out just before the end and we could have been in a precarious position, but it was nice to share in a 200 partnership with Ready and that has put us back on track.

"When we came together we were looking to be positive and push ahead and exert some pressure on them. We were looking for quick runs to give ourselves the maximum opportunity to get the wickets. I suppose we were being a bit more aggressive than normal, but it all played into our hands and things went well."

On his form so far in 2010 Ali said: *"There were a couple of shots today that were pretty sweet and I feel in decent nick and am just a bit disappointed that I haven't scored the runs I should have done in the first couple of games. I felt I played well at Hampshire last week and ok again today."*

He also paid tribute to the Notts seamers. *"They've put the ball in the right place and bowled really well. The wicket has actually done more than perhaps the runs we scored would indicate.*

"Durham have got a few injuries and perhaps we've capitalised on that and taken the game away from them – I fancy our chances tomorrow if we keep putting the ball in the right areas, there's still good bounce and carry and swing and seam."

Close of Play – Durham 88-4 (Rushworth 0*, Blackwell 2*, 32 overs)

13th May – Day Four

Friday the 13th – traditionally a day that proves unlucky for some – and for Durham it marked their first defeat in the County Championship since losing to Hampshire at May's Bounty, Basingstoke in August 2008.

As you would expect, they didn't go down without a fight. Youngster Ben Stokes made it a day to remember for himself, and when the rain twice briefly interrupted proceedings around tea-time you wondered if Notts were going to be denied in the cruellest manner imaginable.

By then, though, they had made sufficient inroads to have Durham nine wickets down and still a long way from safety – and when play did restart after tea it didn't take long for Darren Pattinson to bring the curtain down on the north-easterners unbeaten run.

'Patto' had nipped out Ian Blackwell and the nightwatchman Chris Rushworth during his opening burst, but then 18-year-old Stokes, a flame-haired left-hander, showed some grit and determination to take the fight to the home side.

Stokes fell cheaply in the first innings but made Samit and the rest of the attack work much harder on the final day

He was joined in a stand of 70 for the 7th wicket by Phil Mustard, who fell right on lunch thanks to a brilliant bit of glovework from Chris Read. Standing up to the medium pace of Mullaney, he took a leg side delivery and whipped off the bails in double-quick time to remove his opposite number.

After the interval Stokes found a new ally in Ben Harmison, who hung around for 90 minutes – long enough to witness the youngster reach his maiden hundred.

Having already played for England Under 19s, it was apparent from watching him perform in such adverse conditions – with the game seemingly lost – that Stokes has a big future ahead of him.

Beaten by Samit Patel's flight in the first innings, he exacted some revenge by smiting the spinner for 4-6-6-4 to move from 82 to 102 in just four hits and bring up a well-merited ton from 123 balls, with 15 fours and three sixes.

Another boundary followed, but on 106 he pulled Paul Franks to Mullaney, fielding in the deep. Plunkett went cheaply, also to Franks, whom he edged to Neil 'Safe Hands' Edwards at second slip, and Notts were on the brink of victory with Durham nine down.

Then another twist in a bizarre sort of parlour game; the rains came, went, came and went as the umpires twice took the players to the pavilion before bringing them out again.

Tea brought sanity and an end to the to-ing and fro-ing for a while, but it also brought more amateur weather forecasters out into the open than at the annual meteorological summer barbecue. Will we get any more play or not? They all had an opinion!

The interval was also marked with a simple ceremony which appeared highly significant to those of a Notts persuasion.

For three and a half days the Durham 'County Champions pennant' had fluttered proudly in the breeze high above the pavilion (to the left, the one above the committee room!). During tea it was lowered. Whilst it was obviously just being gathered for the return coach journey to Chester-le-Street, to save a few minutes at the end, the timing was poignant.

Durham were on the brink of an innings defeat to the side that had chased them home as runners-up in the table for each of the last two years. It may not have been an act of surrender but it did appear to be a mark of respect towards – possibly – the new champions-elect!

After scones, jam and cream – and the usual 20 minute break – the players returned to clear blue skies and it took just three more deliveries to end the action

Pattinson, from the Radcliffe Road End, knocked back Ben Harmison's leg stump with the aid of an inside edge Notts had won by an innings and 62 runs – collecting a maximum 24 points in the process.

In completing their fourth straight victory of the campaign, it confirmed Nottinghamshire's best start to a season since 1922, although ominously they finished as runners-up that year having won all of their opening six contests!

Of more immediate importance the side had taken over at the top of the table – nudging eight points clear of Yorkshire and also with a game in hand.

No wonder Mick Newell was delighted with how his troops had performed.

"We spoke at the start of the day about Durham being the best team in the country for the last two years so you don't expect them to fall over – I know Stokes is a talented player because I did some work with him in the winter. We made harder work of it perhaps but you've got to credit Durham with a strong fightback with the bat today.

"We weren't really concerned about the weather interfering too much as we've got enough radars around the ground to know that it wasn't going to rain for very long and luckily the brief break in the game came at a time, around tea-time, when we knew we weren't really losing time.

— 35 —

What Do Points Make?

"The table is interesting now – people will look at that – but the most important thing is to maintain confidence. We should have that, having won four games in a row, but I think most years – or for the last four or five years – we've managed to play well at the start of the season. What we've got to try and do is maintain that consistency.

"Last year we won, I think, three out of the first four, then didn't win again until September. At the moment, with the weather being good and the pitches being a bit more sporting, it's making for more interesting cricket at Trent Bridge than it did at times last season."

With Hashim Amla's brief spell on the Trent Bridge staff now at an end, the Director of Cricket assessed his value to the side.

"To come over in April and May as a batter is a tough ask of anybody and I think he's performed brilliantly. I think he'll play for Notts again – if not this year then certainly in future years because he's developed a nice feeling for the club and we'd be more than happy to have him back. To generate the number of runs he has done in April and May is a fantastic performance."

Chris Read – centurion and winning captain – felt that both sides had shown character on the final day.

"From my point of view I thought it was a fantastic last day and we always knew it wasn't going to be easy. There was always the chance that people would dig in, get scores and build partnerships, but we prevented that with only the young guy, Stokes, going on to get past fifty and all in all I was exceptionally pleased to get it done just after tea."

One of the highlights of the last day was Read's wonderful dismissal of Mustard.

"I was very happy with that stumping because Phil Mustard is a very dangerous character. The relationship a 'keeper builds with his bowlers is important and I'm still learning a little bit about Steven Mullaney, so I was really happy to get that one.

"Four wins out of four means we're going along nicely – it's a dream start to the season – but from here on in we've got to build on that momentum. Momentum is a word that's often used in cricket and it's certainly not an overrated word. We've built that momentum and need to keep it going and it starts again against Hampshire next week."

The skipper also revealed how much Hashim Amla would be missed.

"What a great player he is. I remember watching him when he made his Test debut. I was sat carrying the drinks for England out there in South Africa and he had a very stuttering start to his career, but when I saw that we had managed to sign him I was very excited. At that time he was in the process of scoring a double hundred in India and backed it up with a couple more hundreds!

"I always thought 'This guy is pretty good', but batting at the other end from him he's one of the best I've played with, I think. He will be missed, but hopefully we'll see him at Trent Bridge again at some point in the future."

SCORECARD

Durham first innings		Runs	Balls	Mins	4s	6s
MJ Di Venuto	c Patel b Pattinson	15	38	41	3	-
KJ Coetzer	c Franks b Shreck	3	8	20	-	-
*WR Smith	c Read b Shreck	10	22	29	1	-
DM Benkenstein	b Shreck	36	89	113	6	-
ID Blackwell	c Shafayat b Pattinson	43	72	93	9	-
BA Stokes	st Read b Patel	32	53	68	5	-
+P Mustard	c Read b Franks	31	49	61	6	-
BW Harmison	c Read b Franks	14	31	33	2	-
LE Plunkett	c Shafayat b Patel	3	7	4	-	-
C Rushworth	c Edwards b Franks	9	32	36	-	1
SJ Harmison	not out	4	8	12	1	-
Extras	(4 b, 2 lb, 6 nb, 6 w)	18				
Total	(all out, 269 minutes, 67.4 overs)218					

Fall of wickets: 1-16 (Coetzer, 5.1 ov), 2-32 (Di Venuto, 10.2 ov), 3-36 (Smith, 11.5 ov), 4-117 (Blackwell, 36.1 ov), 5-129 (Benkenstein, 39.4 ov), 6-188 (Stokes, 54.1 ov), 7-188 (Mustard, 55.3 ov), 8-191 (Plunkett, 56.4 ov), 9-205 (BW Harmison, 64 ov), 10-218 (Rushworth, 67.4 ov)

Notts bowling	Overs	Mdns	Runs	Wkts	Wides	No-Balls
Pattinson	17	2	63	2	2	2
Shreck	23	6	73	3	-	-
Franks	15.4	4	38	3	-	-
Mullaney	5	1	21	0	-	1
Patel	7	3	17	2	-	-

Nottinghamshire first innings		Runs	Balls	Mins	4s	6s
NJ Edwards	b Plunkett	33	88	103	3	-
BM Shafayat	lbw b Plunkett	16	30	41	3	-
MA Wagh	c Di Venuto b Rushworth	44	125	164	7	-
HM Amla	c Mustard b BW Harmison	67	78	91	14	-
SJ Mullaney	c Di Venuto b Rushworth	24	30	45	3	-
SR Patel	lbw b Rushworth	4	17	15		
AD Brown	c Mustard b Plunkett	134	121	187	17	3
*+CMW Read	not out	124	181	217	15	1
PJ Franks	c Mustard b SJ Harmison	64	45	47	11	1
DJ Pattinson						
CE Shreck						
Extras	(2 b, 22 lb, 14 nb, 11 w)	49				
Total	(8 wickets, declared, 465 minutes, 118 overs)559					

Fall of wickets: 1-34 (Shafayat, 10.5 ov), 2-91 (Edwards, 27 ov), 3-179 (Amla, 51.4 ov), 4-191 (Wagh, 54.1 ov), 5-199 (Patel), 6-226 (Mullaney, 63 ov), 7-463 (Brown, 104.3 ov), 8-559 (Franks, 118 ov)

Durham bowling	Overs	Mdns	Runs	Wkts	Wides	No-Balls
SJ Harmison	28	4	123	1	1	-
Rushworth	28	4	113	3	-	-
Plunkett	21	1	115	3	3	6
BW Harmison	19	1	86	1	5	-
Blackwell	16	5	39	0	1	-
Stokes	6	0	59	0	1	1

What Do Points Make?

Durham second innings		Runs	Balls	Mins	4s	6s
KJ Coetzer	lbw b Shreck	45	97	121	7	-
MJ Di Venuto	c Edwards b Pattinson	29	37	48	5	-
*WR Smith	c Read b Mullaney	4	17	22	-	-
DM Benkenstein	c Edwards b Franks	8	26	31	2	-
C Rushworth	c Read b Pattinson	6	29	42	1	-
ID Blackwell	c Shreck b Pattinson	15	20	23	2	-
BA Stokes	c Mullaney b Franks	106	126	161	16	3
+P Mustard	st Read b Mullaney	23	76	84	2	-
BW Harmison	b Pattinson	18	68	91	2	-
LE Plunkett	c Edwards b Franks	3	9	5	-	-
SJ Harmison	not out	4	8	14	-	-
Extras	(1 b, 4 lb, 10 nb, 3 w)	18				
Total	(all out, 336 minutes, 85 overs)	279				

Fall of wickets: 1-49 (Di Venuto, 12.5 ov), 2-69 (Smith, 19 ov), 3-84 (Benkenstein, 27.5 ov), 4-86 (Coetzer, 30.4 ov), 5-104 (Blackwell, 36.5 ov), 6-109 (Rushworth, 38.1 ov), 7-179 (Mustard, 61.4 ov), 8-266 (Stokes, 80 ov), 9-269 (Plunkett, 81.3 ov), 10-279 (BW Harmison, 85 ov)

Notts bowling	Overs	Mdns	Runs	Wkts	Wides	No-Balls
Pattinson	21	3	95	4	-	2
Shreck	19	5	30	1	-	-
Franks	21	8	58	3	3	-
Mullaney	12	6	35	2	-	1
Patel	12	3	56	0	-	-

HASHIM AMLA

After the Durham match Hashim Amla prepared to set off to join up with the South African touring party in the West Indies. After he'd said his goodbyes to his team-mates he was asked to reflect on his time with Nottinghamshire.

Hashim: *"The time has gone much quicker than I expected. Fortunately the team performance has been fantastic. I mean I don't think anyone expected us to win four out of four, especially in the time frame we've done it in. It has been a lovely experience. The team has been very welcoming and fortunately I've got a few runs to add to the team's success."*

Q - Have you achieved everything that you wanted to achieve?
Hashim: *"Well, certainly in some respects yes. I knew it was going to be quite difficult batting especially at Trent Bridge and I guess most places in England around this time of the year. It's been great to experience these challenging conditions and get some runs out of it. Certainly I would have loved to have scored a lot more runs. I don't think any batter can ever really be satisfied but on the whole I've been really grateful that things have gone well."*

Q - All of your team-mates have paid warm compliments as to how you have settled in the dressing room and how big an influence you have been. I guess you'll have made a few good friends here during your time here?
Hashim: *"Definitely. The guys have been very warm towards me and very welcoming and that enabled me to settle in quite easily. I think in a professional set up like this I just try to get into the changing room and do my job and contribute on the field in any way I can. Sometimes I would give an idea to the captain or have a word of advice with one of the younger guys. Certainly I've taken a lot of experience out of this. I've learnt a lot of different skills whilst I've been here – that has been the biggest asset for me."*

Q - Mick Newell has openly said that he would love to see you back playing again in Notts ranks before too long. Is there a gap in South Africa's calendar? Is there a possibility, have you looked that far ahead?
Hashim: *"No I actually haven't looked that far ahead. There may be a gap sometime around September or October. I think we have a tour to Dubai and Abu Dhabi against Pakistan. We've got a few games there, so there may be a gap but I haven't looked too far to be able to give exact dates but certainly it would be lovely to come back here if invited and if time permits. I will look forward to whatever challenges lie ahead."*

Q - Finally, have you said goodbye to the new county champions today? Can Nottinghamshire go on and win the County Championship this season?
Hashim: *"Certainly! I think with the start we've had it is more probable than people expected. The bowling has been fantastic and the batting has been outstanding. We've had some tough times but people have stepped in at crucial times and played some fantastic innings in pressure situations. Yes, Notts can go on and win it but it's a long season and you never want to get too complacent in this competition."*

Q - Really enjoyed watching you bat during your time here and hope to see you back in Notts colours before too long.
Hashim: *"Thank you very much – I've really enjoyed it. I've made so many new friends and the supporters have all been very welcoming."*

Match 5

NOTTINGHAMSHIRE v HAMPSHIRE

May 17th, 18th, 19th, 20th 2010 (4 day match)
Venue: Trent Bridge, Nottingham
Toss: won by Hampshire who elected to field
Umpires: B Dudleston & JF Steele
Result: Hampshire won by 2 wickets
Points: Nottinghamshire 5 (Batting 2, Bowling 3)
Hampshire 22 (Batting 3, Bowling 3)

17th May – Day One

Having played a game less than most of the other Division One sides, Nottinghamshire now found themselves in the rather enviable position of being top of the tree after their perfect four in four start.

Critics would point to the fixture list, which had seen them play three of those four matches at home, but no-one could deny that the manner of their win over Durham had been anything less than eye-catching – and with two more home matches up next the possibility of stretching that lead was a very real one.

Worryingly for Notts, they had to make a couple of enforced changes for the return fixture against Hampshire. Hashim Amla had already departed for the Caribbean, leaving a huge gap in the batting line-up with David Hussey not due to return to Trent Bridge for another couple of weeks.

Another key absentee was Mark Wagh, who, already planning for life after cricket, was spending a nervy week taking law exams. Mark's run-scoring during the early weeks had been crucial, especially in the run chases against Somerset and Hampshire, who would have been delighted to see the home side have to make major changes at numbers three and four in their line-up.

The two players to step into the starting eleven were Alex Hales and Andre Adams. Hales had been chomping at the bit for a place in the four day side, having scored 46, 41 and 46 in the three CB40 matches he'd played in 2010, as well as scoring 202 for the Second XI against MCC a week earlier, a knock in which he'd shared in an opening stand of 342 with Akhil Patel, Samit's younger brother.

Adams had recovered from the knee injury which had forced him to miss the last couple of outings and was an obvious candidate to return. Although the absence of the two batsmen did mean that the balance of the side was altered slightly, the fact that Mullaney, Brown, Read and Franks – 5, 6, 7 and 8 on the card – had all scored good runs in the Championship meant that Notts now had even more bowling options at their disposal.

As at Southampton, it was Nic Pothas who won the toss, but this time he elected to give his bowlers first use of the Trent Bridge wicket. Like Notts, the visitors were also without some of their regulars.

Kabeer Ali was still absent after picking up a knock in the first meeting and Michael Carberry had to pull out – initially due to a call-up to represent the England Lions side in a first class match against the touring Bangladeshis at Derby – but then he sustained an injury in the CB40 match the day before and had to miss that match as well.

Additionally, Michael Lumb was still away with the England twenty20 side (who had defeated Australia in the Final a day earlier) and Dimitri Mascarenhas and Simon Jones weren't fit for inclusion.

To say Notts made a poor start would be like saying that social networking has 'caught on a bit'. Neil Edwards went in the fourth over and Hales followed in the next, lbw for nought. Patel and Shafayat both reached double figures – just – but then fell in quick succession to leave the table-toppers in a spot of bother at 29-4, with Cork and Tomlinson taking a couple of wickets apiece.

Yet again it was down to the 'engine room' – the middle order – to make their mark. Steven Mullaney, now elevated to number five and seemingly thriving on the promotion, and Ali Brown took the total beyond three figures.

Both played with a freedom that indicated they weren't too concerned by any scoreboard pressure. Brown's flicked six off his legs from the bowling of Sean Ervine was the shot of the morning, but one over before lunch the Zimbabwean exacted some revenge by trapping his man lbw, although first (and subsequent!) impressions were that Ali had been hit outside the line.

Mullaney brought up his half century (from 87 balls) just after lunch but then was dropped in the slips almost immediately afterwards. Chris Read made 22 before falling, allowing Paul Franks to continue his fine start to the campaign.

Having pulled David Balcombe for a huge six, 'Mull' advanced to 97 before being fed a shocker from the same bowler – a wide half-tracker. Attempting to slash it away high over point for the runs he needed to bring up another hundred, the former Lancs man got a thin tickle instead and Pothas took the catch to send him away, clearly distraught.

Franks took up the attack and reached another half century before Tomlinson wrapped up the innings to claim a five-wicket haul. 270 was significantly greater than Notts could have hoped for, having lost four early wickets, and on a greenish wicket it still looked to be a competitive total.

With Darren Pattinson removing Liam Dawson before the close, there were plenty of positives for the home camp to take from the day, particularly the fine effort from Steven Mullaney.

"I'm a bit gutted not to get three figures again," he said

Steven Mullaney was cruelly denied just short of his century

afterwards. *"But if someone had offered me 97 at the beginning of the day I'd have taken it and it's just pleasing to be able to contribute once again."*

On the short, wide ball that he got out to, Steven said: *"I'm just unfortunate to have nicked it – nine times out of ten I would have hit it for four – but unfortunately this was the one occasion that I nicked it behind. Overall I'm happy to have scored a few and it's even more pleasing considering the position we were in to get up to 270, which I think is a competitive score."*

Having arrived at the crease at 19-3 it could have been a daunting task to go out there so early. *"I want to bat as high up the order as possible. I've been given the chance and I want to take it and make sure I stay in the side. To be fair they bowled well early on and I thought the first four dismissals were as a result of genuinely good deliveries. Sometimes it goes like that and there's not much you can do about it, but we bounced back well and now we're right back in it."*

Close of Day One – Hampshire – 23-1 (9 overs)

18th May – Day Two

Nottinghamshire were made to spend a full day in the field as Hampshire fought to overcome their less than impressive start to the campaign and nudge ahead of the early pace-setters after the first innings.

Nightwatchman James Tomlinson fell early on but Jimmy Adams and Chris Benham then combined with a partnership worth 115 in an attritional period either side of lunch.

Adams looked in good touch to reach a half century, but things didn't go for the home side. The normally reliable Edwards was unable to hang on to a sharp chance offered by the left-hander from the bowling of namesake Andre, and then Benham first survived a confident lbw appeal from Pattinson's bowling and then his nick only found the very tips of Chris Read's gloves.

Charlie Shreck made the breakthrough – knocking Benham's off pole back, heralding the start of a spell which brought three wickets for just 14 runs inside four overs.

Adams, like Mullaney a day earlier, fell within sight of a century. He'd collected 96 when he was caught behind off Franks, who then dismissed Vince in the same over, courtesy of a casual chip to midwicket.

Neil McKenzie put his recent poor form behind him to make 55 and Pothas, Ervine and Cork all got starts before Adams blew away the tail, right on close of play, shortly after Hampshire had established a narrow lead.

Mick Newell admitted that Notts hadn't helped themselves in the field. *"It's disappointing when catches go down, but it's not something I'm particularly worried about because we've got an excellent slip cordon and I rate Chris Read as the best in the world. We bowled well this morning without rewards but I'm pleased with the way we got on top later in the day."*

Close of Day Two – Hampshire 305 all out

The inside story of Nottinghamshire's LV= County Championship success

Great sight for a fast bowler as Charlie Shreck takes out Chris Benham

19th May – Day Three

Alex Hales' maiden first class century lit up the third day of the match, but with only Paul Franks offering too much in the way of support Nottinghamshire's lead was by no means an unassailable one.

Needing 281 from a minimum of 98 overs the visitors had reached seven without loss at the close.

Hales had arrived at the crease after half an hour's play when Shafayat's poor run of scores continued as he drove back to bowler Tomlinson. The catch was taken low down and the umpires conferred before sending 'Billy' on his way.

Neil Edwards and Samit Patel soon followed – both caught behind off Ervine – as Hampshire sensed an opportunity to press home their advantage.

Having been hit for a total of 197 Championship runs in the space of a fortnight by Steven Mullaney, his departure for just 7 boosted the fielding side even more, Dominic Cork's full-throttle appeal finding favour, although the batter had put in a good stride towards the ball.

Brown was quickly into his stride, hitting Tomlinson over the ropes at mid-wicket, and the same bowler was then driven down the ground as Hales brought up his 50.

The 21-year-old had made an early impression around the circuit as a punishing one day batsman, but in an innings of great maturity and responsibility he showed a great deal of common sense and patience.

Despite losing Brown with the score on 125, Alex pushed on, driving sweetly on both sides of the wicket. He brought up his century by using his feet to Rangana Herath and lofting him over the ropes at long on for six. He had occupied the crease for 214 minutes and had faced 194 balls.

Chris Read, in watchful mode, had kept Hales company for more than 30 overs for his 27 before losing his middle stump to Balcombe. The match was still very much in the balance, with the home side ahead by 185 with four wickets left.

Hales was next to go, driving Cork to extra cover for an excellent 136, but Franks, with 45, and Adams, with 26 not out, ensured that his work wasn't wasted.

A terrific three days of cricket had seen the match ebb and flow and no-one was confidently predicting the outcome, although it was easy to name Alex Hales as the man of the day for his splendid century.

"It's been an absolute dream come true today to get my maiden first class hundred in front of the home crowd and it's looking like the team is in a good position, so hopefully with our bowling attack we should be able to win this game."

Release of emotion as Alex Hales reaches three figures

On bringing up his century in such a stylish manner, Alex said: *"With the field up I was always looking to come down the track to him as I thought it would be difficult to pinch a single. I was just delighted to be able to pull it off.*

"At 40-4 there were a few things being said in the dressing room I'm sure, but I feel in good touch and am pleased to have made a contribution in a four day game.

"It was an important partnership with Chris Read in terms of the game and I was pleased that we managed to get through that and hopefully we've put enough runs on the board.

"It'll be key for our bowlers to keep hitting the pitch because it's kept a bit low and a few have bounced a bit – there's plenty of things happening out there, so hopefully we can pull through."

Close of Day Three – Hampshire 7-0 (2 overs)

20th May – Day Four

There can never be any satisfaction in losing a County Championship match but Nottinghamshire fought right until the very end and gave a decent crowd an 'edge-of-the-seat' climax before losing in the tensest of finishes.

Needing another 274 runs at the start of the day the visitors were giving a sound start by openers Adams and Dawson. Even when both fell in quick succession, to leave the chase standing at 52-2, Notts were unable to exert a real stranglehold on proceedings. The next two batsmen, Benham and McKenzie, settled easily and saw it through to lunch on 85-2.

McKenzie's pedigree is undisputed. A seasoned performer in the Test Match arena, he had joined the south coast club as a Kolpak player but hadn't made a half century for them prior to arriving at Trent Bridge. That had been rectified during the first innings and it was soon apparent that his dismissal was key if Notts were to make it a five in five start.

Andre Adams gave the home supporters renewed hope when his inswinger accounted for Benham early in the second session and Paul Franks ensured that James Vince wouldn't recall his contribution with any great fondness when he departed cheaply for the second time.

Although his second 50 of the match had been painstakingly slow (123 balls), McKenzie was still there at tea with his side on 178-4 and another 103 needed.

Sean Ervine went for 26, leg before to Patel, and then Pothas edged to Edwards at second slip off Pattinson. Notts' hopes were increasing – and the atmosphere inside the ground became electric when Dominic Cork fell to the second new ball. Flicking at Adams, he would have landed it on the front row of the Fox Road Stand had Alex Hales, at full stretch, not reached high above his head to make a sensational catch.

At 214-7, with 15 overs left, the match was in the balance. Hampshire needed 67 but only had three wickets remaining. The first of those, David Balcombe, only made 6 before 'Patto' trapped him in front.

Rangana Herath had resembled a walking wicket on the three previous occasions he'd wandered out to the middle against Notts this season and the home side would have felt confident of sending him back quickly.

McKenzie suddenly changed tack. From battling away with self-preservation for almost three and a half hours, he pressed the accelerator and hit Andre Adams for a couple of huge sixes to lift his side to the brink of victory.

Andre had put in a yeoman shift for his skipper, toiling away for hour upon hour on his return from injury. Understandably he began to tire, although with a touch of fortune he would have had Herath, who slashed wildly and lifted the ball high over gully to get a streaky four through the vacant third man area.

With his twelfth boundary McKenzie reached his century, but the celebrations were put on hold for another couple of overs before he finally extinguished home hopes with a six over mid-wicket to win the match with just seven balls remaining.

Despite the defeat Mick Newell remained fairly philosophical. *"I'm always disappointed to lose but we've seen a great game of four day cricket and having won four matches prior to this I can take it in a more relaxed fashion than I would if we'd made a poor start.*

"We worked hard today but Hampshire's top order batted for a long time and made it easier for their lower order with an older ball. We never gave up though and wickets after tea got us right back in it.

"With eight overs to go I thought they would play for a draw, but Neil McKenzie hit one into the stands and they kicked on again."

One touch of good news to end the day arrived via Taunton where Somerset had defeated Yorkshire, meaning that Notts had hung on to their lead at the top of the table.

SCORECARD

Nottinghamshire first innings		Runs	Balls	Mins	4s	6s
NJ Edwards	c Pothas b Cork	4	11	12	1	-
BM Shafayat	c Adams b Tomlinson	14	41	51	2	-
AD Hales	lbw b Tomlinson	0	6	5	-	-
SR Patel	c Pothas b Cork	11	16	17	2	-
SJ Mullaney	c Pothas b Balcombe	97	182	226	14	1
AD Brown	lbw b Ervine	42	46	65	6	1
*+CMW Read	c Pothas b Tomlinson	22	47	51	4	-
PJ Franks	not out	57	107	145	7	-
AR Adams	c Herath b Balcombe	8	17	9	1	-
DJ Pattinson	lbw b Tomlinson	8	38	37	1	-
CE Shreck	c Pothas b Tomlinson	0	1	1	-	-
Extras	(1 b, 2 lb, 4 nb)	7				
Total	(all out, 85 overs)	270				

Fall of wickets: 1-5 (Edwards, 3.2 ov), 2-6 (Hales, 4.5 ov), 3-19 (Patel, 9.4 ov), 4-29 (Shafayat, 12.5 ov), 5-107 (Brown, 28.5 ov), 6-147 (Read, 43 ov), 7-226 (Mullaney, 70.2 ov), 8-238 (Adams, 74.2 ov), 9-270 (Pattinson, 84.5 ov), 10-270 (Shreck, 85 ov)

Hampshire bowling	Overs	Mdns	Runs	Wkts	Wides	No-Balls
Tomlinson	25	7	66	5	-	-
Cork	13	2	43	2	-	-
Balcombe	17	1	92	2	-	1
Ervine	15	4	47	1	-	1
Herath	15	5	19	0	-	-

Hampshire first innings		Runs	Balls	Mins	4s	6s
JHK Adams	c Read b Franks	96	213	250	17	-
LA Dawson	c Read b Pattinson	4	8	22	1	-
JA Tomlinson	c Read b Pattinson	5	28	27	-	-
CC Benham	b Shreck	38	148	179	3	-
ND McKenzie	lbw b Pattinson	55	78	101	12	-
JM Vince	c Mullaney b Franks	0	4	3	-	-
*+N Pothas	lbw b Adams	22	82	102	2	-
SM Ervine	not out	31	45	63	4	-
DG Cork	c Read b Adams	11	10	12	2	-
DJ Balcombe	b Adams	4	14	10	1	-
HMRKB Herath	c Brown b Adams	1	4	14	-	-
Extras	(13 b, 14 lb, 10 nb, 1 w)	38				
Total	(all out, 104.5 overs)	305				

Fall of wickets: 1-21 (Dawson, 6.1 ov), 2-39 (Tomlinson, 14.1 ov), 3-154 (Benham, 64.2 ov), 4-168 (Adams, 67.2 ov), 5-168 (Vince, 68 ov), 6-242 (McKenzie, 90.1 ov), 7-249 (Pothas, 94.1 ov), 8-277 (Cork, 98.1 ov), 9-293 (Balcombe, 101 ov), 10-305 (Herath, 104.5 ov)

Notts bowling	Overs	Mdns	Runs	Wkts	Wides	No-Balls
Pattinson	24	7	58	3	-	5
Shreck	26	9	70	1	-	-
Adams	25.5	8	56	4	1	-
Franks	20	5	57	2	-	-
Mullaney	5	1	15	0	-	-
Patel	4	1	22	0	-	-

The inside story of Nottinghamshire's LV= County Championship success

Nottinghamshire second innings		Runs	Balls	Mins	4s	6s
NJ Edwards	c Pothas b Ervine	23	50	64	3	-
BM Shafayat	c and b Tomlinson	14	21	33	2	-
AD Hales	c Benham b Cork	136	254	290	15	1
SR Patel	c Pothas b Ervine	0	15	13	-	-
SJ Mullaney	lbw b Cork	7	23	36	1	-
AD Brown	lbw b Cork	15	31	52	1	1
*+CMW Read	b Balcombe	27	79	112	2	-
PJ Franks	c Pothas b Cork	45	44	55	10	-
AR Adams	not out	26	22	37	2	2
DJ Pattinson	b Ervine	7	11	15	1	-
CE Shreck	c Vince b Ervine	0	3	2	-	-
Extras	(11 lb, 2 nb, 2 w)	15				
Total	(all out, 92 overs)	315				

Fall of wickets: 1-25 (Shafayat, 8.3 ov), 2-55 (Edwards, 15.5 ov), 3-59 (Patel), 4-79 (Mullaney, 29.3 ov), 5-125 (Brown, 43.1 ov), 6-220 (Read, 74 ov), 7-264 (Hales, 83.2 ov), 8-293 (Franks, 87.5 ov), 9-315 (Pattinson, 91.3 ov), 10-315 (Shreck, 92 ov)

Hampshire bowling	Overs	Mdns	Runs	Wkts	Wides	No-Balls
Tomlinson	23	6	90	1	1	-
Cork	23	2	85	4	-	-
Ervine	15	2	31	4	-	1
Balcombe	18	1	60	1	1	-
Herath	13	3	38	0	-	-

Hampshire second innings		Runs	Balls	Mins	4s	6s
JHK Adams	c Read b Adams	21	57	76	3	-
LA Dawson	c Brown b Franks	21	81	96	3	-
CC Benham	b Adams	45	66	93	7	-
ND McKenzie	not out	115	228	276	13	3
JM Vince	c Read b Franks	8	14	16	2	-
SM Ervine	lbw b Patel	26	54	61	3	-
*+N Pothas	c Edwards b Pattinson	17	38	48	1	-
DG Cork	c Hales b Adams	1	7	5	-	-
DJ Balcombe	lbw b Pattinson	6	20	20	-	-
HMRKB Herath	not out	10	22	39	2	-
JA Tomlinson						
Extras	(4 b, 6 lb, 1 w)	11				
Total	(8 wickets, 97.5 overs)	281				

Fall of wickets: 1-42 (Adams, 20.2 ov), 2-52 (Dawson, 25.5 ov), 3-127 (Benham, 44.5 ov), 4-138 (Vince, 49.4 ov), 5-182 (Ervine, 67.5 ov), 6-213 (Pothas, 82.3 ov), 7-214 (Cork, 83.5 ov), 8-225 (Balcombe, 88.3 ov)

Notts bowling	Overs	Mdns	Runs	Wkts	Wides	No-Balls
Pattinson	21	4	51	2	-	-
Shreck	16	6	38	0	-	-
Adams	29.5	5	118	3	-	-
Franks	16	3	41	2	1	-
Patel	15	7	23	1	-	-

Match 6

NOTTINGHAMSHIRE v ESSEX

May 29th, 30th, 31st, June 1st 2010 (4 day match)
Venue: Trent Bridge, Nottingham
Toss: won by Nottinghamshire who elected to field
Umpires: PJ Hartley & VA Holder
Result: Match drawn
Points: Nottinghamshire 7 (Batting 1, Bowling 3)
Essex 9 (Batting 3, Bowling 3)

29th May – Day One

On a rain-ruined first day play didn't start until 5pm, with Essex batting after Chris Read had won the toss. In the 17 overs play that were then possible the visitors reached 61-2.

Nottinghamshire made two changes to their starting line-up to face Essex in their fifth home Championship match of the season. Mark Wagh returned – available again after taking exams – as did Ryan Sidebottom – now officially a World Champion after playing so successfully for England in the victorious ICC World twenty20 tournament.

Dropping out were Bilal Shafayat, paying the price for a sequence of low scores, and Charlie Shreck, who was the least impressive seamer in the previous match against Hampshire.

Tom Westley and Jaik Mickleburgh opened the innings for Essex and posted 27 in nine overs before Darren Pattinson parted them – Westley, pushing at a good length delivery just outside his off stump, nicked one through to Read.

Mickleburgh then played around a delivery from Andre Adams, bowling from the Pavilion End, and umpire Peter Hartley sent him on his way.

Ravi Bopara and Matt Walker saw it through to the close without any further loss.

Close of Day One – Essex 61-2 (Bopara 13*, Walker 2*, 17 overs)

30th May – Day Two

Nottinghamshire picked up a full compliment of bowling bonus points by dismissing Essex for 329 in their first innings but found themselves held up by the lower order – a characteristic of their own batting performances on so many occasions already this season.

From being 118-5 the visitors bounced back, initially due to a stand of 103 between James Foster and Mark Pettini.

David Masters then enjoyed a fruitful last session, adding 32 with the bat before picking up two late wickets as Notts began their reply.

— 48 —

The inside story of Nottinghamshire's LV= County Championship success

Darren Pattinson made the initial breakthrough on the first two days

The first wicket of the day fell to Darren Pattinson, who dismissed Matt Walker, who played around a full-pitched delivery. Ryan Sidebottom then got Ravi Bopara, also lbw.

Ryan ten Doeschate became the third batsman of the morning to fall to a leg before verdict, although umpire Vanburn Holder seemed to take an absolute age before giving Paul Franks the decision.

Foster and Pettini batted together for two and a half hours, taking the score up to 221 before they were parted. The Essex 'keeper had hit 9 x 4s in a classy 59 before becoming the latest player to pick out Neil Edwards at second slip, from the bowling of Adams.

Pettini, Essex's captain, had struggled for runs during the early weeks of the season but began to find his touch as he powered on past fifty, helped by a lofted straight six off Patel.

Steven Mullaney – full of runs in the previous few matches – showed himself as a useful performer with the ball by dismissing Napier, Masters and Wright in quick succession.

He was then lofted for a maximum by Pettini, who reached 96 with the shot, but when he attempted a repeat it was edged through to Read, giving the bowler career-best figures of 4-31.

After his century in the previous game Alex Hales was promoted to open the innings but fell cheaply. A caught and bowl opportunity to Maurice Chambers was put down, but in the next over he was squared up and a leading edge went straight back to Masters, who comfortably held on.

Pattinson was sent out as nightwatchman but couldn't last the distance, clipping one to Walker in the slips.

At the close Neil Edwards was undefeated on 9 and he gave his assessment of the conditions.

"It's a pretty good wicket, I think. There were a lot of lbws in their innings, which means we've bowled straight. It looks like a good cricket wicket and is perhaps a bit more batter friendly than we've seen at Trent Bridge this season and it's definitely game on tomorrow."

What Do Points Make?

Read, Edwards and Brown are all in agreement

On the way Essex recovered from losing their first five wickets relatively cheaply, Neil said: *"You always find you are going to be up against a big partnership at some point in most matches and it's all about being up for it when it comes along.*

"Foster and Pettini played really nicely and left the ball well. We had the ball swinging and put it in the right areas, but they played time – something we haven't really seen anybody do at Trent Bridge this year, so all credit to them.

"It was a tricky spell at the end of the day – it's never nice as an opening batter, but that's my job, that's what I signed up for. Those eight over sessions are probably a no-win situation because you've got everything to lose and nothing to gain really. I've felt since the first game that a good innings was just around the corner – it's been very frustrating for me personally as I've got out after getting starts and tomorrow will be a big day for me."

Close of Day Two – Nottinghamshire 33-2
(Edwards 9*, Wagh 0*, 8 overs)

31st May – Day Three

For the first time during the season Nottinghamshire weren't able to scramble a recovery after making a poor start and picked up only one batting bonus point. Dismissed for only 217, they were 112 behind on first innings and their hopes of victory had decreased significantly when Essex again did well second time around.

The morning session saw the home side lose four cheap wickets against the visitors all-seam attack, although the overnight pair hung around for a fairly quiet opening hour.

Maurice Chambers, who had been fairly wild and woolly on the second day, then nipped one back to decapitate the off peg of Mark Wagh.

Samit Patel edged Chris Wright into the slip cordon and then Neil Edwards got into an awful mess in trying to avoid a Chambers 'round the wicket' bouncer and he looped it gently back to the bowler.

On the stroke of lunch Ali Brown fell for nought, lbw to Ryan ten Doeschate, making it 88-6. Not for the first time this season it looked as if Ali was on the rough end of a poor decision as he appeared to be hit well outside the line.

A stand of 101 in 18 overs between Steven Mullaney and Chris Read put the brakes on Essex's momentum as each man reached a half century, but then crucially fell in consecutive overs.

Mull's half century had come from 66 balls, with 7 x 4s and a maximum off Chambers, but he couldn't go on, presenting the same bowler with a third wicket as one flew off a length and took a thickish nick through to Pettini at slip.

Read had pulled Graham Napier for a couple of sixes to go to his 50 from 63 deliveries, but he followed his partner straight back to the dressing room by edging to Foster off Masters.

The twin success had left Notts still short of a first batting point and, although Paul Franks – who also hit two legside 6s – took the total beyond 200, he followed Andre Adams in being dismissed as the innings ended in the 59th over for just 217.

Both Franks and Adams were soon back in action with the ball and picked up a wicket apiece as the Essex openers both fell in the 20s, but Ravi Bopara and Matt Walker added an unbroken 82 before the close.

With the visitors holding the initiative after three days Steven Mullaney admitted it hadn't been one of Notts' better performances with the bat.

"We were disappointed with how the day went and did nothing to open anybody's eyes. Myself and Ready got 50 each but then got out after putting 100 on.

"We're playing on the other side of the square to what we've been playing on but 217 all out wasn't good enough – we didn't do ourselves justice. I think it's a decent wicket but we didn't bat well and got out to a few loose shots.

"We've just all had a talk after the game and we've all held our hands up and said it's not been good enough today so we've got to redeem ourselves tomorrow."

Despite Steven's optimism that the final day would bring a brighter showing from the home ranks, there was a less cheery outlook being promised by the weather forecasters – and sadly they were right!

Close of Day Three – Essex 152-2 (Bopara 57, Walker 46*, 43 overs)

1st June – Day Four

No play was possible on the final day of Nottinghamshire's sixth LV= County Championship match of the season, so a draw was added to the opening tally of four wins and one defeat.

It's probably worth remembering that with a potential 96 overs to be played at the start of the day, Essex were 264 runs ahead with eight wickets still in hand.

Speculation about what would have happened is obviously futile, but it rankled a little bit to read in one or two national newspaper reports the following day that 'Essex were denied a certain victory' and that 'Notts were saved by the weather'.

What Do Points Make?

Although I do have a tendency to always look on the optimistic side of things when it comes to Nottinghamshire's fortunes on the cricket field, I suspect that a draw would have been the eventual outcome again with a much better response in their second innings after Essex had batted until just before the lunch interval.

All that supposition was rendered meaningless as soon as dawn broke. Heavy overnight storms had saturated the whole of the East Midlands and a torrential downpour had given way to persistent drizzle.

The entire square and bowlers' run-ups had been adequately protected, but the chance of any play appeared slim from the outset.

To be fair to Peter Hartley and Vanburn Holder, they gave the conditions every chance to improve, thus ensuring that lunch and tea could be prepared (and consumed) before agreeing to call an end to proceedings shortly before four o'clock.

Seven points from the match saw Nottinghamshire move level with Yorkshire on 103 points – although Chris Read's side led the table on matches won – and still with a couple of games in hand on the White Rose county.

Essex collected nine points and left feeling cheated by the weather!

Nottinghamshire's next match was just four days away – against Kent at Tunbridge Wells – and the squad was about to be reinforced by the return of David Hussey to their ranks.

SCORECARD

Essex first innings		Runs	Balls	Mins	4s	6s
T Westley	c Read b Pattinson	17	37	41	-	1
JC Mickleburgh	lbw b Adams	10	29	59	1	-
RS Bopara	lbw b Sidebottom	22	42	68	3	-
MJ Walker	lbw b Pattinson	6	37	42	-	-
RN ten Doeschate	lbw b Franks	26	39	53	3	-
+JS Foster	c Edwards b Adams	59	136	170	9	-
*ML Pettini	c Read b Mullaney	96	209	254	9	2
GR Napier	lbw b Mullaney	12	15	14	3	-
DD Masters	c Patel b Mullaney	32	61	88	5	-
CJC Wright	c Read b Mullaney	0	10	7	-	-
MA Chambers	not out	1	8	8	-	-
Extras	(4 b, 32 lb, 12 nb)	48				
Total	(all out, 102.5 overs)	329				

Fall of wickets: 1-27 (Westley, 9.1 ov), 2-57 (Mickleburgh, 12.4 ov), 3-74 (Walker, 23.1 ov), 4-76 (Bopara, 24.5 ov), 5-118 (ten Doeschate, 36 ov), 6-221 (Foster, 69.3 ov), 7-240 (Napier, 74.3 ov), 8-320 (Masters, 98.3 ov), 9-322 (Wright, 100.4 ov), 10-329 (Pettini, 102.5 ov)

Notts bowling	Overs	Mdns	Runs	Wkts	Wides	No-Balls
Sidebottom	22	4	49	1	-	-
Pattinson	22	2	60	2	-	5
Adams	24	6	82	2	-	1
Franks	17	6	45	1	-	-
Patel	4	0	26	0	-	-
Mullaney	13.5	5	31	4	-	-

Nottinghamshire first innings		Runs	Balls	Mins	4s	6s
AD Hales	c and b Masters	6	14	11	1	-

The inside story of Nottinghamshire's LV= County Championship success

NJ Edwards	c and b Chambers	30	79	133	3	-
DJ Pattinson	c Walker b Masters	2	14	14	-	-
MA Wagh	b Chambers	10	62	76	2	-
SR Patel	c Walker b Wright	12	24	17	2	-
SJ Mullaney	c Pettini b Chambers	53	69	103	7	1
AD Brown	lbw b ten Doeschate	0	10	17	-	-
*+CMW Read	c Foster b Masters	52	64	83	6	2
PJ Franks	c ten Doeschate b Masters	23	17	23	1	2
AR Adams	c and b Napier	1	8	9	-	-
RJ Sidebottom	not out	0	0	5	-	-
Extras	(4 b, 6 lb, 18 nb)	28				
Total	(all out, 58.4 overs)	217				

Fall of wickets: 1-14 (Hales, 2.3 ov), 2-32 (Pattinson, 6.2 ov), 3-65 (Wagh, 26 ov), 4-84 (Patel, 30.2 ov), 5-84 (Edwards, 31.4 ov), 6-88 (Brown, 35.3 ov), 7-189 (Mullaney, 53.5 ov), 8-193 (Read, 54.4 ov), 9-202 (Adams, 57.2 ov), 10-217 (Franks, 58.4 ov)

Essex bowling	Overs	Mdns	Runs	Wkts	Wides	No-Balls
Masters	16.4	6	48	4	-	-
Chambers	15	3	63	3	-	8
Napier	14	3	47	1	-	1
Wright	12	1	44	1	-	-
ten Doeschate	1	0	5	1	-	-

Essex second innings		Runs	Balls	Mins	4s	6s
T Westley	c Edwards b Adams	23	32	44	4	-
JC Mickleburgh	lbw b Franks	25	59	83	3	-
RS Bopara	not out	57	91	114	5	1
MJ Walker	not out	46	76	71	6	1
RN ten Doeschate						
*ML Pettini						
+JS Foster						
GR Napier						
CJC Wright						
DD Masters						
MA Chambers						
Extras	(1 lb)	1				
Total	(2 wickets, 43 overs)	152				

Fall of wickets: 1-36 (Westley, 10.2 ov), 2-70 (Mickleburgh, 21.1 ov)

Notts bowling	Overs	Mdns	Runs	Wkts	Wides	No-Balls
Sidebottom	5	1	24	0	-	-
Pattinson	10	1	33	0	-	-
Adams	9	2	34	1	-	-
Franks	8	1	13	1	-	-
Patel	8	0	30	0	-	-
Mullaney	3	0	17	0	-	-

RYAN SIDEBOTTOM

As the rain continued to fall in Nottingham news came that Mick Newell's plans for that trip were thrown into disarray with Ryan Sidebottom being called back into the England Test squad. Fortunately, I was able to get a first hand reaction to the news from the delighted bowler:

Q – Ryan, as we speak the rain falls heavily over Trent Bridge, but there's cause for yourself to celebrate as you've been recalled into the England Test squad for this week's match against Bangladesh at Old Trafford.

Ryan: *"Yes, it's nice – obviously good news. This game, we're behind the eight ball and I've been pretty disappointed with the way I've bowled actually over the last couple of days, but I've not had much four day cricket so being called up to the Test squad I'm very excited and chuffed to bits. It might be some reward for the way I performed in Barbados with the 20/20.*

"I'm been delighted with my form in that, but four day cricket is a bit different.

"I've always felt that I was bowling a bit of a 20/20 line and length in this game, so hopefully I can improve on that if called in to the eleven that plays."

Q – Do you feel you've got enough work in during this game – you bowled just 27 overs and didn't get a bat?

Ryan: *"Yes and no – the ball is coming out ok and the ball is swinging but I've probably not bowled in the right areas, but that comes with bowling regularly in four-day cricket and I'll have a good bowl this week and we'll see how it's coming out. I'm a bit of a perfectionist and I like to bowl perfect every time I play but realise that's not the way it goes."*

Q – Bangladesh at Old Trafford, is that the ideal opposition and ground that you'd have picked to make your Test return on?

Ryan: *"Hopefully it will be fast and bouncy and Bangladesh are more used to slow, low wickets. I suppose Lord's was ideal for them and they performed really well. England can do better but they won the game so it was job done."*

Q – Tamim Iqbal likes to get the innings off to an explosive start. I guess one of the things is not to let him faze you if he does come at you early.

Ryan: *"No, definitely not – it's difficult. I suppose every bowler would say the same when the batsman are playing like that. It's difficult sometimes because you don't know whether you're bowling good balls or not. If they smack your good balls, where do you go from there? I'm sure we'll have plans for him. We'll see how it goes but its important not to get fazed or flustered by him. If you bowl a good ball and he hits it, then so be it, just carry on and make sure you bowl a good ball the next time."*

Q – Has life changed at all in the last three weeks – now you're a World Cup winner? Many congratulations on that, by the way.

Ryan: *"Thank you, it's been amazing. It's been nice to prove people wrong. People didn't give me a chance of playing when we were going out there, but I suppose I've done that for most of my career. I performed really well and was delighted that I contributed to us winning the world cup. It was a great feeling, absolutely unbelievable. I don't think it's quite sunk in yet what we managed to achieve. It was absolutely amazing"*

The inside story of Nottinghamshire's LV= County Championship success

Q – A lot of players are starting to get pigeon-holed as twenty20 specialists, one day specialists or even players who excel in the longer format. At least you can take satisfaction that you've excelled in all formats.

Ryan: *"I think I'm a little bit older now, maybe my test career is coming towards an end, but in one day cricket and 20/20 cricket I'm still capable. I've proved myself in all forms of the game over my career and I don't think I've anything else to prove now. The icing on the cake would obviously be going to the Ashes and performing in that, but we'll just have to wait and see – that's still too far ahead.*

"With the 20/20 I just like to embrace it – it's only four overs after all."

Q – Talking of the 20/20, the domestic competition is only just around the corner – Notts have assembled a strong squad for this year's tournament.

Ryan: *"Most definitely – like with England, you need to play to your potential and be consistent as a team. Obviously you need to be consistent as a team and your individuals need to play well, but if you play well as a team you can beat anyone."*

Q – You still have International aspirations, but this is your benefit season so it's great to see you keep nipping back into Trent Bridge. How is it going?

Ryan: *"It's going really well – so far we've just had a couple of dinners – people have been amazing, the support I've got has been fantastic. It just shows, maybe it's reward for the way I've played my cricket and the passion I've shown. People have been wonderful and I'd like to thank them all personally. It's just been amazing. I can't say much more than that really."*

I feel very humble to be in this position and Notts have been great to have given me this benefit, so I'd like to say a massive thank you to them as well."

Match 7

KENT v NOTTINGHAMSHIRE

June 4th, 5th, 6th, 7th 2010 (4 day match)
Venue: Nevill Ground, Tunbridge Wells
Toss: won by Nottinghamshire who elected to bat
Umpires: JH Evans & NJ Long
Result: Match drawn
Points: Kent 10 (Batting 5, Bowling 2)
Nottinghamshire 9 (Batting 5, Bowling 1)

4th June – Day One

A capacity crowd and the corporate marquees await the midday start

On a stiflingly hot day Nottinghamshire put themselves within sight of maximum batting bonus points, although they lost rather too many wickets on a docile track.

The opportunity to bat Kent out of the game seemed a possibility when Chris Read won the toss, but far too many players got starts and then fell to injudicious strokes, although Alex Hales again gave confirmation of his growing stature and the skipper also added useful runs towards the end of the day.

From the side that had drawn with Essex three days earlier Mick Newell made a couple of changes. David Hussey was now available to bolster the middle order, having spent a whirlwind few weeks which had incorporated his third stint with the Kolkata Knight Riders in the Indian Premier League, the ICC World twenty20 tournament in the Caribbean and a return to Australia to get married.

To incorporate the return of 'Huss' there was a bit of re-jigging done at the top of the order, with Neil Edwards omitted and Samit Patel invited to open the batting.

The inside story of Nottinghamshire's LV= County Championship success

Ryan Sidebottom's recall to England's Test squad for the match against Bangladesh at Old Trafford (although, infuriatingly for all Notts followers, he was made twelfth man!) also meant a bowling vacancy, which was filled by Graeme White.

The slow left arm spinner had arrived at Trent Bridge during the winter as a rapidly improving bowler, a more than capable batter and an excellent fielder. Graeme himself thought that opportunities for four day cricket during his first season would be limited, but on a dry, dusty surface – with their hosts also going in with two front-line spinners (Tredwell and Herath) – the Notts Director of Cricket handed the 23-year-old a first class debut for his new county.

Edwards' omission was understandable – in part. He had begun the Championship season in fine style, but after eleven innings had only totalled 189 runs at an average of 21. Nine of those innings had been at Trent Bridge however, and anyone who has followed Notts' fortunes over the years will know that it has become increasingly difficult for opening batsmen to succeed there during the early weeks of each season.

Neil's frustration at missing out would have been compounded by the fact that his one decent score (85) had come against Kent – and also that the Tunbridge Wells fixture looked to be one that would favour the batsmen.

Of a more trivial irritation, Edwards had found himself locked neck and neck with Kent's Martin van Jaarsveld as the joint leading catchers in the country, with 15 apiece. At least the return of Hussey gave Notts a more than adequate replacement in the slip cordon.

Samit Patel had also made a poorish start to the first class summer with the bat, and Mick Newell confirmed later that he had also been an option to make way for Hussey but that his ability with the ball had worked in his favour.

Newell had also hoped that Samit would show a little more restraint when elevated to open the batting as impetuosity had got the better of him on too many occasions, and so it proved again when play got under way at the picturesque Nevill Ground.

Although Alex Hales had got off to a bit of a flyer in an opening stand of 43, Samit had looked less at ease and had only made 10 when he chased a wide one from Simon Cook and toe-edged it through to wicketkeeper Geraint Jones.

With the rhododendrons in full bloom and the ground bulging to capacity from early in the morning (many had missed the advance notification that the first day would begin an hour later than normal, at midday, due to Kent's twenty20 floodlit fixture at The Rose Bowl, Southampton, the previous evening) there was a true carnival atmosphere to be enjoyed at this most traditional of festival out-grounds.

The sun-drenched conditions were as far removed from the rain and drizzle which wiped out play at Trent Bridge just a few days earlier and the batsmen seemed determined to make the most of them as a century stand then followed between Hales and Mark Wagh.

Alex Hales had batted superbly – and at a fairly rapid rate. His fifty came off 56 balls in just 67 minutes and a century before lunch looked a possibility. Kent were just about able to check his progress a little however, and he went to the interval on an unbeaten 84 out of a total of 146-1.

It looked as if the home attack would be in for a tough afternoon session, but instead they turned the tables, helped by a mixture of over-confident and ill-disciplined batting – as well as some canny spin bowling.

Unexpectedly, having eased to 44, Wagh fell in a carbon copy fashion to Patel – minimal foot movement and a bottom edge giving Cook another gifted wicket.

What Do Points Make?

Having hit a couple of huge maximums, Hales was on the brink of his second century of the season when he fell five runs short. He'd faced only 121 balls (13 x 4s and 2 x 6s) when he was squared up by Sri Lankan Test leg-spinner Malinga Bandara and a leading edge looped back to the bowler.

Steven Mullaney became the third batsman to fall to the Cook/Jones combination when a delivery jagged back and took an inside edge.

Ali Brown and David Hussey steadied the ship with a stand worth 69 in almost an hour before both fell to spin. Brown was caught behind off Tredwell for 39 and then Hussey, who had sneaked quietly up to 52 and was beginning to look as if he was just about ready to accelerate, tried to pull Bandara away but bottom-edged onto his stumps.

Chris Read and Paul Franks moved the total on to 317 before the latter became the seventh batsman to be dismissed, given out lbw with Tredwell bowling around the wicket.

Andre Adams' eye was in, which was bad news for those enjoying some corporate hospitality as a couple of lusty blows landed amongst the marquees and sent the drinkers scattering.

The second new ball was taken belatedly and it brought Cook a fourth wicket as Adams chopped on, but then Kent suffered a huge blow, with Amjad Khan appearing to pull a hamstring and having to leave the field – Bandara completed an unfinished over for him.

With play going on until seven o'clock, due to the late start, most patrons felt they'd had a full day's entertainment when the players trooped off with Notts on 393-8 and it was so refreshing to observe that Kent – largely due to the amount of work undertaken by their two spinners – had got through 103 overs in the day.

Credit and commiserations were offered to Alex Hales, who had been dismissed just short of his century. *"Obviously if someone had offered me 95 before the game I would probably have taken it so I'm pretty pleased to have scored it but a little bit disappointed not to have got there. I didn't really change the way I played all along so there was not a lot I could have done about it."*

Hales had got into his stride literally from the first ball of the day, which he'd cut away for four. *"I was lucky enough to get a loosener from Amjad Khan first up so was pleased I managed to put it away and from then on I felt in good touch and was happy to be able to cash in."*

Was the elusive century before lunch ever in his sights? *"Tredwell and Bandara are two very experienced campaigners – two good bowlers who are tough to get away, so I thought I'd just try and pick them off and score off the bad balls and I was pleased I managed to do that until I fell just before the hundred."*

It had been the second game in succession in which Alex had been caught and bowled, so did he feel it was an area of concern? *"I've had a couple of jokes about that in the changing room. I don't think it's a problem, I was just a bit lax in the shot and hopefully I can put it right in the second innings.*

"I'm enjoying opening at the moment and that's probably the main spot that's available as we've got such a strong middle order. Opening seems to be the spot that I need to nail down and I feel in good touch and hopefully I can keep it going.

"I think we'd have taken our present score at the start of the day, but having been 150-1 we probably should have been looking for 450 plus in our first innings, but the two spinners have bowled well and Cook's obviously bowled well so I'd say it's fairly even at the moment."

Close of Day One – Nottinghamshire 393-8
(Read 72*, White 6*, 103 overs)

5th June – Day Two

The Nevill Ground – perfect for a lunchtime stroll

Saturday's Tunbridge Wells crowd was just as impressive and again they got full value for their admission price (£20 on the gate – plus £10 for car parking!). The sun continued to beat down, on a bone-hard track, as Nottinghamshire extended their first innings total to 462 but were then made to toil for the five wickets they were able to garner before stumps.

One or two expectant Kent members were overheard before the start of the day's play pronouncing that the last two wickets would be quickly mopped up. As it happened the visitors scored another 69 runs in 21 overs, with Chris Read advancing to his second century of the summer.

His overnight partner, Graeme White, showed some steely determination to ensure his skipper was able to reach three figures. The only surprise was that it actually surprised some people. Graeme had been batting exceptionally well for the seconds prior to his call-up, scoring an unbeaten century in the Trophy, and he looked relatively untroubled before edging Matt Coles to slip for 29.

Read had gone to three figures with a push to mid off, from his 165th delivery, and had reached 112 when the innings ended as last man Darren Pattinson fell to a bat-pad catch on the off side from the bowling of Bandara.

The total looked a useful one – and bore a resemblance to the 456 that Notts had scored when batting first against Kent in the opening match of the campaign. Rob Key's side folded twice on that occasion in the face of some spirited seam bowling.

It looked a tall order to expect something similar to occur on a flat wicket, but visiting supporters were given something to cheer about right at the start of the reply though.

Over the two previous seasons in the annual fixture in the Royal Spa town, opener Joe Denly had scored 0 and 149 in 2008 and 0 and 123 a year later. If it was a sequence of sorts, it continued with the first ball of the innings.

Denly, who had enjoyed a brief spell opening in ODIs for England just a few months earlier, fenced at the first delivery of the innings and steered Pattinson to David Hussey at second slip.

If Notts had needed a lift they'd got one, but that early breakthrough didn't herald a collapse and Geraint Jones put on 53 with his skipper, Rob Key, before he also found the safe hands of 'Huss', this time from the bowling of Andre Adams.

Another solid stand – worth 75 in 20 overs – was broken when Adams found the edge of van Jaarsveld's bat. The former South African Test player had looked in decent touch as he danced down the wicket and plonked Graeme White over the ropes at the Railway End (one of the more unusual End names around the circuit as not a single train was seen or heard during the entire four days!).

Van Jaarsveld always appears to be unready for his next delivery – his bat is held high above his head when in his normal stance – but on most occasions it comes down sweetly to drive the ball away. Just before tea he drove down the wrong line however and a touch of away-wobble from Andre ended his stay out in the middle.

Soon after the break it was four down, and three of them were to Adams, who rushed one through Sam Northeast's tentative push and sent the off stump cartwheeling back towards fine leg.

Key had gone to a painstakingly slow 50 off 135 deliveries, bringing up the landmark with a clubbed six into the marquees off Patel.

Samit got his revenge soon afterwards, though in confusing circumstances. Key attempted a sweep and appeared to be struck on the pad. The bowler appealed excitedly, and after a fair amount of deliberation umpire Llong sent the batsman on his way.

It later transpired however that the ball had taken an edge and flown to Ali Brown at slip and that was the official mode of dismissal!

I assume that Paul Franks was just enquiring about what happened when he found himself in a seemingly heated debate with the Kent captain as he trudged off – either way, the officials seemed keen to end the animated discussion fairly swiftly.

With the top five in their batting order all out, the home county suddenly found themselves in a spot of turmoil – still 286 runs behind.

As elderly Latin scholars and modern-day tattoo artists might suggest, 'Carpe Diem'. But Nottinghamshire weren't able to 'seize the day', the moment or indeed the next few sessions because Darren Stevens and James Tredwell clearly had their own agenda.

By the close the pair had added an unbroken 98 as the sapping conditions began to take their toll on a tiring bowling attack. Stevens advanced past fifty for the sixth time already in the early weeks of the season and he found a reliable partner in the left-handed 'Tredders'.

Close of Day Two – Kent 274-5
(Stevens 80*, Tredwell 35*, 75 overs)

6th June – Day Three

Darren Pattinson and Andre Adams enjoy some batting practice before the start of play

Normally by the time the paying public have entered any sort of entertainment event any behind-the-scenes-wrinkles have been smoothly ironed out. Such was the case on the third morning of this particular contest, but not before there had been a great deal of fluster and concern when umpire Nigel Llong confessed to having taken the key to the match officials' room home with him overnight and forgotten to bring it back.

How far away he'd travelled from Tunbridge Wells wasn't clear, but as time ticked on it was looking like we might have the unusual situation of being ready to start but with an absence of one or two key ingredients – the match ball for starters!

Thankfully, in the nick of time, the groundstaff managed to unearth a spare key and all was well again – and one slightly embarrassed umpire could breathe a huge sigh of relief.

Also spotted on the ground was a former favourite of both participating counties, Mark Ealham, who was clearly enjoying catching up with some old friends, as he told me:

"It's always nice to come down to Tunbridge Wells – it's always been a really good place to visit and when these two teams were put together it seemed a good chance to come along and catch up with a few people. I stayed in the hotel with the Notts boys last night and we went out for dinner together."

Mark had retired from the first class game at the end of the 2009 season.

What Do Points Make?

"Life is very different now – but I'm not missing the training. I'm Head of Cricket at King's School in Canterbury, which is a very different challenge for me. I started in October and am really enjoying things. My main job is to work with the seniors, but I do get to spend a bit of time with the juniors as well, so it's right up from the age of around seven really and right across the age groups. My dad coached there as well and I've been down there for the last couple of winters having a few meetings and putting a few things in place.

"Leaving the first class game as a player I needed to go away and get some experience as a coach and I'm really enjoying working at King's."

A member of Nottinghamshire's title-winning side in 2005, it's no surprise that Mark looks back on his time with the county with great affection.

"I have great memories, especially from the Championship year. After being at Kent for so long and coming close a few times, then to go and win it in just my second year at Notts – and to win it at Canterbury as well – was very special. The boys have made a good start this year, so who knows, they could be on to win it in 2010 as well!"

Sunday's crowd was way down on that of the first two days and those that did come were deprived of a final session when a violent thunderstorm sent the players off for an early tea – and an ultimately early conclusion.

Resuming together, Darren Stevens and James Tredwell batted through the morning session, adding another 125 together with minimum fuss.

Stevens had motored to a splendid century, from just 105 deliveries, and Tredwell had continued to foil the visitors as he moved past fifty.

The stand not only stretched beyond 200, to bring up maximum batting bonus points, but then also broke a new ground record, beating the 233, the highest ever stand at the Nevill, set up by Dickie Mayes and Bill Murray-Wood for Kent against Sussex in 1952.

Notts had spent 65 overs in pursuit of a wicket and Tredwell had reached his third career ton before he chipped one back to Graeme White, who took a sharp catch low down. The stand had been worth 270.

Stevens had moved on to 181 when the impending dark clouds arrived and the players beat a hasty retreat in time to witness a spectacular electric storm, complete with deafening thunder, prolonged lightning and persistent rain.

It had seemed inevitable after the intense humidity of the previous couple of days and most people had left the ground long before the 5pm announcement that play had been abandoned for the day.

Darren Pattinson confirmed that it had been a fairly unresponsive surface for all of the Notts bowlers.

"We rocked up here thinking we could use the spinners to our advantage, but to be fair the wicket's been very good, it hasn't really turned off the good part of the wicket at all.

"We have all been battling pretty hard – we had them 5 down for 176 or something – but they've put on a really good partnership and we've struggled to get wickets since."

Stevens, in particular, had looked very secure out in the middle. *"There's not much else you can do apart from keep trying and come up with ways other than nicking people off to get a wicket. We've tried hard, tried pretty much everything, but still can't get rid of him."*

Patto's recent form had sparked comparisons with that of 2008 when he'd burst into county cricket and been rushed into the Test arena.

"I think I'm almost back to my best. I've worked hard on my fitness and worked hard with Hendo (Mike Hendrick). I think it's imperative you have someone there you can speak to. You don't have to take everything in

that he says, but as long as you get something out of it. He's always there if there's something you want to talk about and it's worked brilliantly so far this season.

"It's pretty difficult, especially being a bowler, to play year in, year out. I think this is my fourth season in a row now without a break. It's pretty tough, but the body's pretty good and sometimes it's more in the mind than anything. You've got to be up for every game – that's the hard part – but I feel I've done OK this year."

Despite appearing to be one of the most in-form seamers around the circuit, Darren admitted he wasn't expecting further international recognition. *"I've had my one go. I'd be very surprised if I played again. It's tough playing in Australia as well as here. I just like to give my best efforts for Notts now."*

The day had also brought a welcome first Championship wicket for his new county for Graeme White, who reflected that maybe it wasn't the ideal track upon which to make an impact.

"We thought it might have turned a little bit more. It's a very good batting deck and its been very hard graft for all the bowlers. The seamers have done especially well for us in this game and I thought Dre (Adams) bowled beautifully.

"It's a tough wicket and you are going to come across tough wickets, but I've enjoyed every minute of it and it's an absolute honour to play for Notts and I'm really enjoying it.

"I was especially glad to get the wicket because they'd put on a very good partnership and made it tough for us – but it was very nice to make the breakthrough as it opened up an end for us."

Close of Day Three – Kent 478-6
(Stevens 181* Coles 11*, 127 overs)

7th June – Day Four

Long before the obligatory 5pm handshake this contest had been consigned to the history books as a draw, but there were a couple of notable final day landmarks for Nottinghamshire players to enjoy first.

Andre Adams collected his first five wicket haul for the county and Samit Patel showed a return to form with the bat on his way to his first Championship half century of the summer.

When play began, in front of a fairly sparse fourth day crowd, home concerns were directed towards Darren Stevens, who was within sight of the third double hundred of his career and also a lifetime best 208.

Neither eventuality was fulfilled as the former Leicestershire man played a rare loose shot, away from his body, and Chris Read took a low catch in front of him. There was an obvious air of disappointment around Stevens as he sloped off, but he'd realised a classy 197 and rescued his side from a poorish start to their reply.

That dismissal had been Adams' fifth of the innings as in the previous over he'd gone round the wicket to the left-handed Matt Coles and angled one into him which surgically uprooted the middle stump.

Paul Franks claimed the two final wickets to fall, but not before Malinga Bandara and Simon Cook had also spent time in the middle, adding 53 for the ninth wicket.

Kent had taken a first innings lead of 108 and on another surface – and on another day – perhaps they may have been able to exert some pressure on the opposition but Notts made 210-3 in the 62 overs before the close.

The scoreboard tells the story as 'Huss' goes through his morning work-out

Alex Hales again started brightly, with three boundaries out of 13 runs, but he then fell to a sucker punch as Matt Coles dropped one in halfway down and 'Bas' obligingly pulled it to deep mid-wicket, where Warren Lee, the substitute fielder, pouched an easy catch.

Mark Wagh and David Hussey played a few aggressive shots in brief cameos worth 34 and 22 respectively, but it was Samit Patel who profited most from this final afternoon 'net' with an impressive 76 not out, which included a huge maximum off Tredwell.

With Nottinghamshire's twenty20 campaign about to start at Worcester in three days' time, it was good to see Samit finding a bit of form with the bat and for the side as a whole to head off into the 'crash, bang, wallop' format of the game knowing they were still top of the Division One table.

So lots of positives for Mick Newell to reflect on.

"It was a good pitch really for batting on – it didn't deteriorate as perhaps people hoped it would and that kind of killed the game a little bit, but we were happy to go away with a draw really.

"There were lots of positives on the batting side – I was pleased with that – but I would have liked us to have made more runs at the top of the order in the first innings, but Samit got an important three hours in the middle there, so hopefully he will be feeling a bit more confident. So, yes, lots of good things and I thought our three seam bowlers did well in the first innings – we had a little sniff when we had them 176-5 but couldn't make it pay."

On Andre's first five wicket haul for the county, the Director of Cricket said: "It's about time – he's had lots of fours and he has made major contributions in a lot of victories so it's a very satisfying personal milestone for him."

Nottinghamshire County Cricket Club – April 2010

Back row: (left to right), Kevin Paxton (Fitness Coach), Akhil Patel, Alex Hales, Andy Carter, Luke Fletcher, Graeme White, Steven Mullaney, Bilal Shafayat, Ross Hollinworth (physio)

Middle row: (left to right), Wayne Noon (Assistant Manager), Samit Patel, Darren Pattinson, Charlie Shreck, Neil Edwards, Alistair Brown, Andre Adams, Matt Wood, Paul Johnson (Club Coach)

Front row: (left to right), Stuart Broad, Ryan Sidebottom, Hashim Amla, Mick Newell (Director of Cricket), Chris Read (Captain), Paul Franks, Mark Wagh, Graeme Swann

The rhododendrons are in full bloom as Notts practise on the outfield at Tunbridge Wells

"Are they talking about us?" Kent's Darren Stevens and James Tredwell return to the crease during their 270 run stand

Above: Out for 95 – Disappointment for Alex Hales as a leading edge carries back to Kent's Malinga Bandara... although these spectators (below) had other priorities

Happy Daze!

Sunshine celebrations against Somerset (above) and Hampshire (below)

"Good name for a stand," muses Marcus Trescothick at first slip – and even the Mexicans came to watch us at Taunton (below)

Plenty of beards around at the start of the season – Bilal Shafayat and Hashim Amla compare notes (above), whilst Andre Adams sports the 'mean look' with umpire Peter Willey watching on (right)

High Five or Low Five? Stuart Broad and Samit Patel find a common ground

Paul Franks leads the team in their own version of the New Zealand 'Haka'

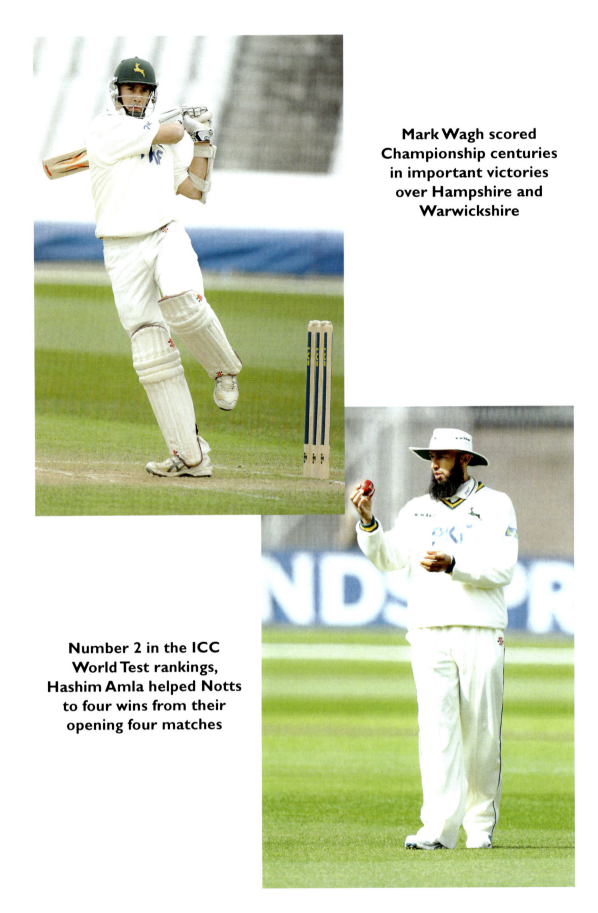

Mark Wagh scored Championship centuries in important victories over Hampshire and Warwickshire

Number 2 in the ICC World Test rankings, Hashim Amla helped Notts to four wins from their opening four matches

Samit Patel bowling in the Trent Bridge win over Durham. Jeff Evans is the umpire

Perfect action – perfect season! 68 County Championship wickets for Andre

You beauty! Luke Fletcher traps Somerset's James Hildreth

Outstanding in his field! Just one Championship appearance for Graeme White but his athleticism ensured he was a regular in the one-day side

Another day at the office – Director of Cricket Mick Newell

Amusement for the naughty boys in the back row!

Done with dignity – Glenn Chapple did his best for Lancashire but concedes defeat at the end of the Trent Bridge match

Paul Franks inspired the fightback against Yorkshire but evidence of the 59 all out remains on the Trent Bridge scoreboard

**"It's all about maintaining your balance."
The skipper gives Ali Brown some coaching tips**

Eyes on the ball? Alex Hales swoops in close

Doing their bit for charity – the players often featured in local matches for good causes. Dirk Nannes (top) gets a game as he prepares for the twenty20 campaign

**David Hussey –
key contributions during the
middle of the season as well
as skippering the side to the
twenty20 Finals Day**

A relaxed and happy dugout

A long way from home! David Hussey and Dirk Nannes beneath the imposing Lumley Castle at Durham

The Outlaws' hopes were washed out on twenty20 Finals Day, but the Mascot Race went ahead. Can you spot Nuts the Squirrel?

The inside story of Nottinghamshire's LV= County Championship success

Mick also admitted that he was pleased with how the first part of the season had gone. *"From the first seven games, to have won four is a tremendous effort. In the last two games we have not made winning chances so you have to live with that sometimes, but it just shows how important it was to win those first four games. The focus now switches to the twenty20 and we'd like to go well in that – we're looking forward to getting stuck into it."*

SCORECARD

Nottinghamshire first innings		Runs	Balls	Mins	4s	6s
AD Hales	c and b Bandara	95	121	147	13	2
SR Patel	c Jones b Cook	10	21	39	2	-
MA Wagh	c Jones b Cook	44	94	90	4	1
DJ Hussey	b Bandara	52	70	100	7	-
SJ Mullaney	c Jones b Cook	1	4	2	-	-
AD Brown	c Jones b Tredwell	39	54	58	7	-
*+CMW Read	not out	112	177	226	9	1
PJ Franks	lbw b Tredwell	17	61	57	2	-
AR Adams	b Cook	35	52	46	3	2
GG White	c Tredwell b Coles	29	77	72	3	-
DJ Pattinson	c Denly b Bandara	5	15	16	1	-
Extras	(4 b, 14 lb, 4 nb, 1 w)	23				
Total	(all out, 124 overs)	462				

Fall of wickets: 1-43 (Patel, 9.5 ov), 2-154 (Wagh, 37.3 ov), 3-172 (Hales, 40.4 ov), 4-173 (Mullaney, 41.4 ov), 5-242 (Brown, 56.5 ov), 6-266 (Hussey, 65.2 ov), 7-317 (Franks, 84.5 ov), 8-386 (Adams, 99.5 ov), 9-444 (White, 119.3 ov), 10-462 (Pattinson, 124 ov)

Kent bowling	Overs	Mdns	Runs	Wkts	Wides	No-Balls
Khan	19.5	3	77	0	-	2
Coles	6	0	37	1	-	-
Cook	22	2	85	4	1	-
Bandara	40.1	5	125	3	-	-
Tredwell	36	4	120	2	-	-

Kent first innings		Runs	Balls	Mins	4s	6s
JL Denly	c Hussey b Pattinson	0	1	1	-	-
*RWT Key	c Brown b Patel	56	156	200	3	1
+GO Jones	c Hussey b Adams	37	60	56	6	-
M van Jaarsveld	c Read b Adams	44	58	80	5	1
SA Northeast	b Adams	12	25	18	1	-
DI Stevens	c Read b Adams	197	238	342	24	2
JC Tredwell	c and b White	115	226	252	19	-
MT Coles	b Adams	22	42	41	2	-
HMCM Bandara	c Hales b Franks	29	39	56	1	1
SJ Cook	not out	26	41	55	2	1
A Khan	b Franks	5	6	3	1	-
Extras	(3 b, 12 lb, 6 nb, 6 w)	27				
Total	(all out, 148.1 overs)	570				

— 65 —

What Do Points Make?

Fall of wickets: 1-0 (Denly, 0.1 ov), 2-53 (Jones, 17.1 ov), 3-128 (van Jaarsveld, 37 ov), 4-142 (Northeast, 44.2 ov), 5-176 (Key, 55.1 ov), 6-446 (Tredwell, 120.1 ov), 7-504 (Coles, 133 ov), 8-511 (Stevens, 134.5 ov), 9-564 (Bandara, 146.3 ov), 10-570 (Khan, 148.1 ov)

Notts bowling	Overs	Mdns	Runs	Wkts	Wides	No-Balls
Pattinson	21	5	89	1	-	1
Adams	31	2	106	5	-	1
White	23	3	104	1	2	-
Franks	28.1	6	75	2	-	-
Mullaney	5	0	33	0	-	1
Patel	37	6	129	1	-	-
Hussey	3	0	19	0	-	-

Nottinghamshire second innings		Runs	Balls	Mins	4s	6s
AD Hales	c sub b Coles	13	18	20	3	-
SR Patel	not out	76	186	198	10	1
MA Wagh	b Tredwell	34	91	111	6	-
DJ Hussey	b Bandara	22	31	21	2	1
SJ Mullaney	not out	48	47	40	8	-
GG White						
AD Brown						
*+CMW Read						
PJ Franks						
DJ Pattinson						
AR Adams						
Extras	(5 b, 10 lb, 2 nb)	17				
Total	(3 wickets, declared, 62 overs)	210				

Fall of wickets: 1-16 (Hales, 4.5 ov), 2-121 (Wagh, 41.1 ov), 3-150 (Hussey, 48.5 ov)

Kent bowling	Overs	Mdns	Runs	Wkts	Wides	No-Balls
Coles	8	1	35	1	-	1
Cook	7	4	9	0	-	-
Bandara	25	7	63	1	-	-
Tredwell	22	1	88	1	-	-

Match 8

ESSEX v NOTTINGHAMSHIRE

July 5th, 6th, 7th 2010
(match scheduled for 4 days but completed in 3)
Venue: The Ford County Ground, Chelmsford
Toss: won by Essex who elected to bat
Umpires: IJ Gould & G Sharp
Result: Essex won by 143 runs
Points: Essex 19 (Bowling 3) Nottinghamshire 3 (Bowling 3)

5th July – Day One

After almost four weeks of twenty20 cup action it's perhaps not altogether surprising that 15 wickets fell on the first day of Nottinghamshire's match with Essex at The Ford County Ground in Chelmsford.

Both sides seemed in an awful hurry to get things moving and by the close Notts had reached 126-5, having dismissed their hosts earlier in the day for just 154.

The visiting line-up showed three changes from the starting eleven that drew at Tunbridge Wells in the previous match. David Hussey, Graeme White and Darren Pattinson were replaced by Bilal Shafayat, Luke Fletcher and Charlie Shreck.

With both Australia and Pakistan sending touring teams to the UK during the summer, it was frustrating for Notts that two twenty20 internationals between the nations would coincide with their return to Championship action. As a regular member of the Aussies side in that format it was inevitable that 'Huss' would be asked to play.

Essex were considered likely to favour a turning pitch and to play two spinners, so

Charlie Shreck bowling on the first morning

Graeme White might again have come into consideration for a place, but in the end Notts again opted for a four-pronged seam attack, with Steven Mullaney and Samit Patel as alternative options. Darren Pattinson had a slight niggle in his ankle, so Fletcher and Shreck returned.

What Do Points Make?

Since the May meeting at Trent Bridge (the one where Essex felt they were robbed by the weather) Mark Pettini had been replaced as captain by James Foster, and when Chris Read called incorrectly it was his opposite number who leapt at the chance to bat first.

Within a short space of time that looked an indifferent decision, although Essex's first casualty was self-inflicted. John Maunders pushed Luke Fletcher out onto the off side. To be fair, the batsman called immediately, sprinted hard and tried to slide his bat in.

Considering those three elements will tell you how bad a run it was because Steven Mullaney, sharpened up by weeks of doing the same thing in white ball cricket, swooped on the ball and threw down the stumps at the non-striker's end – scintillating fielding from one of the best around.

Almost immediately it was 11-2 when Charlie Shreck nipped one through the defences of Jaik Mickleburgh to pick up his 300th first class wicket.

Andre Adams then had a double cause for celebration. Billy Godleman and Matt Walker, both experienced left-handers, could do nothing to prevent the bowler getting them both out in the same over in almost identical fashion – a little bit of bounce and away movement and Chris Read did the rest.

The 'keeper pouched his third victim when Tom Westley was squared up by Paul Franks and the home side were just about able to limp along to the luncheon interval without any further loss, at 58-5.

Read's fourth and fifth catches of the innings both came from the bowling of Shreck, to whom Pettini and Foster had no answer. Tim Phillips hung around to make 46 not out, and support from David Masters, with 20, and Maurice Chambers, who added a career-best 14, saw the innings close on 154 just before the scheduled tea break.

Read had claimed a sixth catch – for the seventh time in his career – when Kaneria had nibbled at one from Franks, who finished with 3-20.

Notts soon discovered that life wasn't going to be any easier for them with the bat. Both openers went quickly to the pace of Maurice Chambers, Shafayat trapped in his crease for 1 and Hales clean-bowled for 9.

Mullaney also fell cheaply to Chambers, lbw, either side of two wickets for Tim Phillips, who dismissed both Wagh and Patel.

Once again it was left to old hands Brown and Read to dig in with a stand of 54 and halt the count of wickets at fifteen for the day.

Afterwards, the Notts skipper assessed the overall situation:

"I think we are marginally in the ascendancy as we're only 28 behind with five wickets still in hand and I'd like to think the last five wickets will do slightly better than the first five.

"It was a tough day for the batsmen. Our bowlers swung the ball around nicely all day and their fellas got some good seam movement out of the pitch. It's not been every ball by any means, it was quite sporadic at times. It's one of those pitches that keep you honest."

On taking six catches in an innings Chris was reminded that Wayne Noon still holds the Notts record with seven, taken in a match against Kent at Trent Bridge in 1999.

"Yes, Wayne has just reminded me of that, but as any keeper knows, it's the bowlers that create dismissals and I was just fortunate to be on the end of them."

The sixth wicket stand between Chris and Ali Brown perhaps holds the key to the size of Nottinghamshire's first innings lead. *"We didn't really want the day to end as we were going along nicely. We need to keep going in the morning, get past them and look to build a decent lead."*

— 68 —

The inside story of Nottinghamshire's LV= County Championship success

Charlie Shreck revealed that he knew he was on the brink of his 300th wicket at the start of play.

"Yes, it's probably one of the only stats I've ever been aware of, but my girlfriend's father told me a couple of games ago and I didn't manage to get a wicket on that occasion. There wasn't really much to it – it was just a stock ball and he inside-edged it onto the stumps, so I can't really claim it was anything special."

Close of Day One – Nottinghamshire 126-5
(Brown 30*, Read 31*, 34 overs)

6th July – Day Two

Essex enjoyed much the better of the second day, ending it 239 runs ahead with six wickets still in hand. They'd made early inroads during the morning session to restrict Notts to a first innings lead of just 26 and then, thanks to John Maunders, Jaik Mickleburgh and Matt Walker, they had created a platform for a formidable, potentially match-winning second innings total.

There's no doubt that Essex's young cricketers can tap into a wealth of experience as they make their way in the game. Aside from head coach Paul Grayson, three veterans of the Test arena were assisting in the pre-start work-outs.

Graham Gooch, 118 appearances at the highest level behind him, Grant Flower, the Zimbabwean all-rounder, and Chris Silverwood, a workhorse who would run in all day for you, were enthusiastically putting the home lads through their paces.

Should anyone wish to recall the sight of Silverwood in his pomp, rhythmically tearing in to terrorise batsmen, then they only need to take a look at the action and aggression of Maurice Chambers.

In the match at Trent Bridge earlier in the season he'd looked out of sorts and unable to get the radar properly locked on the target. On the first day of this match he looked a much more difficult animal to combat. Bowling very sharply, and with almost unplayable lift, he'd taken three of the five Nottinghamshire wickets to fall.

With just his second delivery of the new day – and only the eighth ball of the morning – Chambers was at it again. Chris Read was unable to get inside the line and a thin edge flew through to James Foster.

This was clearly a major set-back for the visitors. Read and Ali Brown had blunted the Essex attack during the final hour of the opening day and would have set their stall out to continue their stand and take the side into a substantial first innings lead.

Worse was to follow: Almost immediately Paul Franks went to another catch behind to give the big fast bowler his fifth wicket, and he was soon followed by Andre Adams, who swished and missed at a straight one from the 22-year-old.

Luke Fletcher joined Brown and the pair nudged the total beyond Essex's 154 to at least establish a first innings lead

Batting positively, Brown reached his half century from 64 deliveries with eight boundaries but then lost the strike and saw his last two partners perish in quick succession.

'Fletch' had made 12 and looked to use his feet to Danish Kaneria, but the Pakistan leg spinner turned one sharply away from a groping lunge and Foster completed a routine stumping.

— 69 —

What Do Points Make?

Settling their differences!
Kevin Paxton puts Mark Wagh through his paces as Bilal looks on

Two deliveries later it was all over as Charlie Shreck played all around the ball and was palpably out leg before wicket. Notts had succumbed in just 47 overs for 180 – so no batting bonus points and only a slender 26-run lead.

Unsurprisingly, Chambers led his team-mates from the field to generous applause for his career best figures of 6-68.

The home side hadn't managed to wipe out their deficit when their openers were parted cheaply for the second time in the match. Billy Godleman guided Shreck to gully where Mullaney safely pouched the catch.

Lunch was taken at 39-1, meaning that the first four sessions of the match had produced 21 wickets, but for the remainder of the second day it was the bat which held sway.

John Maunders and Jaik Mickleburgh posted a century stand for the second wicket as the Notts bowlers struggled to extract the same amount of movement that they'd enjoyed 24 hours earlier.

Shreck broke the stand when Maunders flicked at one that was going a long way down the leg side, but this only allowed Matt Walker to take up the fight. Batting fluently – with shots all around the wicket – he raced to a 59-ball half century, giving immediate payback for having been awarded his county cap earlier in the day.

Maunders had fallen for 70, looking well set for a century. Mickleburgh went even closer, but on 91 he pushed forward to Samit Patel without making contact and was adjudged to be out lbw.

Walker's fine knock came to an end just a couple of overs before the end of play. Trying to whip Franks away to leg, he failed to cope with some late movement and nicked it to Hales at slip.

There was just time for Chambers to make a re-appearance out in the middle – as nightwatchman – before Essex closed the day holding a very healthy advantage at the scheduled halfway point of the contest.

Close of Day Two – Essex 265-4 (Westley 19*, Chambers 0*, 81 overs)

7th July – Day Three

Nottinghamshire's second LV= County Championship defeat of the season – and first on the road – was duly confirmed as Essex wrapped up a convincing 143-run victory an hour before the end of the third day.

Set a target of 309 in almost five full sessions, Notts were again undone by the raw pace of Maurice Chambers and the guile of Danish Kaneria to be hustled out in just 44.3 overs.

Such a crushing defeat had looked improbable as Charlie Shreck and Andre Adams had gone about their morning's work. The tall Cornishman gave Chambers a taste of his own medicine as he fired one through the gate.

Charlie got his fourth wicket when James Foster chipped one straight back to him, and then Andre brought a swift conclusion to the innings by getting rid of Westley, Pettini, Masters and Kaneria to also claim a four-fer. Essex had lost their last five wickets for just 34 runs.

Notts had given themselves plenty of time in which to complete a fourth innings run chase, but clearly they would need to apply themselves much better than they had first time around.

As it transpired the eventual outcome was made crystal clear from very early on. For the second time in the match Alex Hales was undone by the pace of Chambers. The ball may have kept a touch low but the visual effect was impressive as the off stump exploded spectacularly as the ball made impact.

Bilal Shafayat, desperate for a decent score to maintain his place in the side, disappointed again as he inside-edged Masters to the diving 'keeper.

Having made a far from impressive start, Notts' plight then worsened as Samit Patel drove Masters to the gully before Chambers hustled out both Mullaney and Wagh.

Tea was taken at 95-5 and hopes of a dramatic fightback rested with the lower order. For the second time in the contest Ali Brown put bat to ball and counter-attacked impressively, but he received very little in the way of support as Danish Kaneria twirled and whirled his way to four cheap scalps.

'Shining light' – Ali Brown scored half centuries in both innings

What Do Points Make?

Ali Brown – who had offered the most stubborn resistance – fell to David Masters for 62 and Luke Fletcher was last to fall. His bold approach had brought him a couple of well-struck boundaries, but when he tried to hoist Kaneria away for a big six he couldn't quite clear the ropes at deep mid-wicket and picked out Chambers, who gleefully accepted the gift.

In their own fight against relegation this had been a convincing win for James Foster's side and a memorable start to his own reign as skipper. Maurice Chambers had been a revelation. Bowling really quickly and with great control, his match figures of 10-123 tell their own story.

Mick Newell was understandably critical of what he'd witnessed.

"Both times we batted we were pretty awful and the top five have not really been in this game at all. We kept getting out with poor shots, there was some good bowling, but really the top five have got to look at themselves because they've offered nothing in this game.

"If you're going to chase 300 then the top five have got to do the work. We knew Kaneria was going to be difficult for the bottom order, that's part of the game.

"We're missing an overseas player but we seem to have become overly reliant on them, with Hashim and now David Hussey not available.

"It was a disappointing performance on a wicket that, when we turned up here, we thought would suit us. We need to play much better when we come back to this form of cricket in two weeks' time.

"Chambers was excellent in this game and we clearly couldn't cope with him. He was sharp and bowled well and straight, but it was a poor performance from us."

Mick Newell was critical of his batsmen in the defeat by Essex at Chelmsford

The inside story of Nottinghamshire's LV= County Championship success

SCORECARD

Essex first innings		Runs	Balls	Mins	4s	6s
JK Maunders	run out	2	9	13	-	-
BA Godleman	c Read b Adams	15	63	75	1	-
JC Mickleburgh	b Shreck	2	18	14	-	-
MJ Walker	c Read b Adams	13	35	48	2	-
T Westley	c Read b Franks	4	20	23	-	-
*+JS Foster	c Read b Shreck	22	54	79	3	-
ML Pettini	c Read b Shreck	10	34	39	2	-
TJ Phillips	not out	46	79	94	7	-
DD Masters	lbw b Franks	20	20	26	4	-
Danish Kaneria	c Read b Franks	2	11	11	-	-
MA Chambers	c Adams b Mullaney	14	28	32	3	-
Extras	(4 lb)	4				
Total	(all out, 61.5 overs)	154				

Fall of wickets: 1-7 (Maunders, 3.4 ov), 2-11 (Mickleburgh, 8.3 ov), 3-36 (Godleman, 20.1 ov), 4-37 (Walker, 21 ov), 5-45 (Westley, 26 ov), 6-69 (Pettini, 37.2 ov), 7-84 (Foster, 42 ov), 8-114 (Masters, 49.3 ov), 9-120 (Danish Kaneria, 53.2 ov), 10-154 (Chambers, 61.5 ov)

Notts bowling	Overs	Mdns	Runs	Wkts	Wides	No-Balls
Shreck	16	5	40	3	-	-
Fletcher	16	1	50	0	-	-
Franks	12	7	20	3	-	-
Adams	14	4	26	2	-	-
Patel	3	0	13	0	-	-
Mullaney	0.5	0	1	1	-	-

Nottinghamshire first innings		Runs	Balls	Mins	4s	6s
AD Hales	b Chambers	9	19	30	1	-
BM Shafayat	lbw b Chambers	1	5	6	-	-
MA Wagh	lbw b Phillips	20	56	63	2	-
SR Patel	c Godleman b Phillips	25	35	47	5	-
SJ Mullaney	lbw b Chambers	1	3	1	-	-
AD Brown	not out	50	64	111	8	-
*+CMW Read	c Foster b Chambers	32	53	53	3	1
PJ Franks	c Foster b Chambers	4	5	4	1	-
AR Adams	b Chambers	10	17	13	2	-
LJ Fletcher	st Foster b Danish Kaneria	12	27	23	2	-
CE Shreck	lbw b Danish Kaneria	0	3	1	-	-
Extras	(5 b, 1 lb, 10 nb)	16				
Total	(all out, 47 overs)	180				

Fall of wickets: 1-4 (Shafayat, 1.5 ov), 2-13 (Hales, 7.4 ov), 3-61 (Wagh, 18.4 ov), 4-62 (Mullaney, 19.2 ov), 5-72 (Patel, 20.1 ov), 6-127 (Read, 35.2 ov), 7-131 (Franks, 37.1 ov), 8-151 (Adams, 41.1 ov), 9-180 (Fletcher, 46.3 ov), 10-180 (Shreck, 47 ov)

Essex bowling	Overs	Mdns	Runs	Wkts	Wides	No-Balls
Masters	16	4	47	0	-	-
Chambers	15	2	68	6	-	3
Danish Kaneria	10	1	42	2	-	2
Phillips	6	0	17	2	-	-

— 73 —

What Do Points Make?

Essex second innings

		Runs	Balls	Mins	4s	6s
JK Maunders	c Read b Shreck	70	132	154	11	-
BA Godleman	c Mullaney b Shreck	3	23	24	-	-
JC Mickleburgh	lbw b Patel	91	163	202	14	-
MJ Walker	c Hales b Franks	70	114	124	11	-
T Westley	c Read b Adams	32	91	117	5	-
MA Chambers	b Shreck	8	27	33	2	-
*+JS Foster	c and b Shreck	8	22	35	-	-
ML Pettini	b Adams	11	43	49	1	-
TJ Phillips	not out	12	49	62	2	-
DD Masters	c Patel b Adams	0	4	2	-	-
Danish Kaneria	c Patel b Adams	9	6	13	2	-
Extras	(11 lb, 2 nb, 1 w)	14				
Total	(all out, 112.1 overs)	328				

Fall of wickets: 1-15 (Godleman, 6.2 ov), 2-119 (Maunders, 42.1 ov), 3-225 (Mickleburgh, 63.5 ov), 4-263 (Walker, 78.2 ov), 5-276 (Chambers, 87.4 ov), 6-294 (Westley, 94.5 ov), 7-296 (Foster, 96 ov), 8-316 (Pettini, 108.2 ov), 9-316 (Masters, 109 ov), 10-328 (Danish Kaneria, 112.1 ov)

Notts bowling	Overs	Mdns	Runs	Wkts	Wides	No-Balls
Shreck	23	4	81	4	-	-
Fletcher	19	7	57	0	-	-
Adams	25.1	4	57	4	-	-
Franks	17	5	37	1	1	1
Mullaney	4	1	14	0	-	-
Patel	24	7	71	1	-	-

Nottinghamshire second innings

		Runs	Balls	Mins	4s	6s
AD Hales	b Chambers	7	14	13	1	-
BM Shafayat	c Foster b Masters	5	9	19	1	-
MA Wagh	b Chambers	26	85	103	2	-
SR Patel	c Maunders b Chambers	4	13	13	1	-
SJ Mullaney	b Chambers	12	17	16	2	-
AD Brown	c Phillips b Masters	62	81	115	8	-
*+CMW Read	c Mickleburgh b Danish Kaneria	20	25	26	3	-
PJ Franks	c Walker b Danish Kaneria	0	4	6	-	-
AR Adams	b Danish Kaneria	0	3	6	-	-
LJ Fletcher	c Chambers b Danish Kaneria	9	8	14	2	-
CE Shreck	not out	7	11	7	1	-
Extras	(1 lb, 6 nb)	7				
Total	(all out, 44.3 overs)	159				

Fall of wickets: 1-11 (Hales, 3.2 ov), 2-17 (Shafayat, 4.2 ov), 3-22 (Patel, 7.4 ov), 4-42 (Mullaney, 11.5 ov), 5-95 (Wagh, 29.3 ov), 6-126 (Read, 37 ov), 7-134 (Franks, 38.4 ov), 8-142 (Adams, 40.3 ov), 9-144 (Brown, 42 ov), 10-159 (Fletcher, 44.3 ov)

Essex bowling	Overs	Mdns	Runs	Wkts	Wides	No-Balls
Masters	13	2	48	2	-	-
Chambers	13	2	55	4	-	-
Danish Kaneria	15.3	2	51	4	-	3
Phillips	3	1	4	0	-	-

Match 9

WARWICKSHIRE v NOTTINGHAMSHIRE

July 20th, 21st, 22nd 2010
(match scheduled for 4 days but completed in 3)
Venue: Edgbaston, Birmingham
Toss: won by Nottinghamshire who elected to field
Umpires: PJ Hartley & P Willey
Result: Nottinghamshire won by 10 wickets
Points: Warwickshire 6 (Batting 3, Bowling 3)
Nottinghamshire 23 (Batting 4, Bowling 3)

20th July – Day One

Without a win in any of the previous four LV= County Championship matches, Nottinghamshire began the second part of their season with a trip down the M42 to face Warwickshire.

For the first time Mick Newell had the luxury of having all three England players at his disposal and, unsurprisingly, Ryan Sidebottom and Stuart Broad returned to the team alongside Graeme Swann, who was making his first 4-day appearance for the county since April 2009.

Additionally, David Hussey, now free from his commitments with Australia, was also available to bolster the batting. The four players who missed out having featured against Essex in the previous game were Bilal Shafayat, Charlie Shreck, Luke Fletcher and, perhaps unluckily, Paul Franks.

Having inserted the opposition at the start of the day Chris Read saw his formidable attack exerted fully before eventually dismissing Warwickshire for 313 just before the close. Neil Carter had turned the day around for the home side before being cruelly stranded on 99 not out. Notts responded with 18 without loss by the close.

Ryan Sidebottom made the initial breakthrough, inducing the left-handed Ant Botha to push at a beauty which moved away from him. Read took the catch in his usual composed style and had another one shortly afterwards when the dangerous Jonathan Trott fell to his international team-mate Stuart Broad.

Bears' skipper Ian Westwood was next to fall, driving at a widish delivery from Adams he only found the reliable Hussey at second slip. Just before lunch Jim Troughton became Read's third victim when he did well to get anything on a sharply turning off spinner from Swann.

Lunch was taken with the score on 96-4, but Warwickshire lost their fifth batsman straight after the resumption. Darren Maddy had played a couple of nice extra cover drives but couldn't resist pulling a short ball from Broad and holed out to Sidebottom at long leg.

The innings appeared to be in sharp decline when Adams dismissed Clarke and Woakes in quick succession to bring Carter to the middle on 157-7.

— 75 —

Used to opening the batting in the shortened format of the game, Neil Carter can be a dangerous opponent when set. A powerful hitter, with a good eye for the ball, his assessment of Warwickshire's predicament was that it was a good moment to go on the offensive.

He chanced his arm from the word go, and on 16 had a couple of lives as the unfortunate Sidebottom saw Read (legside) and Hales (slip) fail to grasp sharp opportunities.

There was some reward at the other end as Ambrose fell to Broad, but the same bowler was then savaged for three maximums by the Cape Town-born Carter as he brought up his 50.

Imran Tahir appeared to be inspired by Carter's assault as he hit Swann away for a couple of slog sweep sixes on his way to a rapid 29, but his departure brought Nottinghamshire their third bowling point and at 266-9 the end appeared within sight.

Carter had other ideas however and twice hit Sidebottom over the ropes, and with Boyd Rankin as his final partner took the total beyond 300.

Only once before had he reached three figures but a worthy second career century seemed inevitable as he moved on to 99. Disaster then struck from a Warwickshire point of view. Carter worked Adams away to square leg but straight to Graeme Swann. The alert fielder's smart pick up and throw ran out Rankin at the non-striker's end as the big Irishman tried to recover his ground having backed up a touch too far.

A John Cleese-type moment followed as Carter put his head in his hands before trudging off, leaving Rankin laying face down on the Edgbaston turf. It had taken a brilliant piece of fielding to end the innings and there was some comedy value in the news that the two batsmen were house-sharing at the time. "Coffee Neil?" "I'll get it myself!"

Having lost seven of their first ten Championship matches, Warwickshire's season had been spiralling towards inevitable relegation when they had been 157-7, but even despite Carter's heroics Notts will have been satisfied to dismiss their hosts inside a day.

Close of Day One – Nottinghamshire 18-0
(Hales 16*, Patel 1*, 7 overs)

21st July – Day Two

For the second season in a row Mark Wagh returned to his former stomping ground to help himself to a century. His innings really was like 'a game of two halves'. A stodgy, watchful, indeed almost painful, first 50 eventually arrived after three hours fifty minutes of batting and from 157 balls faced. His second appeared to have been scored by a different player – one shorn of responsibility and burden. He raced from 50 to 100 in 37 minutes with a flurry of perfectly executed strokes and from just another 59 deliveries.

Wagh's effort ensured a first innings advantage of at least 60 for his side as they closed the day on 373-9, with the centurion having moved on to 127 and with Ryan Sidebottom unbeaten on six alongside him.

The star of the opening day, Neil Carter, was soon making more headlines. In just the first over of the morning Samit Patel chopped on to his leg stump for just a single. That brought Wagh to the crease, but it was a watching brief initially as Alex Hales played his shots at the other end.

Eight boundaries in a 52-ball half century confirmed that Alex was in extremely good touch, so it was a gratifying moment for the home support when he chased a wide one from Carter and bottom-edged it to slip. 61-2 with Hales out for 53 tells its own story!

Mark Wagh, imperious against his former county

David Hussey, who had made 34 and 33 on the same ground a week earlier for his country in two twenty20 internationals against Pakistan, only made eight for his county, also guilty of being unable to resist a wide one from Carter.

123-3 at lunch, Notts lost Steven Mullaney shortly afterwards as he got the thinnest of edges when trying to pull Boyd Rankin, who followed it up by uprooting Ali Brown's off stump.

Wagh remained at the crease – a model of concentration. Interspersed with long passages of defiance were fleeting samples of textbook driving, but again he found a partner who was prepared to put bat to ball.

Chris Read had scored two centuries and two fifties in the opening half of the season and was soon on his way to another half century. Despite giving Wagh a 36-over start, the Notts skipper beat him to the landmark, from his 80th delivery in just 85 minutes, with 7 x 4s.

Clubbing Imran Tahir back over his head for his fifth boundary, Wagh reached his own 50 just before tea but then began to kick on. The pair added 156 together in 42 overs before Carter again induced a batsman – this time Read – to chase a wide one and bring the slip cordon into play. Read's 83 had undoubtedly changed the context of the match.

Graeme Swann went cheaply before Wagh pushed Carter into the off side for a couple to bring up his 31st career century. Stuart Broad failed to score, but Andre Adams took Notts into a first innings lead with an exhilarating cameo which brought him 37 from only 26 balls with six fours and a six.

At the close Notts had only an outside chance of securing maximum batting points, requiring a further 27 in just 7 overs but with only one wicket standing. Nevertheless, they had enjoyed the better of the day, with handy contributions from Hales and Adams topping up the splendid partnership between Mark Wagh and Chris Read.

Close of Day Two – Nottinghamshire 373-9
(Wagh 127*, Sidebottom 6*, 103 overs)

22nd July – Day Three

A career best analysis of 8-52 by Stuart Broad was the cornerstone of a dramatic Warwickshire collapse, which enabled Nottinghamshire to secure a 10 wicket three-day victory over their hosts.

Broad's consistent line and length, coupled with steepling bounce and a little away movement, was too much for a side that had struggled with confidence over the past few matches.

Nottinghamshire's victory took them to 138 points, just six behind Yorkshire in the Division One table but with two games in hand.

The day began with Mark Wagh looking to dominate the strike in pursuit of the 27 more runs needed for maximum batting points, but having added only 12 to his overnight 127 he flashed hard at Neil Carter and was held at backward point by Jim Troughton.

Wagh's magnificent knock quite rightly earned him a standing ovation, whilst there was also generous applause for the yeoman efforts of Carter, who finished with figures of 5-116 to go with his unbeaten 99 earlier.

Warwickshire, or rather 'Cartershire', had kept themselves in contention throughout this 'top v bottom' game and were 'only 76' adrift after the first innings. The situation then altered dramatically when they began their second innings at just after twenty past eleven.

By lunch-time – 1pm – the contest was as good as over. From the 17 overs of play the home side had been reduced to 36-7, totally decimated by Broad, who had taken all of the wickets to fall.

The first three, Westwood, Trott and Botha, fell to slip catches, Troughton lost his middle stump to a ball angled in from around the wicket, and it became 18-5 next ball when Clarke was beaten for pace and adjudged lbw.

At that stage Broad had figures of 5-15 having bowled just 26 deliveries. Maddy and Woakes also went cheaply – to catches by Mullaney (point) and Adams (3rd slip) respectively. Nottinghamshire ate wondering if Broad could pick up all ten wickets – you don't imagine that there would have been too much chatter in the Warwickshire half of the players' dining room.

There was still Neil Carter, of course, and batting at number nine he again threatened to hold up the Nottinghamshire victory charge. He'd cracked five boundaries in his 27 and got his side within two runs of extending the game into a fourth innings when he carved Andre Adams out to the cover fence where Mullaney picked up his second catch of the day.

The dismissal ensured that Broad couldn't become the first Notts bowler since Ken Smales in 1956 to take all ten wickets in an innings, but he did claim his eighth scalp when Ambrose fell in the next over.

Imran Tahir and Boyd Rankin ensured that Notts would have to bat again with a last wicket partnership of 25 – ended with another run out as Mullaney threw down Tahir's stumps. Warwickshire's 100 was their lowest all-out score for a decade and meant that only 25 were needed.

It took Alex Hales and Samit Patel just three overs to knock off the required runs, with each batsman hitting a brace of boundaries to confirm a very emphatic victory, Nottinghamshire's first since the win over Durham in mid-May.

The inside story of Nottinghamshire's LV= County Championship success

A career best 8-52 for Stuart Broad at Edgbaston

SCORECARD

Warwickshire first innings		Runs	Balls	Mins	4s	6s
*IJ Westwood	c Hussey b Adams	17	37	54	3	-
AG Botha	c Read b Sidebottom	1	6	9	-	-
IJL Trott	c Read b Broad	21	16	17	5	-
JO Troughton	c Read b Swann	25	68	80	4	-
DL Maddy	c Sidebottom b Broad	21	60	83	4	-
R Clarke	c Hussey b Adams	27	41	53	3	1
+TR Ambrose	c Read b Broad	34	103	117	3	-
CR Woakes	b Adams	13	28	25	3	-
NM Carter	not out	99	123	129	10	5
Imran Tahir	lbw b Swann	29	27	33	3	2
WB Rankin	run out	5	12	34	1	-
Extras	(8 b, 9 lb, 4 nb)	21				
Total	(all out, 86.4 overs)	313				

Fall of wickets: 1-1 (Botha, 2.3 ov), 2-28 (Trott, 7.3 ov), 3-54 (Westwood), 4-92 (Troughton), 5-98 (Maddy), 6-135 (Clarke), 7-157 (Woakes), 8-200 (Ambrose), 9-266 (Imran Tahir), 10-312 (Rankin, 86.4 ov)

Notts bowling	Overs	Mdns	Runs	Wkts	Wides	No-Balls
Sidebottom	20	3	81	1	-	-
Broad	19	1	79	3	-	1
Adams	17.4	7	35	3	-	-
Swann	26	5	88	2	-	1
Mullaney	4	1	13	0	-	-

Nottinghamshire first innings		Runs	Balls	Mins	4s	6s
SR Patel	b Carter	1	22	25	-	-
AD Hales	c Clarke b Carter	53	53	60	8	-
MA Wagh	c Troughton b Carter	139	279	382	15	1
DJ Hussey	c Maddy b Carter	8	13	16	2	-
SJ Mullaney	c Ambrose b Rankin	31	66	70	4	-
AD Brown	b Rankin	1	14	14	-	-
*+CMW Read	c Clarke b Carter	83	133	154	12	-
GP Swann	c Trott b Woakes	1	5	5	-	-
SCJ Broad	c Rankin b Woakes	0	8	10	-	-
AR Adams	b Imran Tahir	37	26	36	6	1
RJ Sidebottom	not out	6	17	32	1	-
Extras	(8 b, 16 lb, 4 nb, 1 w)	29				
Total	(all out, 105.4 overs)	389				

Fall of wickets: 1-25 (Patel, 8 ov), 2-61 (Hales, 15.3 ov), 3-69 (Hussey, 19.4 ov), 4-127 (Mullaney, 40 ov), 5-131 (Brown, 44 ov), 6-287 (Read, 85.1 ov), 7-288 (Swann, 86.2 ov), 8-298 (Broad, 88.4 ov), 9-347 (Adams, 97 ov), 10-389 (Wagh, 105.4 ov)

Warwickshire bowling	Overs	Mdns	Runs	Wkts	Wides	No-Balls
Woakes	18	5	59	2	-	-
Carter	27.4	3	116	5	-	1
Maddy	12	4	22	0	-	-
Rankin	10	2	49	2	1	1
Imran Tahir	26	5	79	1	-	-
Clarke	7	0	25	0	-	-
Botha	5	1	15	0	-	-

The inside story of Nottinghamshire's LV= County Championship success

Warwickshire second innings		Runs	Balls	Mins	4s	6s
*IJ Westwood	c Hales b Broad	0	5	3	-	-
AG Botha	c Brown b Broad	4	19	29	1	-
IJL Trott	c Hales b Broad	4	7	10	1	-
JO Troughton	b Broad	9	15	28	2	-
DL Maddy	c Mullaney b Broad	8	23	40	1	-
R Clarke	lbw b Broad	0	1	1	-	-
+TR Ambrose	c Adams b Broad	22	44	58	4	-
CR Woakes	c Adams b Broad	0	2	5	-	-
NM Carter	c Mullaney b Adams	27	18	22	5	-
Imran Tahir	run out	17	12	18	2	-
WB Rankin	not out	8	7	10	2	-
Extras	(1 lb)	1				
Total	(all out, 25.3 overs)	100				

Fall of wickets: 1-0 (Westwood, 0.5 ov), 2-4 (Trott, 3 ov), 3-9 (Botha, 6.2 ov), 4-18 (Troughton, 8.5 ov), 5-18 (Clarke, 9 ov), 6-29 (Maddy, 14.5 ov), 7-33 (Woakes, 16.1 ov), 8-74 (Carter, 21.5 ov), 9-75 (Ambrose, 22.3 ov), 10-100 (Imran Tahir, 25.3 ov)

Notts bowling	Overs	Mdns	Runs	Wkts	Wides	No-Balls
Broad	13	3	52	8	-	-
Sidebottom	8	4	14	0	-	-
Adams	4.3	0	33	1	-	-

Nottinghamshire second innings		Runs	Balls	Mins	4s	6s
SR Patel	not out	10	12	11	2	-
AD Hales	not out	10	6	11	2	-
MA Wagh						
DJ Hussey						
SJ Mullaney						
AD Brown						
*+CMW Read						
GP Swann						
SCJ Broad						
AR Adams						
RJ Sidebottom						
Extras	(5 w)	5				
Total	(no wicket, 3 overs)	25				

Warwickshire bowling	Overs	Mdns	Runs	Wkts	Wides	No-Balls
Woakes	2	0	15	0	5	-
Carter	1	0	10	0	-	-

Match 10

SOMERSET v NOTTINGHAMSHIRE

July 29th, 30th, 31st 2010
(match scheduled for 4 days but completed in 3)
Venue: The County Ground, Taunton
Toss: won by Somerset who elected to bat
Umpires: MA Gough & JW Lloyds
Result: Somerset won by 10 wickets
Points: Somerset 24 (Batting 5, Bowling 3)
Nottinghamshire 5 (Batting 3, Bowling 2)

29th July – Day One

A richly entertaining first day at the County Ground, Taunton, ended with Somerset on 423-6. James Hildreth, with 142, his fourth Championship century of the summer, and 19-year-old Jos Buttler, who added 88, put on 210 for the fifth wicket after the Notts attack had removed the top four batsmen for 126.

Nottinghamshire were forced into a number of changes from the side that completed the ten wicket victory over Warwickshire. Added to the enforced absences of both Graeme Swann and Stuart Broad, due to Test match duty, were Steven Mullaney, who injured an ankle in practise the previous day, and Ryan Sidebottom, who tweaked a knee shortly before the start of play. Paul Franks, Darren Pattinson and Charlie Shreck all returned to the seam bowling ranks, whilst Matt Wood earned a first Championship start of the season against his former county.

**10.15am – just a few moments later Ryan (centre)
had to pull out with a knee injury**

The inside story of Nottinghamshire's LV= County Championship success

Nottinghamshire made a dream start, dismissing Marcus Trescothick with the first ball of the match. The Somerset left-hander missed a full-pitched delivery from Darren Pattinson which uprooted his leg stump. Having been on the receiving end of scores of 99, 97 and 98 from the former England opener in his last three matches against them, there was no disguising the joy and celebration of Chris Read's side.

Attacking field placings and a sportingly short boundary on the western side of the ground contributed to a flurry of early runs before Pattinson struck again, having Nick Compton taken by David Hussey at second slip for 17 – a routine chance, although Hussey tumbled over backwards in celebration.

Arul Suppiah, who had hit 151 in this fixture twelve months earlier, perished on 30 this time. Pushing at Andre Adams, he nicked the ball straight to Alex Hales at first slip. 77-3, having chosen to bat first, the home county were up against it as Notts celebrated their first bowling bonus point.

Zander De Bruyn had reached 44 by lunch, having survived a drop by Ali Brown at slip from the bowling of Adams. However, with the first ball of the afternoon session he fell lbw to Pattinson – umpire Jeremy Lloyds upholding the confident appeal to give the bowler his second consecutive perfect start to a session.

From then on it became really tough going for Notts as James Hildreth and Jos Buttler produced a flurry of attacking strokes on both sides of the wicket. Read rotated his bowlers but neither seam nor spin could slow the scoring rate as the pair raced to tea at 280-4.

Hildreth reached his century from 128 deliveries, with 13 boundaries, whilst his younger partner produced the more eye-catching strokeplay, which also included a majestic straight six from the bowling of Samit Patel.

Patel eventually got his man though, Buttler falling in the 79th over after trying one extravagant shot too many. The stand had been worth 210 runs and came in just under three hours and from 46 overs.

Steven Mullaney on crutches after his scan, flanked by former Somerset openers Matt Wood and Neil Edwards

The second new ball was taken one over later and Pattinson, with his first delivery of the post-tea session, induced Hildreth to pull a short delivery straight to Mark Wagh at deep square leg.

At 347-6 Notts sensed an opportunity to make further inroads, but they were frustrated by another stand that threatened to take the game away from them. Craig Keiswetter (43 not out) and Peter Trego (36 not out) continued to profit against a tiring attack in the final half hour of the day to ensure that Somerset picked up maximum batting points from their first innings.

Notts' skipper Chris Read admitted it had been a tough day for his side. *"We had to work hard for those wickets. It's slightly disappointing we didn't get a couple more out but it's a big day tomorrow. We need to work hard in the first session and get these last four wickets fairly cheaply – then we need to score well. The key is for us to be still in the game at the halfway stage."*

Close of Day One – Somerset 423-6
(Kieswetter 43*, Trego 36*, 96 overs)

30th July – Day Two

Thanks to an unbroken stand of 148 between Samit Patel and Chris Read, Nottinghamshire recovered from the perilous position of 130-5 to reach 278-5 by the close of Day 2, still 239 runs behind Somerset's all out first innings total of 517.

Under slate-grey clouds, Somerset began looking to build on their overnight score of 423-6.

Craig Keiswetter and Peter Trego both passed their half-centuries, although Trego had a life when he was dropped on 38 by Matt Wood at long leg.

Trego was the first to fall, flailing at a wide ball which went to Mark Wagh on the off side fence and gave Pattinson his first five wicket haul of the season.

Samit Patel then gained sufficient turn to clean bowl Keiswetter, who had looked impressive up to that point in advancing to 73, and Charlie Shreck picked up a well-deserved first wicket when he trapped Murali Kartik in front of his stumps. Shreck then hung on to a skier to dismiss last man Charl Willoughby off Patel. Alfonso Thomas remained unbeaten on 30 not out.

Alex Hales and Matt Wood, Nottinghamshire's fifth different Championship opening pair of the season, had a six-over, 20-minute spell before lunch, which they safely negotiated whilst adding 15 runs.

Wood lit up the start of the post-lunch session with a sequence of boundaries, but the introduction of spin parted the openers. Alex Hales fell during Kartik's first over, nudging the Indian Test spinner to Trescothick at slip and Mark Wagh perished soon afterwards, lured into driving Peter Trego to Zander de Bruyn at short extra cover to leave Notts on 48-2.

Joined by Samit Patel, Wood continued to caress the ball to the off side boundary with great regularity and reached his 50 from 87 deliveries, including 9 x 4s.

Obviously eager to make an impression, Wood remained the dominant partner in a stand of 71 with Patel before edging Arul Suppiah to give Trescothick his second catch of the innings. It was a tame end to a very good knock from the former Somerset man and the County Ground gave him an appreciative round of applause as he made his way from the field.

At tea Notts were 128-3, but they were rocked when they lost both David Hussey and Ali Brown in Charl Willoughby's first over after the resumption. Hussey had made just four when he edged to Trescothick and two balls later Brown emulated Mark Wagh's dismissal by driving straight into the grateful hands of de Bruyn.

Patel and Read then embarked on a two hour stand of the highest quality, despatching anything short or wide on either side of the wicket. Samit lofted Kartik high over the Marcus Trescothick Stand and into the River Tone for the first maximum of the innings. The necessary ball change was certainly to the delight of the Notts skipper, who hit Suppiah for three consecutive boundaries with the replacement.

There were eight boundaries and the one six in Samit's 50, which came off 103 deliveries, but he was in danger of being caught up by the free-scoring Read, who passed fifty for the sixth time in the Championship this season with his 11th boundary and from just 58 balls faced.

Another Patel maximum put him in touching distance of three figures before the close, but he ended on 92 not out with his partner on 75.

Samit admitted afterwards that he was eyeing up the opportunity of getting to his hundred during the last few minutes of the day. *"Yes, I fancied it and asked the skipper if it was on, but he told me to reign it in a little bit and go on again tomorrow."*

The batsman admitted he was aware that he hadn't scored a Championship ton since hitting 135 against Surrey at The Oval in September 2008. *"I'm probably the only one of the top order that hasn't hit one since then, so I'd not only like to do it but also go on and beat my career best of 167."*

Having claimed three wickets himself during Somerset's knock, Samit was only too aware of the danger that Murali Kartik posed. *"On that wicket he is going to be a great danger and I was very circumspect against him to begin with, but the longer you're out there the easier it becomes. It's one of those tracks where you have to play the percentages."*

Close of Day Two – Nottinghamshire 278-5
(Patel 92*, Read 75*, 76 overs)

31st July – Day Three

Nottinghamshire succumbed to their third LV= County Championship reverse of the season, going down to a ten wicket defeat. Asked to follow-on, they subsided to 190 all out in their second innings, leaving the home side to knock off the required 13 runs for a maximum 24-point haul.

After a spot of very light early morning drizzle, the conditions were much fresher at the start of the day as Samit Patel and Chris Read looked to build on Notts' overnight 278-5.

The second new ball was taken as soon as it became available and Willoughby struck immediately with Read edging behind to fall for 80.

Samit had reached his century earlier in the same over, hitting the South African-born left armer for two boundaries and a single, but was then trapped in front of his stumps by Alfonso Thomas. Despite having reached his first Championship century since September 2008, the batsman was clearly disappointed at not having gone on and built a substantial individual score.

Willoughby then quickly wrapped up the innings, Adams edging behind attempting an expansive drive, Franks trapped in his crease and Shreck losing his off stump.

Luxury apartment or deck chair? Plenty of good vantage points as Notts warm up at Taunton

Darren Pattinson ended on 7 not out and had the pleasure of hoisting Murali Kartik away for a huge maximum on the leg side. Willoughby finished with figures of 6-101.

Notts had fallen for 339 – 29 runs away from avoiding the follow-on, but perhaps more significantly just eleven away from the 350 mark and the extra bonus point that would have lifted them to the top of the table.

Marcus Trescothick and Arul Suppiah then fooled everyone by sprinting off the field as if to prepare themselves for batting, but once inside the pavilion the decision to make Notts bat again was confirmed.

The decision looked justified when Matt Wood, after his first innings heroics, fell first ball lbw to Willoughby.

Alex Hales and Mark Wagh took the visitors to lunch at 28-1, but the opener fell shortly afterwards, edging Kartik behind before Patel quickly followed.

Wagh and David Hussey looked to counter-attack, with the former hitting Willoughby for four exquisite boundaries in succession, but he was then sent on his way by umpire Lloyds despite pushing forward to a de Bruyn delivery.

Hussey had reached 30 before shouldering arms to the same bowler and losing his off stump, leaving Ali Brown and Read to guide Notts to tea on 155-5.

Any hope of extending play into the fourth day quickly evaporated as Alfonso Thomas ripped through the lower order to finish with a five-wicket haul.

The inside story of Nottinghamshire's LV= County Championship success

Notts had scraped their way past the 178 target needed to make their hosts bat again, but when Shreck lost his off stump for the second time in the day it meant that only 13 were required for victory.

Marcus Trescothick and Nick Compton, deputising for the injured Suppiah, knocked off the required runs against the new ball attack of David Hussey – bowling seam up from a long run – and Alex Hales.

An understandably disappointed Mick Newell admitted his side hadn't done well enough but felt that Somerset executed their game plan perfectly.

"We knew what they would be about. Prepare a dry pitch and hope to bat first and get Kartik into the game later on. We didn't make a good enough fist of it in our first innings."

With only five points accumulated from the contest, Nottinghamshire ended the match just behind Yorkshire in the table, with an away fixture against the White Rose county up next.

"We should have certainly made this an exercise in points gathering," said Mick. *"Had we been able to save the follow-on then I'm sure we would have saved the game and got at least ten points out of the match. Everyone keeps talking up the Yorkshire game, but Somerset are now right in the picture and Durham and Lancashire will also think they can go on and win the title also. I'm just happy that after ten games played we have gained more points than any other side."*

On individual performances the Notts Director of Cricket praised Samit Patel, Matt Wood and Chris Read for their first innings batting but agreed that an all-round improvement would be expected the following week.

"There are a number of players who haven't given us enough in this game and they will need to improve at Headingley on Tuesday."

SCORECARD

Somerset first innings		Runs	Balls	Mins	4s	6s
*ME Trescothick	b Pattinson	0	1	1	-	-
AV Suppiah	c Hales b Adams	30	58	79	6	-
NRD Compton	c Hussey b Pattinson	17	37	40	3	-
Z de Bruyn	lbw b Pattinson	44	63	74	9	-
JC Hildreth	c Wagh b Pattinson	142	187	211	18	-
JC Buttler	b Patel	88	129	158	12	1
+C Kieswetter	b Patel	73	121	138	10	-
PD Trego	c Wagh b Pattinson	54	65	90	8	-
AC Thomas	not out	30	37	51	5	-
M Kartik	lbw b Shreck	7	15	14	1	-
CM Willoughby	c Shreck b Patel	5	5	4	1	-
Extras	(8 b, 5 lb, 14 nb)	27				
Total	(all out, 118.3 overs)	517				

Fall of wickets: 1-0 (Trescothick, 0.1 ov), 2-44 (Compton, 10.5 ov), 3-77 (Suppiah, 20.1 ov), 4-126 (de Bruyn, 32.1 ov), 5-336 (Buttler, 78.1 ov), 6-347 (Hildreth, 80.1 ov), 7-460 (Trego, 105.1 ov), 8-489 (Kieswetter, 113 ov), 9-504 (Kartik, 117.2 ov), 10-517 (Willoughby, 118.3 ov)

Notts bowling	Overs	Mdns	Runs	Wkts	Wides	No-Balls
Pattinson	20	3	95	5	-	7
Shreck	29	5	101	1	-	-
Adams	26	4	121	1	-	-
Franks	15	2	50	0	-	-
Patel	18.3	0	93	3	-	-
Hussey	10	1	44	0	-	-

Nottinghamshire first innings		Runs	Balls	Mins	4s	6s
AD Hales	c Trescothick b Kartik	6	37	42	1	-
MJ Wood	c Trescothick b Suppiah	72	132	134	12	-
MA Wagh	c de Bruyn b Trego	4	18	19	1	-
SR Patel	lbw b Thomas	104	185	221	17	2
DJ Hussey	c Trescothick b Willoughby	4	6	6	1	-
AD Brown	c de Bruyn b Willoughby	2	2	1	-	-
*+CMW Read	c Kieswetter b Willoughby	80	119	131	17	-
PJ Franks	lbw b Willoughby	15	25	46	3	-
AR Adams	c Kieswetter b Willoughby	20	19	22	2	1
DJ Pattinson	not out	7	13	13	-	1
CE Shreck	b Willoughby	0	2	1	-	-
Extras	(12 b, 1 lb, 6 nb, 6 w)	25				
Total	(all out, 92.3 overs)	339				

Fall of wickets: 1-41 (Hales, 11.5 ov), 2-48 (Wagh, 18.3 ov), 3-119 (Wood, 40 ov), 4-128 (Hussey, 42.2 ov), 5-130 (Brown, 42.4 ov), 6-287 (Read, 81 ov), 7-297 (Patel, 83.1 ov), 8-332 (Adams, 88.5 ov), 9-339 (Franks, 92.1 ov), 10-339 (Shreck, 92.3 ov)

Somerset bowling	Overs	Mdns	Runs	Wkts	Wides	No-Balls
Willoughby	22.3	3	101	6	-	-
Thomas	13	3	68	1	-	1
Kartik	33	15	59	1	1	-
Trego	6	1	17	1	-	-
Suppiah	11	2	48	1	1	-
de Bruyn	7	1	33	0	-	2

The inside story of Nottinghamshire's LV= County Championship success

Nottinghamshire second innings		Runs	Balls	Mins	4s	6s
AD Hales	c Kieswetter b Kartik	28	44	51	5	-
MJ Wood	lbw b Willoughby	0	1	2	-	-
MA Wagh	lbw b de Bruyn	45	85	105	7	-
SR Patel	c Trescothick b Thomas	1	5	1	-	-
DJ Hussey	b de Bruyn	30	68	95	5	-
AD Brown	lbw b Thomas	47	83	90	7	-
*+CMW Read	c de Bruyn b Thomas	4	21	24	-	-
PJ Franks	c Hildreth b Thomas	1	5	10	-	-
AR Adams	lbw b Kartik	10	11	15	1	1
DJ Pattinson	not out	7	21	22	1	-
CE Shreck	b Thomas	3	10	11	-	-
Extras	(1 b, 9 lb, 4 nb)	14				
Total	(all out, 58.4 overs)	190				

Fall of wickets: 1-1 (Wood, 0.4 ov), 2-41 (Hales, 13.2 ov), 3-42 (Patel, 14.1 ov), 4-93 (Wagh, 28.5 ov), 5-134 (Hussey, 40.2 ov), 6-162 (Read, 48.1 ov), 7-168 (Franks, 51 ov), 8-175 (Brown, 52.2 ov), 9-179 (Adams, 55.1 ov), 10-190 (Shreck, 58.4 ov)

Somerset bowling	Overs	Mdns	Runs	Wkts	Wides	No-Balls
Willoughby	13	1	52	1	-	-
Thomas	14.4	4	40	5	-	-
Kartik	26	3	64	2	-	-
de Bruyn	5	1	24	2	-	2

Somerset second innings		Runs	Balls	Mins	4s	6s
*ME Trescothick	not out	4	8	5	1	-
NRD Compton	not out	5	5	5	1	-
AV Suppiah						
Z de Bruyn						
JC Hildreth						
+C Kieswetter						
JC Buttler						
PD Trego						
AC Thomas						
M Kartik						
CM Willoughby						
Extras	(4 nb)	4				
Total	(no wicket, 1.5 overs)	13				

Notts bowling	Overs	Mdns	Runs	Wkts	Wides	No-Balls
Hussey	1	0	8	0	-	2
Hales	0.5	0	5	0	-	-

— 89 —

Match 11

YORKSHIRE v NOTTINGHAMSHIRE

August 3rd, 4th, 5th, 6th 2010 (4 day match)
Venue: Headingley Carnegie, Leeds
Toss: won by Yorkshire who elected to bat
Umpires: RJ Bailey & NJ Long
Result: Match Drawn
Points: Yorkshire 5 (Bowling 2) Nottinghamshire 11 (Batting 5, Bowling 3)

3rd August – Day One

Having had an unexpected day off after their comprehensive defeat to Somerset just three days earlier, Notts had been sent away to rest up and re-group by Mick Newell before arriving in Leeds with their 'game heads' on to play the side considered by many to be one of their main challengers for the crown

Nottinghamshire bossed the opening three sessions of this match to such an extent as to leave their opponents looking more than a little shell-shocked by the close.

The new Headingley Carnegie Pavilion was in use for its first county game

Yorkshire's predicament was, to an extent, self-induced as they'd won the toss and elected to bat first. To be skittled out for just 178 against one of your fiercest rivals was clearly not part of Andrew Gale's thinking when he'd made his decision and he would have hoped for more than three wickets when his bowlers had their turn in the second part of the day.

The wheels had certainly come off the bus as far as Notts' title charge was concerned when they succumbed to Kartik, Willoughby, Thomas and co in the west country, but Mick Newell was able to freshen his side up with the availability of Ryan Sidebottom, who'd shaken off the niggle he'd picked up just before the start of play at Taunton. Charlie Shreck was the luckless bowler to miss out.

Sidebottom, of Yorkshire stock and still regarded as one of their own whenever he reappears at Headingley – or Headingley Carnegie to give it its proper title – had entered the contest to a backdrop of unresolved contract talks, but none of that seemed to matter as he kicked off proceedings from the Football (Rugby League) Stand End.

The inside story of Nottinghamshire's LV= County Championship success

Like so many of the major grounds in the modern era, extensive work always seems to be going on at Headingley and this match was the first county game in which the new pavilion at the Kirkstall Lane End was properly in use.

For the press it meant coming to terms with interminable secure doors for which pass keys and swipe cards were essential, university briefing suites to work in rather than traditional media rooms and, perhaps most importantly (I'm joking – ish), not too much in the way of sustenance at lunch-time. Teething problems only, I'm sure!

Nevertheless, traditional Yorkshire hospitality and good humour were in plentiful supply in all other parts of the ground until that first over. Overhead conditions seemed to favour swing bowling and many were doubting whether Gale had done the right thing in batting, but there was a lot of confidence around, particularly with regards the openers.

Adam Lyth looks to be a genuinely high-class top order batsman with a bright future ahead of him. Almost exactly a month earlier (4th July), he had become the first batsman in the country to reach 1,000 first class runs for the season. He – to put it bluntly – had been in great nick.

It took Ryan just five balls to dismiss him though with an absolute beast of a delivery that pitched just outside off and did enough to shave the outside edge on its journey through to Chris Read.

Only five runs had been scored when Yorkshire netted their second own goal of the morning. Jacques Rudolph had also been in imperious touch with the bat and had reached his own 1,000-run landmark. To get rid of both him and Lyth so early was pivotal for Notts and clearly detrimental to the home effort.

Pushing Darren Pattinson into the off side, Anthony McGrath initially looked set for a sharp single. Certainly his partner Rudolph responded immediately, but having got halfway down he would have been alarmed to see that 'Mags' had gone back. Rudolph was stranded and the quick-thinking Ali Brown realised this and didn't even have the anxiety of having to make an accurate throw as he just jogged in from a widish mid off to flip off one of the bails.

McGrath and Gale moved the total along to 36 before Paul Franks was brought into the attack and trapped the Yorkshire skipper lbw with just his second delivery.

Andre Adams was the fourth bowler to be used on this occasion and he enjoyed a double success, removing both McGrath and Gerard Brophy to send the home side in to lunch on 89-5.

Pattinson had made his only Test appearance on this ground in 2008 and picked up the first wicket of the afternoon session, rapping Rashid on his pads in front of middle, and then Jonny Bairstow, who'd looked impressive on his way to 45, fell to a beauty from Sidebottom as the ball just came back enough to kiss the off bail.

Franks had Shahzad caught at the wicket and the introduction of Samit Patel into the attack was timed to perfection as he took out the last two batsmen in quick succession.

Notts were jubilant but lost Alex Hales for 2 when they began their reply after tea. The opener chased a ball he could have comfortably left and paid the price as a thin contact flew to the 'keeper.

With Tim Bresnan away on Test duty for England, much depended on Yorkshire's other international opening bowler, Ajmal Shahzad, but on the way back from an ankle injury he looked far from fit and appeared to go through the motions in two short spells before disappearing from the attack.

Matt Wood looked in good touch for Notts, punishing the Yorkshire bowlers on either side of the wicket with a succession of boundaries. With the score on 52 he lost partner Mark Wagh, who'd made just 4 from 35 deliveries, tucked up by one from Oliver Hannon-Dalby.

Wood's half century came from 68 balls but he fell shortly afterwards, for 59, when Patterson was given the verdict after a confident lbw shout.

Samit Patel and David Hussey put on 50 together in the last hour of play to take Notts within 31 of the Yorkshire total. It had been a good day for the visitors.

Former Yorkshire and England opener Geoffrey Boycott had been in attendance and he was quick to criticise the decision of the home captain after Australia's Ricky Ponting had done something similar a few days earlier and then seen his side bowled out on the same ground for just 88 by Pakistan.

Writing on his own website, Geoffrey said:

"And blow me, with similar conditions, the same thing goes and happens again this week when Yorkshire won the toss in their table-topping match against Nottinghamshire. Andrew Gale is a young and very talented captain, but he made a major mistake – a miscalculation. The overcast conditions were there again for the ball to swing and seam, as it does at Headingley, and Nottinghamshire took advantage when Andrew chose to bat. After the second roller the wicket was as flat as a pancake – my mum could certainly have batted on it…even I, at my age, would have fancied a go!"

Close of Day One – Nottinghamshire 147-3
(Patel 37*, Hussey 35*, 37 overs)

4th August – Day Two

Just occasionally you are fortunate enough to witness a sporting accomplishment of the highest calibre – a piece of skill so breathtaking you'll talk about it forever, or a sustained spell of excellence the likes of which has rarely been seen before: Tiger shooting a 61 in difficult conditions, a breathtaking individual goal, or a stunning 147 from O'Sullivan – all genius in their execution and a delight to behold.

At Headingley Carnegie on Wednesday 4th August 2010 those present were able to observe one of the truly great County Championship innings.

Whilst true cricket aficionados would never admit to having witnessed a dreary passage of play, it has to be admitted that occasionally some sessions aren't as riveting as others. On this particular day David Hussey played an exceptional knock and was still unbeaten at the close and threatening to inflict even more punishment on the weary bowlers.

The prospect of anyone performing at all seemed in doubt as daybreak brought the sight of a very wet morning. Heavy overnight rain had given way to steady drizzle and, although the forecast was for things to clear later, it didn't look good initially.

Eventually, thanks to some excellent work by the groundstaff, play was able to start after lunch, with Hussey and Patel looking to strengthen Notts' hold on the game.

For a while Samit matched his partner run for run but was then left behind as Hussey brought up his 50 with an eighth boundary as Notts moved into a first innings lead.

The Australian accelerated away, clubbing 18 from one over of spin from David Wainwright, including a huge six over long on.

Samit had looked in good order in registering a ton at Taunton in the previous game and brought up his own fifty with a single off Rashid. His innings had been a perfect foil for Hussey, who continued to blaze away at the other end.

The inside story of Nottinghamshire's LV= County Championship success

There was one brief moment of consternation when Hussey was on 93. Clipping the ball to mid-wicket, he was looking for two but was rightly sent back by Patel. Had Wainwright not fumbled McGrath's return as he attempted to break the wicket then Yorkshire would have ended the partnership there and then.

Hussey's 100 came up from just 106 deliveries, with 14 x 4s and that six off Wainwright, and Patel should have followed suit but mistimed a drive off Rashid and Rudolph hung on to a sharp one-handed chance at slip.

The 4th wicket partnership had been worth 184, a record for the fixture. Chris Read joined Hussey for another productive stand, with the pair adding 114 in 27 overs as Notts looked to ensure a full haul of batting points and establish a huge advantage over their title rivals.

Barring a miraculous U-turn in the contest, and an unlikely Yorkshire victory, Notts had already assured themselves of going back to the top of the table, having picked up more bonus points than their opponents.

The full compliment of batting points was achieved, but not before a slight middle order wobble. Read fell with the score on 395 and Ali Brown went cheaply five runs later. It was later confirmed that Ali had been feeling unwell throughout the day – hence his demotion in the order behind his skipper.

Hussey's 150 had come at better than a run a ball, but on 168 he gave the home side another half chance to dismiss him, drilling a ball straight back at Hannon-Dalby, but the power of the shot went clean through the bowler's hands, into his chest and down. At least it saved four runs!

Paul Franks continued the positive approach and was on hand to congratulate the brilliant Australian as Hussey brought up his double-ton with a majestic extra cover boundary off Rashid.

With uncertainty about the weather holding for the remainder of the contest, both batsmen really went to town against a tiring attack in the last hour of the day. Franks also passed 50, and the pair nudged Notts to within three of 500 by the close – an overall lead of 319.

With understated modesty David Hussey played down the quality of his performance.

"It was a pretty satisfying innings to be honest, but it's a good wicket and always good to get runs against Yorkshire at Headingley. They always want to get stuck in at you and I think it's a really good place to play cricket. I was fortunate that I saw the ball very early on and lucky enough to hit a few in the middle and take it from there."

Close of Day Two – Nottinghamshire 497-6
(Hussey 222*, Franks 57*, 112 overs)

5th August – Day Three

Despite heavy cloud cover from dawn to dusk, the full allocation of overs was played out with Yorkshire fighting back strongly in their second innings. Facing a deficit of 367, they showed immense character in battling their way to 272-2 by the close, still 95 runs adrift.

Jacques Rudolph had led the way, hitting a classy 141, after David Hussey had moved his overnight score to 251 before Chris Read had declared the Nottinghamshire innings closed.

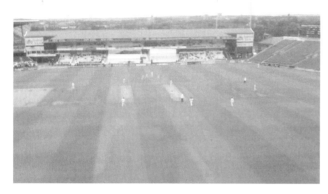

It was tough going on the third afternoon for Notts

There was some speculation that the visiting captain might 'pull the plug' on his side's overnight score, but he elected to bat on for a further 20 minutes, which saw Paul Franks fall to Shahzad for 61 and Hussey bludgeon a straight six off the same bowler before reaching the 250 milestone.

The prospect of a three day defeat would have loomed large as the Yorkshire openers took guard for a second time, but they safely negotiated the new ball and had only lost Lyth – caught smartly by Adams off Franks – by lunch, which was taken at 73-1.

Clearly any communication issues that led to the first innings mix-up had been resolved by Rudolph and McGrath as they then took occupation of the crease in a stand that was eventually worth 211.

Both batted beautifully and with great application and would have met with the approval of the likes of Brian Close, Raymond Illingworth and the rest of the successful Yorkshire side of the 1950s, who were present to enjoy a reunion and watch the day's proceedings.

Rudolph, rumoured to be considering turning his back on county cricket in an attempt to force his way back into South Africa's international reckoning, punished anything short or wide, whilst McGrath defended stoically in a supporting role.

Rudolph's ton duly arrived – off 155 deliveries, although the second 50 had come from just 56. Patel nearly saw him off, but Brown spilt the chance at slip before Pattinson eventually broke the stand, thanks to another fine low catch from Adams.

Yorkshire sent out Steven Patterson as nightwatchman and he shielded McGrath through to the close.

Samit Patel revealed there hadn't been too much in it for the bowlers.

"It's got pretty flat out there. This place is like the new Taunton – it's going to be very difficult for any side to get 20 wickets on there.

"There's not much in the wicket so all you can do is try and build pressure with a few dot balls.

"Rudolph and Mags played very well and we missed a chance when we put Rudolph down, but if we can have a good early morning session and get a few quick wickets we can still win this."

Close of Day Three – Yorkshire 272-2
(McGrath 78*, Patterson 3*, 91 overs)

6th August – Day Four

Conjecture and speculation, although futile, would presume that Nottinghamshire were denied the opportunity of defeating Yorkshire when the threatened heavy rain arrived during the tea interval and wiped out the final session. At that stage the home side were 39 runs ahead with just two wickets left standing and 34 overs still to be bowled.

A maximum haul of bonus points had already ensured that Chris Read's side would take their place back on top of the Division One table, but it was the Yorkshire supporters who were metaphorically 'Singin' in the Rain' at the end.

The morning session was attritional – Notts striving for wickets; their opponents equally keen to deny, particularly nightwatchman Steven Patterson, who batted obdurately for almost two and a half hours.

With the second new ball still relatively fresh, Darren Pattinson struck a major blow for his side in getting rid of McGrath early on.

The normally free-scoring Andrew Gale hung around for 82 minutes in making just 14 before falling on the stroke of lunch. Ryan Sidebottom's vicious inswinger brought him a return catch off a combination of bat and instep. As Notts celebrated Gale hobbled off, clearly in discomfort.

Having survived the entire morning session, Patterson then fell just after the resumption. Patel, bowling from the Football Stand End with an attacking field, got the benefit as a bat/pad catch was taken at silly point by Mark Wagh.

Patterson was clearly not happy with the verdict – or maybe, like most observers, he was just confused as to what 'Waggy' was doing so close to the action!

Notts now had half of the wickets down and were still 41 ahead and they were soon given a further lift when Bairstow played around one from Pattinson.

As the afternoon wore on there were as many glances skywards as towards the action. It was getting blacker and blacker overhead. Brophy and Rashid put on 62 for the 7th wicket, but with tea approaching Sidebottom picked up two quick wickets.

Brophy was caught behind and then, with the final ball before the interval, Andre Adams took a blinder of a chance at third slip to dismiss Shahzad. There was no disguising the euphoria amongst the fielding side as they made their way off the field at the fall of that wicket.

Yorkshire's resistance had been commendable but the momentum was now with Notts and surely they would have been able to remove the last two obstacles with plenty of time remaining to knock off the winning runs.

Alas, no sooner had the players reached the sanctuary of the dressing rooms, torrential rain fell and almost immediately you knew that it wouldn't relent in time for a re-start.

The umpires gave as much time as they could before making the inevitable announcement that the conditions wouldn't improve and that the match had reached a soggy and unsatisfactory conclusion, to leave Mick Newell understandably frustrated.

"By tea-time we'd got ourselves into a very good position with Yorkshire eight down and only thirty-odd ahead, so had we had the last 34 overs we would have expected to win the game but the weather came in and that closed out the match."

Nevertheless, the result had seen Nottinghamshire return to the top of the table.

"It's important we got 11 points from the match, which is a good return from a drawn match, and the fact that Yorkshire didn't get many points is good for us but it doesn't leave us with much of a lead. Somerset, Lancashire and maybe one or two other counties will still fancy their chances of getting into the top couple."

SCORECARD

Yorkshire first innings		Runs	Balls	Mins	4s	6s
A Lyth	c Read b Sidebottom	0	5	4	-	-
JA Rudolph	run out	1	10	26	-	-
A McGrath	c Read b Adams	29	62	94	4	-
*AW Gale	lbw b Franks	24	29	33	5	-
JM Bairstow	b Sidebottom	45	81	115	9	-
+GL Brophy	b Adams	5	18	15	-	-
AU Rashid	lbw b Pattinson	13	16	13	2	-
A Shahzad	c Read b Franks	17	41	61	2	-
DJ Wainwright	not out	20	48	70	2	-
SA Patterson	lbw b Patel	10	31	38	-	-
OJ Hannon-Dalby	lbw b Patel	2	12	6	-	-
Extras	(3 b, 3 lb, 4 nb, 2 w)	12				
Total	(all out, 58.3 overs)	178				

Fall of wickets: 1-0 (Lyth, 0.5 ov), 2-5 (Rudolph, 5.5 ov), 3-36 (Gale, 13.2 ov), 4-82 (McGrath, 22.2 ov), 5-89 (Brophy, 26.5 ov), 6-104 (Rashid, 31.4 ov), 7-136 (Bairstow, 40.5 ov), 8-144 (Shahzad, 45.1 ov), 9-176 (Patterson, 56.1 ov), 10-178 (Hannon-Dalby, 58.3 ov)

Notts bowling	Overs	Mdns	Runs	Wkts	Wides	No-Balls
Sidebottom	15	6	25	2	-	-
Pattinson	12	1	61	1	-	2
Franks	14	3	40	2	2	-
Adams	14	3	44	2	-	-
Patel	3.3	1	2	2	-	-

Nottinghamshire first innings		Runs	Balls	Mins	4s	6s
AD Hales	c Brophy b Patterson	2	13	22	-	-
MJ Wood	lbw b Patterson	59	77	102	7	-
MA Wagh	b Hannon-Dalby	4	35	42	-	-
SR Patel	c Rudolph b Rashid	96	153	182	16	-
DJ Hussey	not out	251	250	343	29	3
*+CMW Read	c Rashid b Shahzad	42	89	104	5	-
AD Brown	b Patterson	2	8	5	-	-
PJ Franks	c Bairstow b Shahzad	61	68	62	10	1
AR Adams	not out	13	10	13	-	1
RJ Sidebottom						
DJ Pattinson						
Extras	(5 b, 5 lb, 2 nb, 3 w)	15				
Total	(7 wickets, declared, 117 overs)	545				

Fall of wickets: 1-22 (Hales, 5.4 ov), 2-52 (Wagh, 16.4 ov), 3-97 (Wood, 24.4 ov), 4-281 (Patel, 65.5 ov), 5-395 (Read, 93.1 ov), 6-400 (Brown, 94.4 ov), 7-511 (Franks, 113.4 ov)

Yorkshire bowling	Overs	Mdns	Runs	Wkts	Wides	No-Balls
Shahzad	21	1	115	2	1	-
Patterson	29	3	110	3	-	1
Hannon-Dalby	22	1	104	1	1	-
Rashid	23	0	104	1	-	-
Wainwright	11	1	57	0	-	-
McGrath	10	1	32	0	-	-
Lyth	1	0	13	0	-	-

The inside story of Nottinghamshire's LV= County Championship success

Yorkshire second innings		Runs	Balls	Mins	4s	6s
A Lyth	c Adams b Franks	37	42	58	7	-
JA Rudolph	c Adams b Pattinson	141	241	311	19	-
A McGrath	c Read b Pattinson	80	263	283	8	-
SA Patterson	c Wagh b Patel	26	116	143	1	-
*AW Gale	c and b Sidebottom	14	73	82	-	-
JM Bairstow	b Pattinson	7	24	34	-	-
+GL Brophy	c Read b Sidebottom	37	79	91	6	-
AU Rashid	not out	34	69	98	5	-
A Shahzad	c Adams b Sidebottom	3	15	15	-	-
DJ Wainwright						
OJ Hannon-Dalby						
Extras	(6 b, 12 lb, 8 nb, 1 w)	27				
Total	(8 wickets, 153 overs)	406				

Fall of wickets: 1-58 (Lyth, 13.1 ov), 2-269 (Rudolph, 88 ov), 3-276 (McGrath, 95.1 ov), 4-322 (Gale, 117.3 ov), 5-326 (Patterson, 124.5 ov), 6-336 (Bairstow, 127.3 ov), 7-398 (Brophy, 148.3 ov), 8-406 (Shahzad, 153 ov)

Notts bowling	Overs	Mdns	Runs	Wkts	Wides	No-Balls
Sidebottom	29	9	66	3	-	1
Pattinson	24	3	78	3	-	2
Franks	26	11	61	1	1	1
Adams	29	11	68	0	-	-
Patel	41	6	104	1	-	-
Hussey	4	0	11	0	-	-

DAVID HUSSEY – 13th BEST

Nottinghamshire's Championship match at Headingley Carnegie ended in disappointment, with heavy rain wiping out the final session with the visitors closing in on a deserved victory. Amongst a number of outstanding performances, in a game which served as a sharp reminder of just how compelling four day cricket can be, was David Hussey's magnificent 251 not out.

The Australian came to the wicket late on the first evening and was 35 not out at the close. During the 76 overs available during a rain-affected second day, he raced to 222 and the following morning, in the 20 minutes before Chris Read declared Notts' first innings closed, he advanced to 251 not out.

Conveniently for those who like a good stat or two, it was David's 100th first class innings for the county he joined in 2004 and the 22nd time he had reached three figures for them. He made his Notts' First Class debut on 21st April 2004 away at Durham and showed his intent by scoring 76 in an innings victory. His first ton for his new county came in his fifth match, 125 against Yorkshire at Headingley. This was the start of a particularly impressive run of scores against the White Rose county. After his 2010 effort he now boasts an average of 138.66 against them, having hit four centuries – 832 runs – from just eight visits to the crease. There must also be something about the Leeds air that agrees with him as he now boasts an average of 198 at Headingley, with three tons from just five innings.

On three previous occasions 'Huss' has reached 200. The first was for Victoria against New South Wales, a match-winning 212 not out as his state chased down a fourth innings 455 in a Pura Cup fixture in January 2004. His previous other two 'doubles' both came for Nottinghamshire at Trent Bridge, 232 not out against Warwickshire in August 2005 was followed in May 2007 when he recorded 275 against Essex.

David joins Notts greats William 'Dodger' Whysall, Derek Randall, Tim Robinson, Clive Rice and Kevin Pietersen, who all hit three double centuries during their time with the county, with only seven other players having hit more. Other footnotes to attach to his 251 not out are that it's the 13th highest individual score for Nottinghamshire and the 39th century of his career.

At the close of the second day at Headingly David did hope that he'd be allowed the time to go on and beat his previous best (275) but confirmed that the team effort would always come before individual milestones. Brother Mike Hussey scored three triple centuries during his stint in county cricket with Northamptonshire – so don't rule out David having another attempt to reach that landmark!

The 13 highest individual scores for Nottinghamshire in first class cricket are:

312* WW Keeton v Middx 1939
296 AO Jones v Gloucs 1903
294 JR Gunn v Leics 1903
275 DJ Hussey v Essex 2007
274 AO Jones v Essex 1905
272 J Iremonger v Kent 1904
268* JA Dixon v Sussex 1897
267 A Shrewsbury v Middx 1887
267 A Shrewsbury v Sussex 1890
266 J Hardstaff jnr v Leics 1937
261 WW Keeton v Gloucs 1934
254* KP Pietersen v Middx 2002
251* DJ Hussey v Yorkshire 2010

Match 12

NOTTINGHAMSHIRE v WARWICKSHIRE

August 16th, 17th 2010
(match scheduled for 4 days but completed in two)
Venue: Trent Bridge, Nottingham
Toss: won by Nottinghamshire who elected to bat
Umpires: NL Bainton & RA Kettleborough
Result: Nottinghamshire won by an innings and 55 runs
Points: Nottinghamshire 22 (Batting 3, Bowling 3) Warwickshire 3 (Bowling 3)

16th August – Day One

Notts batting on day one with Chris Woakes bowling to David Hussey

Although this was the twelfth County Championship game of the season, it was only the second time that Nottinghamshire had selected the same starting eleven from the previous match. For reasons of form, fitness, international availability or even law exams, Mick Newell had been unable to have any continuity with team selection, but having come so close to defeating Yorkshire it was, at last, a case of 'same again'.

Much had happened though since the side had left Headingley Carnegie – notably the huge disappointment of losing a rain-ruined semi final against Somerset at the twenty20 Finals Day just 48 hours earlier. If the side were a little deflated by the experience no-one could really blame them.

Warwickshire arrived at Trent Bridge fortified by a seven wicket victory at Southend over Essex, another side desperately scrapping to avoid relegation.

Chris Read won the toss and decided to have first use of a wicket that did have a greenish tinge to it and may well have given him food for thought as to whether it would assist his bowlers more than his batters on the opening day.

As it transpired, Notts were dismissed for just 328 in 87.5 overs but it looked an above-par total, provided the home attack bowled well during the remainder of the contest. Most batsmen got starts, although only Ali Brown, with 76, and Mark Wagh, 54, passed fifty. Warwickshire's openers saw it through to the close, having survived a nervy six overs.

Hales and Wood again fell with modest scores at the top of the order, but then Wagh, Patel, Hussey, Brown and Read all made handy contributions as Notts reached tea on 253-6 from 64 overs.

Wagh had again delivered against his old side and appeared well set before nicking Woakes to slip, where Darren Maddy took a fine low catch. Chris Read fell to the same bowler for 45, having hit Boyd Rankin for two sixes.

Brown batted almost 50 overs for his 76, but it was a gritty effort and he held the innings together before flicking Rankin straight to Chopra on the square leg boundary.

A useful 18 not out from Ryan Sidebottom saw Notts up to 328, at which point last man Pattinson edged Rankin to slip. Bears skipper Ian Westwood and Varun Chopra made it safely through to stumps.

Close of Day One – Warwickshire 13-0
(Westwood 10*, Chopra 3*, 6 overs)

17th August – Day Two

For the second time in a month Warwickshire's batsmen subsided against Nottinghamshire's seamers. At Edgbaston it had been Stuart Broad's eight-fer that had sliced through their second innings – on this overcast Tuesday they were dismissed twice in a day, with Ryan Sidebottom and Andre Adams leading the way with 15 wickets between them. Paul Franks picked up the remainder, and so rarely will a bowler have taken five wickets in a day and been outshone by two of his colleagues.

There was no indication that this would be anything other than a tough day in the field for Notts when play began and Westwood and Chopra survived the initial half hour with assurance.

Sidebottom parted them, the left-handed Westwood taken low down by Read with the score on 32. The introduction of Adams into the bowling attack from the Radcliffe Road End heralded the start of an astonishing spell which saw him produce 53 consecutive deliveries without conceding a run. Additionally, he picked up three wickets during that time, Chopra and Troughton lbw and Maddy well taken by Hales at slip.

The inside story of Nottinghamshire's LV= County Championship success

From 32-0 and 53-1 the visitors were now in freefall and Paul Franks helped them on their way as he also began his spell in miserly fashion. Six consecutive maidens included the wickets of Clarke, who was caught behind, and youngster Ateeq Javid, who fatally left one alone and turned to find only one stump remaining in the ground.

Sidebottom returned to mop up Ambrose, for a duck, and then Keith Barker – and at 98-9 it looked as if Warwickshire wouldn't get beyond the century again, having been dismissed for exactly 100 in the fixture at Edgbaston four weeks earlier.

A late slog by Chris Woakes and Boyd Rankin managed to get the total up to 121 before Adams struck again, collecting his fourth wicket with the help of a diving catch from Sidebottom. Extras, with 22, had been the top scorer!

Midway through the day it wasn't the greatest of surprises when Read invited his guests to follow-on, 207 behind. Once more, things looked well to begin with as Westwood and Chopra this time batted for 17 overs in compiling a partnership worth 48.

Westwood went first, clean bowled by Adams for 14, but it appeared as if a stubborn rearguard would ensure the match went into a third day at least as Chopra and Maddy took the total up to 87-1.

From then on it was carnage as nine wickets fell for just 65. Sidebottom claimed five of them in a devilishly impressive spell which confirmed that for as long as he remained a Notts player then he would be sure to give of his best. Not only did he bowl with pace and late movement, he was visibly enjoying his work. Fist-pumping, high-five celebrations followed the fall of each wicket as victory drew closer.

After Adams had dismissed Maddy, clipping straight into the hands of Matt Wood at mid-wicket, Ryan took over – like a cat toying with a mouse, he teased and tormented the Warwickshire batters before putting Chopra, Clarke and Troughton out of their misery in rapid succession and then trapping Ambrose plum in front of his stumps first ball. The former England wicketkeeper, in fairly wretched form for most of the summer, had been dismissed for a pair in a day.

Even at 'swing-friendly' Trent Bridge this was extraordinarily controlled bowling against a side that suddenly appeared to lose the will to fight any longer.

For the second time Ateeq Javid was bowled not offering a shot as Adams grabbed his third wicket of the innings. Sidebottom sent back Barker to secure his five-fer, and at 132-8 Read asked for the extra hour to complete the victory.

In the fifth of the final eight overs Paul Franks nipped one back through the gate to send Imran Tahir's middle stump leaping for freedom and in the penultimate over of the extra allocation Woakes slashed the same bowler to David Hussey at second slip to wrap up the innings victory inside two days.

Andre Adams confessed that it wasn't the first time he'd begun a session with eight consecutive maidens.

"I've done it once before back in New Zealand a couple of years ago. The whole idea was just to try and create pressure and make sure they weren't going anywhere. If the wickets came, the wickets came!

"We just wanted to put the ball in the right areas and we felt that if we did that for long enough then wickets would come."

'Dre's recent performances had brought comparisons with another former Kiwi and Trent Bridge favourite, Sir Richard Hadlee, a likeness which brought a big smile – and a confession. *"I was actually looking at Paddles' record today and he took 97 wickets at 11 when they won the Championship here – so I'm a fair way behind that – but to bowl a spell where you get compared to the great Richard Hadlee is very nice indeed."*

What Do Points Make?

For David Hussey it marked the end of yet another period with Nottinghamshire.

"What a way to go out, 20 wickets in a day. The boys bowled superbly and hopefully they will now go on to win the Championship. Hopefully I'll be back next year because I love playing here – I get along with everyone here and hopefully there'll be enough gaps in the calendar for me to return.

"Unfortunately I've got to go back to a pre-season camp up in Darwen. I'm rapped to be captain of Victoria but it means I've got to miss out on a couple of games here so will miss the chance to help Notts win the Championship, but I'll be keeping in touch with everyone – lots of texts and there'll be lots of internet action so I can follow what's going on."

Fifteen wickets between them in the day, Ryan and Andre celebrate

SCORECARD

Nottinghamshire first innings		Runs	Balls	Mins	4s	6s
AD Hales	c Ambrose b Rankin	9	14	16	2	-
MJ Wood	c Ambrose b Woakes	15	28	36	2	-
MA Wagh	c Maddy b Woakes	54	109	155	8	-
SR Patel	c Javid b Maddy	34	42	52	7	-
DJ Hussey	b Woakes	32	46	50	6	-
AD Brown	c Chopra b Rankin	76	138	172	9	-
*+CMW Read	b Maddy	45	52	67	4	2
PJ Franks	lbw b Imran Tahir	17	29	50	2	-
AR Adams	b Clarke	6	16	12	-	-
RJ Sidebottom	not out	18	40	51	4	-
DJ Pattinson	c Maddy b Rankin	6	17	15	1	-
Extras	(8 lb, 8 nb)	16				
Total	(all out, 87.5 overs)	328				

Fall of wickets: 1-19 (Hales, 4 ov), 2-45 (Wood, 8.3 ov), 3-105 (Patel, 22.1 ov), 4-146 (Hussey, 35.4 ov), 5-165 (Wagh, 44 ov), 6-248 (Read, 62.2 ov), 7-279 (Franks, 69.4 ov), 8-292 (Adams, 83.3 ov), 9-322 (Brown, 83.3 ov), 10-328 (Pattinson, 87.5 ov)

Warwickshire bowling	Overs	Mdns	Runs	Wkts	Wides	No-Balls
Woakes	18	4	59	3	-	-
Rankin	14.5	0	66	3	-	1
Barker	9	1	35	0	-	-
Clarke	11	1	53	1	-	-
Maddy	17	3	52	2	-	2
Imran Tahir	18	1	55	1	-	1

Warwickshire first innings		Runs	Balls	Mins	4s	6s
*IJ Westwood	c Read b Sidebottom	19	44	60	4	-
V Chopra	lbw b Adams	15	89	117	1	-
DL Maddy	c Hales b Adams	8	35	34	1	-
JO Troughton	lbw b Adams	0	5	4	-	-
R Clarke	c Read b Franks	15	48	52	3	-
A Javid	b Franks	5	32	47	-	-
+TR Ambrose	c Adams b Sidebottom	0	8	10	-	-
KHD Barker	c Hussey b Sidebottom	4	17	21	-	-
CR Woakes	not out	19	29	44	4	-
Imran Tahir	c Adams b Franks	1	3	2	-	-
WB Rankin	c Sidebottom b Adams	13	16	17	2	-
Extras	(13 b, 7 lb, 2 nb)	22				
Total	(all out, 54.1 overs)	121				

Fall of wickets: 1-32 (Westwood, 15 ov), 2-53 (Maddy, 25.3 ov), 3-53 (Troughton, 27.2 ov), 4-58 (Chopra, 29.3 ov), 5-83 (Clarke, 41.4 ov), 6-84 (Javid, 43.1 ov), 7-86 (Ambrose, 44.1 ov), 8-97 (Barker, 48.2 ov), 9-98 (Imran Tahir, 49.2 ov), 10-121 (Rankin, 54.1 ov)

Notts bowling	Overs	Mdns	Runs	Wkts	Wides	No-Balls
Sidebottom	18	5	37	3	-	-
Pattinson	12	3	35	0	-	1
Adams	13.1	9	14	4	-	-
Franks	11	6	15	3	-	-

What Do Points Make?

Warwickshire second innings (following on)		Runs	Balls	Mins	4s	6s
*IJ Westwood	b Adams	14	57	60	2	-
V Chopra	b Sidebottom	54	103	125	8	-
DL Maddy	c Wood b Adams	11	31	50	2	-
JO Troughton	c Read b Sidebottom	13	23	29	3	-
R Clarke	b Sidebottom	4	2	1	1	-
A Javid	b Adams	1	19	33	-	-
+TR Ambrose	lbw b Sidebottom	0	1	1	-	-
KHD Barker	c Read b Sidebottom	10	18	21	2	-
CR Woakes	c Hussey b Franks	20	32	42	3	-
Imran Tahir	b Franks	11	23	24	-	1
WB Rankin	not out	0	5	8	-	-
Extras	(10 lb, 4 nb)	14				
Total	(all out, 52 overs)	152				

Fall of wickets: 1-48 (Westwood, 17 ov), 2-87 (Maddy, 30 ov), 3-91 (Chopra, 32.3 ov), 4-95 (Clarke, 32.5 ov), 5-108 (Troughton, 36.5 ov), 6-108 (Ambrose, 37 ov), 7-118 (Javid, 41.1 ov), 8-122 (Barker, 43 ov), 9-151 (Imran Tahir, 49.4 ov), 10-152 (Woakes, 52 ov)

Notts bowling	Overs	Mdns	Runs	Wkts	Wides	No-Balls
Sidebottom	16	4	35	5	-	-
Pattinson	5	1	34	0	-	2
Adams	16	7	37	3	-	-
Patel	4	2	16	0	-	-
Franks	11	3	20	2	-	-

Match 13

NOTTINGHAMSHIRE v LANCASHIRE

August 24th, 25th, 26th, 27th 2010 (4 day match)
Venue: Trent Bridge, Nottingham
Toss: won by Lancashire who elected to bat
Umpires: MJD Bodenham & MA Gough
Result: Nottinghamshire won by 3 wickets
Points: Nottinghamshire 20 (Batting 1, Bowling 3)
Lancashire 6 (Batting 3, Bowling 3)

24th August – Day One

Alone with his thoughts – what a big part Shivnarine Chanderpaul was about to play in Nottinghamshire's season

Having run into the stubborn defiance of Shivnarine Chanderpaul for most of the first day of this match, Nottinghamshire were suddenly reprieved with a flurry of late wickets as the away side closed on 300-6. The West Indian had scored an unbeaten century last season against Chris Read's team for his previous county, Durham, and went close again, but his departure for 92 heralded a spell of four wickets for just 17 runs to inspire what had looked a weary-looking bowling unit.

Notts had been forced into one change from the side that had ruthlessly destroyed Warwickshire in the previous game. To replace David Hussey, who had returned to an Australian 'boot camp' helping his Victorian Bushrangers side prepare for their impending Champions League twenty20 duties in South Africa, was Steven Mullaney – chomping at the bit having missed the last three four-day games and keen to make an impression against his former employers.

Lancashire began the match in fourth place in the table, 31 points behind leaders Notts, but the sides also had to meet at Old Trafford in September, so two victories for the Red Rose county would alter things significantly in their favour.

Glenn Chapple won the toss for the visitors and opted to bat first on a greenish wicket and was rewarded as both openers passed 50 before lunch, which was taken on 118-1. Paul Horton had advanced to a 53-ball half century before Andre Adams nipped one back off the seam to trap him lbw.

Adams should have enjoyed further success, but both Smith, on 41, and Chilton, on 1, were put down in consecutive overs in the slips before eventually a catch was taken – Hales clinging on to a sharp one to his left to despatch Smith off Sidebottom's bowling.

A near 50-over stand between Chanderpaul and Mark Chilton then monopolised the rest of the day's play. As a spectacle it was less than riveting – though purists would have enjoyed the way Lancashire ground their way towards a healthy total.

There can't be many more infuriating batsmen around than Chanderpaul. His stance would appear to be at odds with convention, but he's so light on his feet and his timing so crisp he rarely gives the bowlers any hint of encouragement.

His fifty came from 88 balls faced, whilst Chilton eventually reached his own half century from 143 as the pair seemed intent on batting through to the close. The taking of the new ball altered the shape of the first day though. Sidebottom finally breached the West Indian's defences as umpire Martin Bodenham upheld the appeal for leg before.

Shortly afterwards bad light drove the players from the field and many spectators left the ground believing that, as it was almost six o'clock, play had been concluded for the day. Moments later the filthy black clouds parted and a ray of sunshine beamed down on West Bridgford, allowing time for four more overs to be delivered.

In that time Notts picked up a further three wickets – and another priceless point. Sidebottom snared Stephen Croft, helped by a superb low catch from Adams, who then ended the day on a hat-trick, getting nightwatchman Gary Keedy and Gareth Cross with the final two balls of the day.

Notts' fightback had been spectacular as Lancashire crumbled from 280-2 to 300-6 in the face of some penetrative bowling from Ryan and Andre – and also a little bit of help from above!

<h2 style="text-align:center">Close of Day One – Lancashire 300-6
(Chilton 61*, Sutton 2*, 93 overs)</h2>

25th August – Day Two

Nottinghamshire enjoyed much the better of a rain-shortened second day against Lancashire and closed it on 178-4, just 141 runs adrift, after skittling the visitors in quick fashion during the opening session and then rebounding after losing three early wickets themselves.

The day had begun with Andre Adams foiled in his bid for a hat-trick, but he wasn't long in sending Luke Sutton back, thanks to a fine catch at third slip from Samit Patel.

In the next over Mark Chilton's vigil was over and he would have been disappointed to battle hard for more than five hours and then be dismissed not playing a shot to Ryan Sidebottom.

Adams, continuing his superb form from the previous match, appeared to have the ball on a string as he then wasted little time in sending Sajid Mahmood and Kyle Hogg back for his 50th and 51st first class wickets of the season and to finish with county best figures of 6-79. Sidebottom took the other four wickets to fall, also at a personal cost of 79.

Lancashire's collapse had been spectacular. From 280-2 they had lost eight wickets for 39 runs and their last seven wickets had fallen in the space of just 56 deliveries.

Even allowing for the fact that it should have been much more, 319 was still a respectable first innings total on a surface that provided the seam bowlers with plenty of assistance and Lancashire soon had the home side in difficulties at 37-3.

Matt Wood was caught behind in the first over and Mark Wagh and Samit Patel soon followed as Notts reached the lunch interval on 38-3.

Alex Hales went to his 50 off 97 balls and with Ali Brown stemmed the Lancs tide with a stand of 57 before the latter fell to Mahmood for 28.

Chris Read then offered staunch support to Hales and by tea Notts were closing in on their first batting point. The rains, which had been threatening all day, then began to fall heavily during the tea interval and it quickly became apparent that play would be washed out for the remainder of the day.

Close of Day Two – Nottinghamshire 178-4
(Hales 87*, Read 35*, 53 overs)

26th August – Day Three

Remember those long hot balmy summers of our youth when it didn't rain for the whole of the cricket season? Well, slight exaggeration perhaps, but Thursday 26th August would have been considered a safe bet for a decent spot of weather most years, but, sadly, not in 2010. It rained all night long and continued for most of the morning.

Early in the piece the umpires announced that there would be no play before lunch. Then it was a case of "We'll have a look when it stops" and then "We'll give it time to brighten up as the forecast isn't so bad for later in the day". Eventually, once tea had been consumed, common sense kicked in and everyone headed off for home with play officially abandoned at around 4.30pm.

What Do Points Make?

The timing of these things is never great, but at 5pm it was officially announced via a Trent Bridge Press release that Ryan Sidebottom would be leaving Notts at the end of the season "after the two parties had failed to agree terms on a new contract".

In truth the news wasn't totally unexpected, although it was a bit of a 'downer' at the end of an utterly frustrating day spent watching the rains fall, and with only the prospect of Nottinghamshire batting on for bonus points on the final day to look forward to – or would there be a twist?

'Wet wet wet' – Trent Bridge in August.

Close of Day Three – No play. Nottinghamshire still 178-4

27th August – Day Four

Nottinghamshire gave themselves a golden chance of winning the 2010 LV= County Championship title when they pulled off a three wicket victory over Lancashire in one of the most thrilling day's cricket you could ever hope to see.

Desperate for a victory themselves, the visitors had agreed to 'make a game of things' on the final day in the hope of bowling Notts out in two sessions, and to be fair to them, they came much closer to doing it than their critics would later give them credit for.

As a regular 'early-bird' at most cricket venues, the 90 minutes or so before the start of play usually follows a similar pattern. One or two batsmen like to have an early net session, then there's the protracted catching, fielding and bowling drills, stretching exercises and then perhaps a game of football or touch-rugby.

The inside story of Nottinghamshire's LV= County Championship success

On this (thankfully dry and sunny) Friday morning it was readily apparent that Lancashire captain Glenn Chapple was a man on a mission. He'd been one of the first on the outfield and stood alone, close to the playing strip, for around ten minutes. Eyeing the pavilion doors, he suddenly set off walking briskly to greet his opposite number, Chris Read.

The two then distanced themselves (over in front of the Hound Road Stand) and engaged in earnest conversation for several minutes before each joined up with the rest of their team-mates. Although it had been strongly reported in the press beforehand that Lancashire would try and give themselves the best chance they could of beating Notts and getting back into Championship contention, it didn't seem likely that the table-toppers would agree to anything that may turn the supposed three-horse race (Somerset and Yorkshire were just behind Notts going into this round of matches, although both had played a game more) into a four-horse one!

Glen Chapple (right) headed straight for Chris Read to offer a final day run-chase

Batting points were surely the way forward for Chris Read's side. They had Alex Hales well set and could bat all day if they wanted to try and get as close as they could to 400.

That seemed the plan from the outset as a couple of quiet overs were safely negotiated. Hales and Read both like to score their runs at a decent lick so an increase in the tempo was not surprising, but it proved to be the undoing of the younger man, who'd reached 98 when he flicked at Kyle Hogg and was caught behind.

Alex's dismay at being so close to a second career ton was surely magnified when Read then hit a boundary to bring up the 200 and promptly declared.

Rarely has there been such a transformation over a Trent Bridge crowd. Seemingly set for a soporific day in the sun and only the occasional boundary to distract them from their sudokus, they quickly came to terms with what had just taken place.

Notts had thrown away the opportunity of some guaranteed batting points to engage in a run-chase which could potentially bring another side back into contention for the title.

It's fair to say they weren't all in agreement with Read's decision and that depth of feeling was intensified as Alex Hales, Ali Brown and Matt Wood shared 13 overs of less-than-testing bowling, whilst Andre Adams and Ryan Sidebottom remained unemployed.

In the light of the previous evening's announcement about his future, Ryan perhaps welcomed the opportunity of a leisurely graze down at long-leg, although his true feelings were carefully shielded behind his sunglasses.

Leading up to lunch Lancashire put their toe down and reached 143-1 by the interval – Steven Mullaney opened the bowling and clean bowled Horton for just 4, but Tom Smith and Mark Chilton went along at the required tempo before a declaration which meant that Notts had 64 overs in which to chase down 260.

Even those who had pooh-poohed the suggestion of entering into a run-chase realised that this had been a good bit of business by Read – provided his batters came good!

The wicket clearly still offered some assistance if the bowlers put it in the right areas and Wood, for 2, and Wagh, 3, went quickly. Had Gary Keedy not made a right horlicks of a chance down at long leg and spilled Samit Patel early on then the home side would have been in desperate straits at 24-3.

Reprieved, Samit helped Hales add 86 in sixteen and a half overs for the third wicket before Mahmood got him with one which appeared to keep very low.

Having looked crestfallen earlier in the day, when he'd gone for 98, Hales seemed to have erased it from his mind as he brought up his 50 with his tenth boundary from just 58 deliveries.

Ali Brown joined him in a stand of 84 which appeared to have taken the game completely away from Chapple's side, but there was a further twist when they picked up two wickets in quick succession.

Hales created an unwanted piece of cricketing trivia when he was dismissed in the 90s for the second time in a day, again to a catch behind but this time off the slow left arm spin of Gary Keedy. If it was humanly possible to look even more distraught than he'd been during the morning session then Alex achieved it as he trudged off for 93. For the second time in the match though he had batted superbly and reinforced the viewpoint of many that an international career will eventually beckon.

Barely had the applause for his innings subsided when Chris Read went to the same bowler for 2. Suddenly it was game on – with half the side out and still 61 needed.

Brown calmed any nerves with a majestic 65, and even though he fell to Kyle Hogg, as did Paul Franks next ball, Steven Mullaney's 34 not out paved the way for Andre Adams to bludgeon a couple of boundaries to take Notts to their victory target.

The win had been achieved with more than eight overs to spare and three wickets in hand and had surely swung the title in Notts' direction as they moved 16 points clear of Somerset, with Yorkshire a further three points behind.

Lancashire's challenge had now firmly been eradicated, and although they came in for a fair amount of stick from some supporters up and down the country for agreeing to leave Notts just 260 to get, they gave themselves the only chance they had of staying in the Championship race. Had Keedy caught Patel it may have been different – and although Hales and Brown took the major batting plaudits the match had initially swung when the visitors collapsed so dramatically in the first innings.

Having been dismissed twice in one day in the 90s, Alex Hales reflected on a fairly bizarre few hours.

"I've obviously got mixed emotions. I'm really disappointed that I didn't cross the hundred mark on both occasions, but at the same time it's a really good win for the lads and it's put us in a really good spot to hopefully win the Championship this year.

"They had an in-out field for me at the start of the day and there were plenty of ones on offer and all I needed were a couple of singles!"

Alex didn't have much time to hang about as he was soon back on the field, bowling!

"It's not often I get the chance to have a bowl and it's the first time I've bowled seam up for about five years, but all credit to Lancashire for wanting to set the game up.

"I was then even more determined to get my head down in the second innings but still couldn't get over the line. I felt in great shape, but again was just very disappointed to get out. I could sense the crowd were with me – they've been brilliant all season and I just hope we can reward them with some silverware this year."

The inside story of Nottinghamshire's LV= County Championship success

SCORECARD

Lancashire first innings		Runs	Balls	Mins	4s	6s
PJ Horton	lbw b Adams	51	57	76	8	-
TC Smith	c Hales b Sidebottom	61	111	134	8	-
MJ Chilton	lbw b Sidebottom	67	211	308	10	-
S Chanderpaul	lbw b Sidebottom	92	171	183	13	-
SJ Croft	c Adams b Sidebottom	9	26	26	2	-
G Keedy	lbw b Adams	4	3	2	1	-
GD Cross	c Hales b Adams	0	1	1	-	-
+LD Sutton	c Patel b Adams	11	15	22	1	-
SI Mahmood	lbw b Adams	4	2	6	1	-
*G Chapple	not out	0	1	5	-	-
KW Hogg	c Read b Adams	0	5	2	-	-
Extras	(4 b, 7 lb, 6 nb, 3 w)	20				
Total	(all out, 100 overs)	319				

Fall of wickets: 1-87 (Horton, 17.5 ov), 2-129 (Smith, 34.1 ov), 3-280 (Chanderpaul, 84.2 ov), 4-292 (Croft, 91 ov), 5-297 (Keedy, 92 ov), 6-297 (Cross, 92.1 ov), 7-311 (Sutton, 98 ov), 8-319 (Chilton, 99 ov), 9-319 (Mahmood, 99.2 ov), 10-319 (Hogg, 100 ov)

Notts bowling	Overs	Mdns	Runs	Wkts	Wides	No-Balls
Sidebottom	26	7	79	4	-	-
Pattinson	15	3	61	0	1	3
Adams	26	6	79	6	1	-
Franks	17	4	40	0	1	-
Mullaney	8	2	16	0	-	-
Patel	8	1	33	0	-	-

Nottinghamshire first innings		Runs	Balls	Mins	4s	6s
AD Hales	c Sutton b Hogg	98	176	228	16	-
MJ Wood	c Sutton b Chapple	0	5	2	-	-
MA Wagh	c Smith b Mahmood	6	28	30	-	-
SR Patel	c Sutton b Hogg	10	26	35	1	1
AD Brown	lbw b Mahmood	28	32	42	5	-
*+CMW Read	not out	49	82	106	8	1
SJ Mullaney	not out	0	4	3	-	-
PJ Franks						
AR Adams						
RJ Sidebottom						
DJ Pattinson						
Extras	(1 b, 3 lb, 8 nb)	12				
Total	(5 wickets, declared, 58.1 overs)	203				

Fall of wickets: 1-1 (Wood, 1 ov), 2-14 (Wagh, 9.1 ov), 3-37 (Patel, 18.1 ov), 4-94 (Brown, 29.1 ov), 5-199 (Hales, 57.2 ov)

Lancashire bowling	Overs	Mdns	Runs	Wkts	Wides	No-Balls
Chapple	13	3	41	1	-	-
Mahmood	15	4	43	2	-	-
Hogg	12	2	47	2	-	2
Smith	13	1	49	0	-	2
Keedy	5.1	1	19	0	-	-

What Do Points Make?

Lancashire second innings		Runs	Balls	Mins	4s	6s
TC Smith	not out	76	79	89	11	1
PJ Horton	b Mullaney	4	2	5	1	-
MJ Chilton	not out	49	64	82	6	-
SJ Croft						
GD Cross						
S Chanderpaul						
+LD Sutton						
*G Chapple						
SI Mahmood						
KW Hogg						
G Keedy						
Extras	(2 lb, 2 nb, 10 w)	14				
Total	(1 wicket, declared, 24 overs)	143				

Fall of wickets: 1-4 (Horton, 1.2 ov)

Notts bowling	Overs	Mdns	Runs	Wkts	Wides	No-Balls
Pattinson	3	1	11	0	1	-
Mullaney	8	0	45	1	-	1
Hales	5	1	21	0	-	-
Brown	7	0	53	0	1	-
Wood	1	0	11	0	-	-

Nottinghamshire second innings		Runs	Balls	Mins	4s	6s
AD Hales	c Sutton b Keedy	93	125	169	14	-
MJ Wood	c Cross b Mahmood	2	14	21	-	-
MA Wagh	c Smith b Chapple	3	7	3	-	-
SR Patel	b Mahmood	37	57	69	7	-
AD Brown	c Smith b Hogg	65	86	110	7	-
*+CMW Read	c Croft b Keedy	2	8	8	-	-
SJ Mullaney	not out	34	34	37	3	2
PJ Franks	c Horton b Hogg	0	1	1	-	-
AR Adams	not out	8	3	1	2	-
RJ Sidebottom						
DJ Pattinson						
Extras	(4 b, 5 lb, 6 nb, 2 w)	17				
Total	(7 wickets, 55.2 overs)	261				

Fall of wickets: 1-20 (Wood, 5.1 ov), 2-23 (Wagh, 6.2 ov), 3-109 (Patel, 23 ov), 4-193 (Hales, 43.1 ov), 5-199 (Read, 45.3 ov), 6-252 (Brown, 54.3 ov), 7-252 (Franks, 54.4 ov)

Lancashire bowling	Overs	Mdns	Runs	Wkts	Wides	No-Balls
Chapple	17.2	4	67	1	-	-
Mahmood	16	1	77	2	-	1
Smith	5	0	31	0	-	2
Hogg	3	0	20	2	-	-
Keedy	14	0	57	2	2	-

Match 14

DURHAM v NOTTINGHAMSHIRE

August 31st, September 1st, 2nd, 3rd 2010 (4 day match)
Venue: Emirates Durham ICG, Chester-le-Street
Toss: won by Durham who elected to bat
Umpires: TE Jesty & NA Mallender
Result: Durham won by 210 runs
Points: Durham 23 (Batting 4, Bowling 3)
Nottinghamshire 6 (Batting 3, Bowling 3)

31st August – Day One

Having already experienced twenty20 and CB40 victories at Durham earlier in the season, Nottinghamshire were made to struggle on the first day of their County Championship fixture at Chester-le-Street as the home skipper, Phil Mustard, made an unbeaten century and the defending champions closed on 347-6.

Chris Read's side had ended Durham's long unbeaten sequence when they won at Trent Bridge in May and now appeared set to take over their mantle as four day champions, especially after the uplifting victory in the previous match against Lancashire.

Once more Mick Newell had to tinker with the Notts starting line-up as he welcomed an old face back into the side.

For the third consecutive season Adam Voges had accepted an invitation to jump on an airplane and succeed Hashim Amla and David Hussey as the third overseas player of the summer in Championship cricket.

Adam had arrived in Nottingham three days earlier and had already played twice – hitting 71 not out against Leicestershire before being unluckily run out for 2 against Durham in a couple of CB40 outings.

The Durham game, astonishingly, had been played the previous day – at Trent Bridge. Both sides had then travelled north for a four day encounter 150 miles away – a totally bizarre and unnecessary piece of fixture scheduling that should never have been approved.

Voges' place in the side had been created by the omission of Matt Wood. Four Championship games had produced 148 runs for Matt from six innings, but the 0 and 2 sustained against Lancashire had put paid to his chances of keeping possession of a starting berth.

There was one other change from the previous match, but confusion was high on the agenda when the side was announced at the toss, with twelve names included amongst the Notts ranks.

Over the course of the last couple of years it has become common practice for players to be pulled from a Championship game, on a whim, to join up with the national side. The opening day of the Durham match was a Tuesday and England had a twenty20 international

— 113 —

scheduled for the forthcoming Sunday. However, the side wasn't going to be announced until Wednesday. (Confused?)

As such, the ECB had permitted Notts to begin the game with Ryan Sidebottom, but if he were to be selected for his country then he would have to leave the north east after the end of the second day's play to join up with the rest of the England party.

Mick Newell, deciding that Ryan's release was virtually inevitable, opted to include Luke Fletcher from the start and to give Darren Pattinson a couple of days' rest before bringing him in for the final two days of the contest. (Best laid plans etc!)

The opportunity to get Sidebottom in the game from the start was handed to Notts when Phil Mustard, the Durham skipper, won the toss and decided to bat first.

With just the sixth ball of the match Ryan ripped one into the pads of Michael Di Venuto and umpire Jesty sent the Tasmanian on his way back to the pavilion.

Luke Fletcher had bowled 35 overs without a wicket in his previous Championship game, at Chelmsford, but he soon broke that sequence as Gordon Muchall guided the ball straight to Patel at gully.

Dale Benkenstein was caught behind in Andre Adams' first over and Ben Harmison fell cheaply to Paul Franks. Four wickets down by lunch made Mustard's decision to bat look a little suspect.

A patient 67 from Mark Stoneman, one of seven left-handers in the Durham line-up, eased home nerves, and with Ian Blackwell adding a controlled 59, the innings gained some impetus in the afternoon sunshine before both fell to the trusty Adams.

As the wicket flattened and the ball deviated less run-scoring became easier, although Notts should have made further in-roads before tea with both Phil Mustard and Scott Borthwick getting lives.

On 22 Mustard appeared to be a touch fortunate when a delivery from Sidebottom appeared to be deflected through to Read. The entire fielding unit went up as one to celebrate and the bowler looked aghast when the decision didn't go his way.

Shortly afterwards Borthwick edged the left-armer, but Read, diving across in front of his slips, couldn't hang on and parried it away for a couple of runs to third man.

Those two opportunities were the last to be presented as the pair batted through the final session, with Mustard reaching his fourth career century and his younger partner passing his half century.

Close of Day One – Durham 347-6
(Mustard 117*, Borthwick 54*, 96 overs)

1st September – Day Two

Nottinghamshire fought back well on the second day to wrap up Durham's first innings in quick fashion and respond with a fighting 257-6 by the close.

Andre Adams had again eclipsed his colleagues to take the bowling honours. His five wicket haul meant he'd picked up 18 Championship wickets in the last four innings in which he'd bowled.

Half centuries from Ali Brown and Chris Read, plus 48 from Adam Voges, had ensured that Notts had remained competitive with the bat.

The inside story of Nottinghamshire's LV= County Championship success

**Pencils sharpened! The scorers are ready for their duties
– Notts' Brian Hewes on the right**

Mustard and Borthwick added a further 15 runs in the morning session before they were parted. The stand had put on 174 for the seventh wicket when Sidebottom had the Durham skipper caught behind – retribution of sorts for the previous day's not out verdict against the same batsman, but it had cost Nottinghamshire a considerable amount of runs.

Typically, after a lengthy stand Liam Plunkett fell to the next delivery, and when Adams removed Mich Claydon and then ended Scott Borthwick's stay, four wickets had fallen in five overs for just ten runs.

In the hour's batting before lunch Nottinghamshire lost both openers, Samit Patel for 4 and Alex Hales for 13.

Mark Wagh's was the only wicket to fall during the afternoon session, but Voges, Brown and Read all appeared set for really big scores before their post-tea dismissals.

Read fell with two overs remaining in the day and Ryan Sidebottom went out to join Steven Mullaney as nightwatchman. Earlier in the day Ryan had, as expected, been selected to join the England squad for forthcoming twenty20 combat against Pakistan, so at the close he was classed as 'Retired Not Out' with Darren Pattinson to take his place at the start of the third day.

**Close of Day Two – Nottinghamshire 257-6
(Mullaney 23*, Sidebottom 5*, 90 overs)**

2nd September – Day Three

As with Durham 24 hours earlier, Nottinghamshire failed to capitalise on a decent overnight position and were unable to push on towards maximum batting bonus points. They were eventually dismissed for 343, a first innings deficit of 29, but then spent the remainder of the day trying to stem the flow of runs from the home side's top order.

Going into the match, the reigning county champions retained only the slimmest of mathematical possibilities that they could hang on to their crown, but clearly team spirit remained strong as they fought to deny Nottinghamshire an easy passage to the title.

By the close of the third day Phil Mustard's team had an overall lead of more than 300 with five wickets still in hand. The prospect of Nottinghamshire being given an inviting target to chase on the final day looked slim, but with the wicket likely to assist spinners Ian Blackwell and Scott Borthwick some staunch defiance would be needed to ensure valuable draw points.

Perhaps uniquely, a player who hadn't yet participated in the match walked out to bat at the start of play. Darren Pattinson, given a couple of days' rest in what seemed like a canny piece of team selection by Mick Newell, assumed Ryan Sidebottom's place in the side, replacing him as a not out batsman alongside Steven Mullaney.

Mullaney's hopes of a lengthy knock with the lower order were quickly snuffed out when he fell in the first over of the morning. Having added a couple to his overnight 23 he was squared-up by a delivery from Liam Plunkett and edged it to third slip.

A 40 minute period of consolidation produced a stand of 37 between Pattinson and Paul Franks before the latter chased a wide one from 'young Harmy' and was caught behind for 26.

Andre Adams made 10 and Luke Fletcher, fresh from a debut career century earlier in the week for the second team, enjoyed himself with a lusty 23, which included a powerfully-clubbed six off Borthwick.

Pattinson was last out for 19, but the innings had already lasted for 113 overs so any disappointment at their total was tempered by the fact that they hadn't been in a position to get any further batting points.

The day coincided with Darren Pattinson's 31st birthday and he'd celebrated by making a handy contribution with the bat, having stayed in the middle for more than 90 minutes. Had he been able to hang on for just a little while longer then perhaps events may have turned out differently.

There was still time for 15 minutes batting before lunch and 'Patto' was given the new ball from the Finchale End. As he released his first delivery he appeared to go over on his ankle and fall away dramatically to his left. Clearly the footholds hadn't been true and the bowler was in obvious pain as he left the field, with Adams completing the over.

Andre followed up his first innings five-wicket haul by dismissing both Durham openers early in the afternoon session. Round the wicket (of course) he trapped each of the left-handers, Di Venuto and Stoneman, comprehensively in front of all three stumps.

Gordon Muchall and Dale Benkenstein then began to dominate the proceedings. Driving, cutting and pulling at every opportunity, they rattled along, adding 144 in just under 30 overs.

A brief re-appearance from Pattinson proved ineffective. Clearly still troubled by the ankle injury, he went for 26 runs from two laboured overs before hobbling away for further treatment. Indeed, with Neil Edwards as fielding substitute and the side's resources stretched due to the 2nd XI's commitments, fitness coach Kevin Paxton was stripped and ready for action should any more injuries occur.

It was good to see Neil back in the ranks. After losing his place in the side he'd hoped to regain some form with the 2nd XI but had suffered a broken hand when batting down at The Rose Bowl. A popular and engaging member of the squad, he may yet have a productive time ahead of him as a Trent Bridge opener.

Muchall's half century came from just 52 balls, whilst Benkenstein made his at a more sedate pace, from 72, as the pair reached tea on 170-2.

Benkenstein is a class act, of that there is no doubt. As his innings prospered there were more and more home supporters relishing the fact that he was compiling these runs against Notts. When the two counties had met in the twenty20 competition, earlier in the season on the same ground, a boundary catch taken by Alex Hales had been strongly disputed by the home fans.

'Benks' had taken the word of the fielder that it had been 'clean' and walked off. Hales and Notts received some unwarranted abuse and, although the two sides remained professionally cordial, some snide comments from over the boundary boards persisted into the 4-day match.

The fact that Samit Patel extracted enough turn and bounce to end Benks' innings on 58, and that he followed it up by dismissing Ben Harmison and Gordon Muchall, was of dubious benefit with Durham possessing a couple of front line spinners in their line-up.

Muchall's ton had been impressive, from 126 balls faced and with 16 x 4s, but his work wasn't wasted with Blackwell also going to his own 50 before the close.

There was much for Mick Newell to ponder on at the close of play, with Darren Pattinson's injury uppermost in his thoughts.

"He's turned his ankle in the foot marks and won't play much further part in this game, other than batting, for which he should be OK. He's pretty doubtful now for Saturday (Warwickshire away in the CB40) but hopefully he'll be fit for next Tuesday.

"We wanted to rest him up in this game and get him going for next week without Ryan being around – but he's obviously a doubt now."

On the match situation, Mick felt Notts had done well in the early part of the day.

"We wanted to be as close to Durham as we could be; we wanted to use as many overs as we could to keep our second innings as short as possible and that went OK. It was an unusual supply of runs, with Fletch getting 20 odd – but I thought 340 was a pretty decent effort."

After a decent start to Durham's second innings, the match shifted back towards the hosts.

"I thought for the first 15-18 overs we did well. At 35-2 we had a little sniff there but the next half an hour's cricket was pretty ordinary and we let Durham get away and we sort of had to keep holding them back after tea as well.

"We bowled six or seven overs that were pretty hopeless really – if you bowl halfway down you are going to get hit around the ground. You can't bowl that short to good players on a good wicket.

"It wasn't that Durham came out with an overly-aggressive intent – we gave them the runs and after that we had to claw it back, which I thought we then did reasonably well but for half an hour it was pretty shabby stuff from us."

Mick agreed that Durham had batted positively.

Sign please! Mark Wagh obliges, with birthday boy Darren Pattinson next in line

"Gordon Muchall played very well – hit the bad balls away and played with some urgency and ran between the wickets with some intent so you've got to give him credit – and Benkenstein we know is one of the best players in the country."

Despite Samit Patel picking up three wickets with his slow left armers, the Notts Director of Cricket didn't think he'd received too much assistance. "I don't think the pitch is taking a huge amount of spin, but we'll see when Blackwell and Borthwick bowl tomorrow – it might be a different proposition. I expect them to do a lot of bowling as and when Durham eventually declare.

"If I was betting man I'd expect Durham will bat on for another 10-12 overs – maybe give themselves around 80 to bowl us out, with us needing a total of 350, which realistically will be difficult for us to get so it may be a question of survival, but we'll have to see how we start and it will also depend on what Durham leave.

"It's in their hands – they are very much dominant in the game and it's up to them to decide when they've had enough of batting."

Close of Day Three – Durham 279-5
(Blackwell 50*, Mustard 13*, 70 overs)

3rd September – Day Four

After competing well with their hosts for around three quarters of the contest, Nottinghamshire subsided meekly on the final afternoon and were eventually beaten by more than 200 runs.

Set an impossible target of 391 to win, the opportunity of some extended batting practice was tossed aside by the visitors, who were exposed by a burst of three wickets in four balls from Ben Harmison which altered the context of the day and heralded the onset of a crushing defeat.

For the third time in the match a wicket fell in the first over of the day, with Blackwell failing to add to his overnight 50 as he guided Luke Fletcher into the gloves of Chris Read.

Mustard and Borthwick then added some lustre to the total with a quickfire stand of 79 in 15 overs before the Durham skipper decided that he'd got enough runs and declared with a lead of 390 and with 78 overs remaining in the day.

From the outset Notts sprung a surprise, with Paul Franks walking out to open the batting alongside Alex Hales.

This was the sixth different opening combo that Notts had tried throughout the campaign, with Edwards, Shafayat, Hales, Patel, Wood and now Franks all having a go, and although this pairing added 31, it again couldn't be trumpeted as an outstanding success.

Paul had already survived a huge lbw appeal against the bowling of Mitch Claydon before the same bowler trapped him in front for 8.

With Mark Davies already off the field and unable to bowl, Durham's woes intensified when Liam Plunkett limped off as well. Ben Harmison was brought into the attack much sooner than he would have expected and was expensive in four overs before lunch.

He worked with the coaching staff through much of the lunch break and was allowed to continue when play re-started, with devastating effect. Hales had been timing the ball sweetly and a draw seemed the only logical outcome when 'Big Ben' swung the match.

Hales snicked him into the hands of Di Venuto at second slip and then Adam Voges got a faint touch on the next delivery. Samit Patel worked the hat-trick ball away for a couple but was then given out as the next ball clipped his back pad. It may have been a trifle harsh but up went the finger to transform the scoreboard from 52-1 to 54-4 in the space of four deliveries.

Not for the first time Nottinghamshire had been undone by a Harmison – only this time it wasn't injured absentee Steve who had caused the havoc but his younger sibling.

Mark Wagh and Ali Brown established an element of control again with a stand of 30, but when both fell to Blackwell, either side of Read's duck which gave Hamison a fourth victim, the omens didn't look good.

That the innings stretched into the final session – although not the final hour – was down to Steven Mullaney. Taking the opportunity to put bat to ball in a seemingly lost cause, he built on his form of the first innings to reach a very punchy 64 at better than a run a ball before he was last out. Attempting to hit Borthwick away to leg the ball ballooned up and was held by Mustard running at speed back towards fine leg.

Champions-elect in most people's eyes at the start of the week, Notts had under-performed to such an extent that the national media began to speculate on their ability to get over the finishing line.

Despite the defeat, there were still 22 points separating the leaders from nearest rivals Somerset, with Yorkshire – due up next at Trent Bridge – a further three points adrift.

After the disappointment Mick Newell revealed the thinking behind the new opening partnership. *"Our opening situation is well known as we're struggling to find someone to bat with Hales with any great consistency. Franksy is a decent player against quick bowling – that's probably more his strength than to bat against spin and we thought there'd be a lot of spin bowling later in the day.*

"It also gave us the option of pushing Samit back to number five and to hope that he'd bat for a longer period of time, but unfortunately it didn't work out like that."

Mick praised the efforts of Ben Harmison, who changed the course of the afternoon.

"If you look back at that over you'll see there were two or three quite special deliveries that were bowled and you've got to give him some credit for that. For the most part, for all of the seamers' bowling on that wicket there hadn't been a great deal happening, but that over completely transformed the game and within that session we lost six wickets, so by tea-time we were just about done."

The only plus point from the final passage of play was Steven Mullaney's knock.

"He's hitting the ball nicely and the situation meant he could play with a bit of freedom, with the field fairly well spread. He's hit the ball well all season and is one of the successes of our season, there's no doubt about that."

Looking to the upcoming game against Yorkshire, the Director of Cricket added: *"There haven't been many draws at Trent Bridge and hopefully we can force a result this time. It's a huge opportunity for us – win the game and we win the Championship."*

SCORECARD

Durham first innings		Runs	Balls	Mins	4s	6s
MJ Di Venuto	lbw b Sidebottom	0	6	4	-	-
MD Stoneman	lbw b Adams	67	141	204	11	-
GJ Muchall	c Patel b Fletcher	13	28	36	2	-
DM Benkenstein	c Read b Adams	13	14	15	1	-
BW Harmison	c Read b Franks	2	20	22	-	-
ID Blackwell	b Adams	59	108	144	5	-
*+P Mustard	c Read b Sidebottom	120	166	185	17	-
SG Borthwick	c Mullaney b Adams	68	117	185	12	-
LE Plunkett	c Read b Sidebottom	0	1	1	-	-
ME Claydon	c Read b Adams	1	5	5	-	-
M Davies	not out	5	17	16	1	-
Extras	(15 lb, 8 nb, 1 w)	24				
Total	(all out, 416 minutes, 103.5 overs)	372				

Fall of wickets: 1-4 (Di Venuto, 1 ov), 2-29 (Muchall, 9.4 ov), 3-53 (Benkenstein, 13.3 ov), 4-76 (Harmison, 20.2 ov), 5-163 (Stoneman, 50 ov), 6-188 (Blackwell, 57.2 ov), 7-362 (Mustard, 98.2 ov), 8-362 (Plunkett, 98.3 ov), 9-363 (Claydon, 99.2 ov), 10-372 (Borthwick, 103.5 ov)

Notts bowling	Overs	Mdns	Runs	Wkts	Wides	No-Balls
Sidebottom	27	3	100	3	-	1
Fletcher	22	4	85	1	-	1
Adams	27.5	6	92	5	-	2
Franks	18	4	48	1	1	-
Patel	7	1	15	0	-	-
Mullaney	2	0	17	0	-	-

The inside story of Nottinghamshire's LV= County Championship success

Nottinghamshire first innings		Runs	Balls	Mins	4s	6s
AD Hales	c Mustard b Davies	13	34	45	-	-
SR Patel	c Borthwick b Claydon	4	5	3	1	-
MA Wagh	b Plunkett	30	99	112	5	-
AC Voges	lbw b Davies	48	146	162	5	-
AD Brown	c sub (MA Wood) b Borthwick	52	112	133	5	-
*+CMW Read	c Mustard b Plunkett	56	92	97	7	1
SJ Mullaney	c Benkenstein b Plunkett	25	53	59	3	-
RJ Sidebottom	retired not out	5	7	9	1	-
DJ Pattinson	c sub (GR Breese) b Claydon	19	68	93	2	-
PJ Franks	c Mustard b Harmison	26	27	39	3	-
AR Adams	c Di Venuto b Harmison	10	10	9	2	-
LJ Fletcher	not out	23	29	36	2	1
Extras	(4 b, 15 lb, 8 nb, 5 w)	32				
Total	(all out, 409 minutes, 113 overs)	343				

Fall of wickets: 1-5 (Patel, 1 ov), 2-23 (Hales, 11.1 ov), 3-71 (Wagh, 32.3 ov), 4-146 (Voges, 58.5 ov), 5-196 (Brown, 73.1 ov), 6-252 (Read, 90 ov), 7-259 (Mullaney, 90.4 ov), 8-296 (Franks, 101.1 ov), 9-306 (Adams, 103.5 ov), 10-343 (Pattinson, 113 ov)

Durham bowling	Overs	Mdns	Runs	Wkts	Wides	No-Balls
Claydon	21	2	78	2	-	2
Davies	15	11	10	2	-	-
Benkenstein	7	2	31	0	-	-
Plunkett	25	5	66	3	-	2
Blackwell	21	8	33	0	-	-
Borthwick	20	2	78	1	-	-
Harmison	4	0	28	2	1	-

Durham second innings		Runs	Balls	Mins	4s	6s
MD Stoneman	lbw b Adams	13	29	51	2	-
MJ Di Venuto	lbw b Adams	15	32	34	2	-
GJ Muchall	lbw b Patel	111	141	170	17	-
DM Benkenstein	st Read b Patel	58	92	109	7	1
BW Harmison	b Patel	11	12	9	2	-
ID Blackwell	c Read b Fletcher	50	77	91	7	-
*+P Mustard	not out	51	93	108	4	-
SG Borthwick	not out	43	41	56	6	-
LE Plunkett						
ME Claydon						
M Davies						
Extras	(5 lb, 2 nb, 2 w)	9				
Total	(6 wickets, declared, 324 minutes, 86 overs)	361				

Fall of wickets: 1-20 (Di Venuto, 8.3 ov), 2-35 (Stoneman, 13 ov), 3-179 (Benkenstein, 42.5 ov), 4-191 (Harmison, 45.2 ov), 5-242 (Muchall, 55.3 ov), 6-282 (Blackwell, 71 ov)

Notts bowling	Overs	Mdns	Runs	Wkts	Wides	No-Balls
Fletcher	20	3	67	1	1	1
Pattinson	2.1	0	26	0	-	-
Adams	15.5	1	76	2	1	-
Franks	13	1	51	0	-	-
Patel	30	3	113	3	-	-
Voges	1	0	2	0	-	-
Mullaney	4	0	21	0	-	-

What Do Points Make?

Nottinghamshire second innings		Runs	Balls	Mins	4s	6s
AD Hales	c Di Venuto b Harmison	36	61	76	7	-
PJ Franks	lbw b Claydon	8	18	31	2	-
MA Wagh	c Mustard b Blackwell	18	75	97	2	-
AC Voges	c Mustard b Harmison	0	1	1	-	-
SR Patel	lbw b Harmison	2	2	2	-	-
AD Brown	lbw b Blackwell	29	42	66	5	-
*+CMW Read	c sub (GR Breese) b Harmison	0	11	12	-	-
SJ Mullaney	c Mustard b Borthwick	64	62	69	11	1
AR Adams	c Blackwell b Claydon	9	17	23	2	-
LJ Fletcher	c Muchall b Blackwell	5	23	25	1	-
DJ Pattinson	not out	0	13	12	-	-
Extras	(5 b, 2 lb, 2 w)	9				
Total	(all out, 216 minutes, 54.1 overs)	180				

Fall of wickets: 1-31 (Franks, 7.3 ov), 2-52 (Hales, 18.2 ov), 3-52 (Voges, 18.3 ov), 4-54 (Patel, 18.5 ov), 5-84 (Wagh, 31.2 ov), 6-97 (Read, 34.4 ov), 7-103 (Brown, 36 ov), 8-128 (Adams, 42.5 ov), 9-170 (Fletcher, 49.5 ov), 10-180 (Mullaney, 54.1 ov)

Durham bowling	Overs	Mdns	Runs	Wkts	Wides	No-Balls
Plunkett	2	0	8	0	1	-
Claydon	15	4	61	2	-	-
Harmison	15	2	70	4	1	-
Blackwell	19	13	23	3	-	-
Borthwick	3.1	0	11	1	-	-

Match 15

NOTTINGHAMSHIRE v YORKSHIRE

September 7th, 8th, 9th 2010
(match scheduled for 4 days but completed in 3)
Venue: Trent Bridge, Nottingham
Toss: won by Yorkshire who elected to field
Umpires: MA Gough & RT Robinson
Result: Yorkshire won by 5 wickets
Points: Nottinghamshire 3 (Bowling 3) Yorkshire 21 (Batting 1, Bowling 4)

7th September – Day One

A shell-shocked Mick Newell left Trent Bridge almost as soon as the final ball of the day had been bowled after seeing his side turn in an insipid performance to record their lowest Championship score for 22 years.

Given the importance of the contest – a win would all but guarantee the title – and the fact that the opposition was one of only two sides left who could still deny them the crown, it was an abject display from Nottinghamshire to be skittled out for just 59.

Andrew Gale, the Yorkshire skipper who felt the heat after electing to bat first when the sides had met at Headingley Carnegie a month earlier, this time chose wisely on a lush green track.

Gale's bowlers did him proud and then he successfully took up the challenge of batting on a seaming wicket by hitting an unbeaten 147 by the close as the White Rose county manoeuvred themselves into a position of strength.

With Darren Pattinson now having recovered from the ankle injury which forced him out of the action at Durham and Ryan Sidebottom still on England duty, Notts selected the same side that had completed that match.

It had been a harrowing few days for Chris Read's side. Defeat at Durham had raised questions about whether there was enough 'bottle' in the dressing room to clinch the biggest prize in domestic cricket, and then a loss to Warwickshire at Edgbaston in front of the TV cameras had curtailed the Outlaws' involvement in the CB40 competition.

So, with two pieces of silverware now out of reach, only the LV= crown remained a target as a huge Tuesday morning crowd assembled for a really crucial encounter. After Gale had done his bit at the toss, Ajmal Shahzad, looking 100% fitter than the shell of a bowler who was making his way back from injury in the previous encounter, ripped out both openers.

It has to be admitted that he had some help, with rash strokes contributing to the early downfall of Hales and Franks – opening together again after the Chester-le-Street 'trial run' in the second innings there.

Youngster Moin Ashraf, making his Championship debut at just 18, looked equipped for the task and picked up a notable first scalp as he breached the defences of Adam Voges.

— 123 —

Recovering from early setbacks had become something of a Nottinghamshire speciality all season, but when Patel fell for 0 and both Brown and Read followed to leave them 47-6 at lunch, the situation looked perilous.

Immediately afterwards Mullaney became the third consecutive batsman to fall lbw to Oliver Hannon-Dalby to inspire one or two pessimists to begin searching their record books for low totals.

In 1977 a Wayne Daniels and Mike Selvey-inspired burst had routed Notts for just 57 in 18.4 overs at Trent Bridge, but that had been a final day run chase in pursuit of 311 and Mike Harris had 'retired hurt' early in the piece.

That modest effort was surpassed – but only just! Mark Wagh's 22 was the top score in the innings, but both he and Adams fell to Shahzad, who claimed four wickets, as did Hannon-Dalby, who got Pattinson for nought – the fifth duck of an innings which had lasted for just 33.2 overs.

Adam Lyth and Jacques Rudolph responded with 30 from eight overs but then both fell to Adams. Gale apart, batting continued to look a precarious occupation as the bowlers held sway.

The visitors had established a lead of just one when Franks removed McGrath, but the Yorkshire skipper was superb, bringing up his 50 from 48 balls before tea.

He continued in the same vein afterwards, an innings totally out of character with everything that had happened around him all day. His third century of the summer – and surely the most crucial – arrived from just his 85th delivery.

Support from Jonny Bairstow was worth 36 before Adams got him, and when Gerard Brophy departed soon afterwards, 15 wickets had fallen in the day.

Any concerns over the pitch inspectors coming in and docking points because of the first day surface were being nullified by Gale's progress and, although he lost Rashid, Shahzad and Patterson late in the day, he remained defiant to close on 147 not out.

Mark Wagh confirmed that the day's events had left a slightly sombre mood in the home dressing room.

"From any point of view it was as bad as it could have gone, but it's still day one so we'll have to see what happens.

"The ball certainly moved around a hell of a lot in that first session and you needed a fair amount of luck just to stay in. They put the ball in good areas but it was a very helpful surface and when you are on a surface like that you become a little hesitant as a batter – it was hard work there's no doubt about it

"The conditions were very conducive to seam bowling in that session – pitches often seam around here, which is fine but there was a great deal of movement today."

On Andrew Gale's innings Mark said: *"It was a true captain's knock. He'd obviously come out looking to play positively and decided he would attack as much as he could and he really played well and has put them in a strong position – but you never quite know how these matches are going to turn out. There's a lot of cricket left to be played in this one yet."*

Close of Day One – Yorkshire 260-8
(Gale 147*, Hannon-Dalby 0*, 60 overs)

8th September – Day Two

Having 'cleared the air' with a few home truths being spoken in the dressing room, Nottinghamshire fought like demons to get themselves back into the match on the second day.

Yorkshire's last two wickets were only allowed to add four more runs before a spirited home response threatened to turn the game completely on its head.

Substantial scores from Mark Wagh, Paul Franks and Adam Voges took their side into an overall lead which had been stretched to 152 by the end of the day, with still four wickets left to fall.

Despite missing two matches early in the season, Andre Adams had already overtaken Gemaal Hussain of Gloucestershire as the leading wicket-taker in the country and he took his haul to 64 when he polished off the Yorkshire tail inside the first few minutes of the morning's play. His figures of 6-82 meant a third five-wicket haul in as many matches.

Only four more runs had been added meanwhile, a boundary to Andrew Gale which elevated him to 151 not out – a sumptious innings.

Behind by 205 runs, Nottinghamshire batted again and in their 15th Championship match of the summer they produced an opening partnership which stretched beyond 50 for the first time.

In the confines of team meetings and player huddles one can imagine that a number of huge characters like to have their say. As in all walks of life opinions matter from those that are prepared to put their heads above the parapet and 'do their bit' when it's most needed.

When the chips had been down for Notts at various stages of the 2010 campaign Paul Franks had come out fighting. As vice-captain he was a valued and trusted ally to Chris Read and was on his way to his best all-round season ever – with his highest number of first class runs and more wickets than he'd taken for a decade.

The 'Farnsfield all-rounder' had more than justified Mick Newell's faith in him and you can imagine 'Franksy' pleading for the chance to open the innings and get Notts back into this game.

For 19 overs he helped Hales negate the swing and seam movement before the younger man was caught behind off Ashraf for 24. The stand had been worth 56 but neither Franks, nor his new partner Mark Wagh, were prepared to let the bowlers build on their solitary success.

With some of the most fluent and positive batting seen on the ground all summer they put on 131 in 25 overs. Spin was Franks' undoing as he edged Rashid to slip for 79, but then Adam Voges maintained the impetus with another exhilarating exhibition of strokeplay.

Notts' Championship credentials had been questioned overnight and clearly the players had some answers – what a shame they hadn't produced such a performance on the opening morning.

Wagh sped beyond 50 and went from 84 to 90 with a huge blow into the Radcliffe Road Stand off Rashid, but then mistimed another attempted big hit and holed out.

Voges had also moved beyond 50 but suddenly was hit with a new wave of responsibility as Patel and Brown came and went quickly. Yorkshire's fightback intensified just before the close when the second new ball accounted for the Australian for a splendid 72 to leave the game very much in the balance.

What Do Points Make?

72 for Adam Voges in the second innings

Despite scoring 79 at the top of the order Paul Franks admitted he'd been looking for even more runs.

"I'm definitely disappointed at not getting a hundred but delighted to have done the job and given the team a bit of a platform.

"It was nice to get a few at the start. Much has been made of the fact that we hadn't had a 50 opening partnership all season and I'm sure that it's played on a few of the lads' minds and it doesn't make life easy playing cricket under any sort of pressure."

Having spent time in the middle on both days of the match Paul assessed the state of the wicket: "I think we saw less swing today – consistent swing anyway. I think the ball went through phases when it swung for a little bit and then not so. I'm not trying to build up hopes but I think there's still a little bit there for the bowlers. It's now important that when we bowl we make them work hard for the runs and who knows what might happen?"

On his side's first innings showing Paul pulled no punches. "There's no excuse for performing as poorly as we did yesterday and to be bowled out for 59 is not good enough, there's no hiding from that.

"The important thing is we showed character when we bowled and we showed some character when we batted second time round.

"I went home feeling pretty down yesterday – it was one of the hardest days of my fifteen years here and I wanted to come back and try and do something about it and I think we've got ourselves in a position where we can be happy with what we've done today. The dressing room is a different place from what it was 24 hours ago and we don't want to toss away what we've achieved so far this season."

Away from the action Nottinghamshire announced that neither Matt Wood nor Bilal Shafayat, two batsmen who had failed to make a significant impact when given chances in the County Championship side, would be offered new contracts and would be leaving Trent Bridge at the end of the season.

Close of Day Two – Nottinghamshire 357-6
(Read 24*, Pattinson 20*, 87 overs)

9th September – Day Three

Nottinghamshire's second home defeat of the season, and fifth in all, confirmed that the LV= County Championship wouldn't be decided until the final week of the season and meant that Yorkshire had now put themselves into a strong position to lift their first title since 2001.

Although the Tykes were made to fight hard for their victory, the home side just didn't quite score enough runs on the third morning to make the target a formidable one. Considering where they were after the first innings of the match Mick Newell's side had shown commendable strength of character to haul themselves back into the contest and that – and bucket loads of spirit and good fortune – would be needed if the final outcome to the season was to be a positive one.

Chris Read fell early on the third morning

Nightwatchman Darren Pattinson had again proved himself to be no mug with the bat when he extended his innings as far as 27 before being dismissed by Steven Patterson.

Steven Mullaney – batting as low as nine – came in next and helped Chris Read add 32 for the next wicket, but then both fell inside the space of six deliveries.

Luke Fletcher hit two boundaries in his 8 but then totally misread a slower one from Shahzad and was bowled. Almost criminally, Andre Adams was 0 not out – what a difference a quickfire 20 or 30 from him could have made.

What Do Points Make?

Yorkshire's target was 209 and it would take only inspired bowling or the pressure of the situation to prevent them from getting there in more than five sessions.

The task looked a routine one as Lyth and Rudolph helped themselves to 70, but then Pattinson, in one of his most inspired spells of the season, got them both, either side of McGrath, to make it 91-3 and open up the possibilities of a comeback win.

Those possibilities began to intensify when Adams clean-bowled Gale. The majority of the crowd were baying for more wickets, but Bairstow and Brophy counter-attacked and put on 97 to blunt the Nottinghamshire sword.

Although Adams got Brophy eventually, for 41, the end was in sight and it was confirmed when Bairstow worked Patel away to the leg side to move on to 63 not out and see his side over the finishing line.

Despite the loss Mick Newell remained upbeat when he spoke after the match.

"It was a vitally important game that we wanted to win and we haven't been able to do so. I think the toss was important, although you can't say we lost the game because we lost the toss. The first two hours of the match were important as it was difficult to bat then, but Yorkshire have bowled better than anyone else has bowled here this season, so fair play to them.

"The wicket was prepared in exactly the same way as all the other pitches have been here this season and the same amount of grass was left on. It does swing and seam at Trent Bridge and I've no complaints.

"After being bowled out so cheaply we stressed to the players that we had to somehow try and fight back and win the game because we'd got so few bonus points in the first innings and I thought we did very well in the second innings and gave ourselves a chance.

"We're still top – after 15 matches – and it's not a fluke because we've got the most points and played the best cricket over the course of the season – we've just chosen a bad time to have a bad game so now we've got to go to Old Trafford and play well and it's a ground we'll be looking to win at."

Old Trafford
16th September, 2010

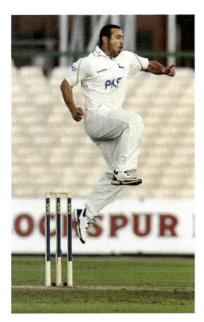

Left: Two wickets down, one to go – Andre celebrates the fall of Mark Chilton's wicket

Above: 'He's nicked it' – Waggy and Patto start the celebrations as Shiv departs

Left: Caught you! His team-mates eventually catch up with Andre and the title is won

Won it! There's no disguising the joy of the Nottinghamshire players as they celebrate in front of the Old Trafford pavilion

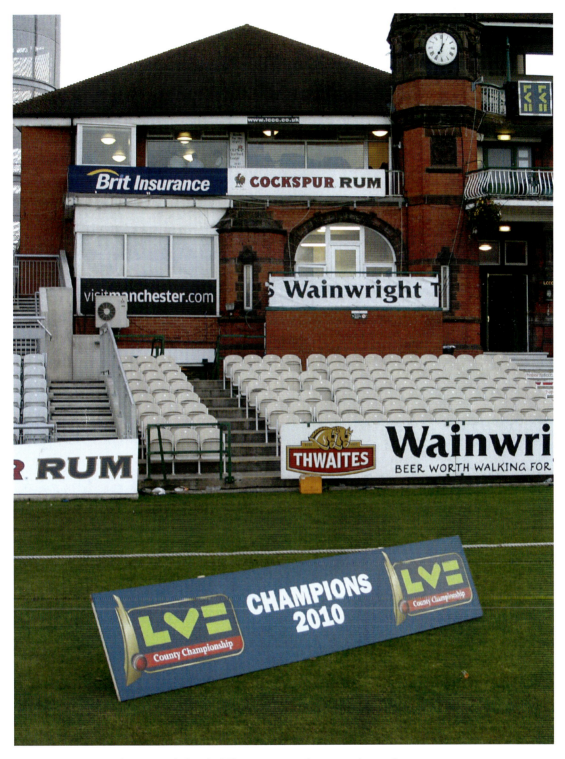

Seven o'clock. The season is over but the party is just beginning inside the away dressing room

A dream fulfilled for captain Chris

"What do points make?" says Franksy. Not a bad suggestion for a title!

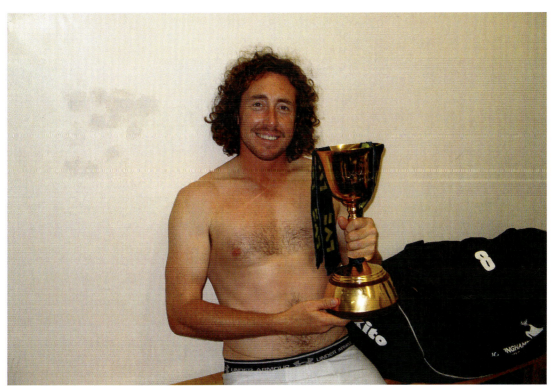

Job done! Nottinghamshire's beneficiary
reflects on a fitting end to the season

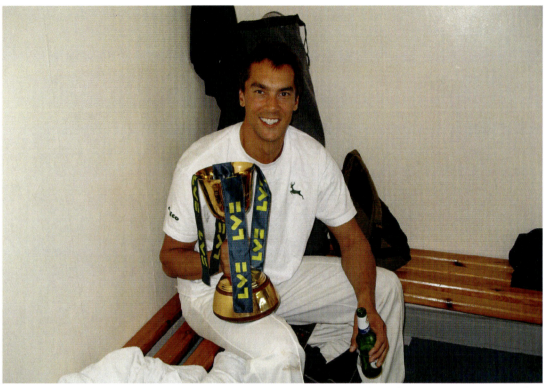

Above: "This was definitely one of the better days," said Mark afterwards

Below: A well-earned drink for two of the last day heroes – a century for Adam and two quick wickets for Andre

No letting go! 96 and the decisive catch for Samit

Still going strong – Ali Brown adds another title win to his collection

"Cheers," says Fletch

**Take a bow young man!
A fine low catch from Alex Hales brought the dream closer**

"Anyone for a party?" Fletch (hidden) and Patto are in the mood!

Graeme White: "It wasn't like this at Northampton"

Played their part – Ross Hollinworth and Wayne Noon share the moment

On 19th October 2010 Nottinghamshire's players, officials and staff were invited to Buckingham Palace to receive their Championship medals from His Royal Highness, the Duke of Edinburgh. Chris Read receives the trophy (above), whilst Charlie Shreck is introduced (below)

Graeme Swann and Chris Read proudly display their medals

Suited and booted! Some of the players and staff outside Buckingham Palace

Graeme Swann at the Palace – the Duke of Edinburgh wished him well for the forthcoming Ashes tour

The inside story of Nottinghamshire's LV= County Championship success

SCORECARD

Nottinghamshire first innings		Runs	Balls	Mins	4s	6s
AD Hales	c Rashid b Shahzad	3	24	29	-	-
PJ Franks	c Bairstow b Shahzad	0	4	4	-	-
MA Wagh	c Rudolph b Shahzad	22	83	121	1	-
AC Voges	b Ashraf	8	25	36	1	-
SR Patel	c Brophy b Ashraf	0	7	7	-	-
AD Brown	lbw b Hannon-Dalby	16	34	31	1	-
*+CMW Read	lbw b Hannon-Dalby	0	2	5	-	-
SJ Mullaney	lbw b Hannon-Dalby	0	4	3	-	-
AR Adams	c Lyth b Shahzad	3	6	10	-	-
LJ Fletcher	not out	6	8	11	-	1
DJ Pattinson	c Brophy b Hannon-Dalby	0	3	2	-	-
Extras	(1 lb)	1				
Total	(all out, 33.2 overs)	59				

Fall of wickets: 1-1 (Franks, 1 ov), 2-4 (Hales, 7 ov), 3-18 (Voges, 16.5 ov), 4-18 (Patel, 19 ov), 5-41 (Brown, 28 ov), 6-47 (Read, 29.2 ov), 7-47 (Mullaney, 30 ov), 8-49 (Wagh, 30.3 ov), 9-52 (Adams, 32.4 ov), 10-59 (Pattinson, 33.2 ov)

Yorkshire bowling	Overs	Mdns	Runs	Wkts	Wides	No-Balls
Shahzad	11	4	21	4	-	-
Patterson	7	2	8	0	-	-
Ashraf	6	4	11	2	-	-
Hannon-Dalby	9.2	4	18	4	-	-

Yorkshire first innings		Runs	Balls	Mins	4s	6s
A Lyth	c Voges b Adams	19	31	35	3	-
JA Rudolph	c Brown b Adams	10	25	28	1	-
A McGrath	c Adams b Franks	10	21	35	1	-
*AW Gale	not out	151	176	216	22	-
JM Bairstow	lbw b Adams	36	51	69	6	-
+GL Brophy	b Adams	5	13	16	1	-
AU Rashid	c Fletcher b Patel	11	11	22	2	-
A Shahzad	c Read b Franks	7	26	32	1	-
SA Patterson	c Read b Franks	0	4	4	-	-
OJ Hannon-Dalby	lbw b Adams	0	15	14	-	-
MA Ashraf	c Patel b Adams	0	3	8	-	-
Extras	(8 lb, 6 nb, 1 w)	15				
Total	(all out, 62.1 overs)	264				

Fall of wickets: 1-30 (Rudolph, 8 ov), 2-31 (Lyth, 9.1 ov), 3-60 (McGrath, 16.5 ov), 4-171 (Bairstow, 33.4 ov), 5-195 (Brophy, 38 ov), 6-228 (Rashid, 44.3 ov), 7-251 (Shahzad, 54 ov), 8-251 (Patterson, 55.4 ov), 9-260 (Hannon-Dalby, 60.4 ov), 10-264 (Ashraf, 62.1 ov)

Notts bowling	Overs	Mdns	Runs	Wkts	Wides	No-Balls
Fletcher	8	0	39	0	1	-
Pattinson	10	2	58	0	-	2
Adams	20.1	3	82	6	-	-
Franks	15	3	58	3	-	1
Patel	9	1	19	1	-	-

What Do Points Make?

Nottinghamshire second innings		Runs	Balls	Mins	4s	6s
AD Hales	c Brophy b Ashraf	24	79	76	3	-
PJ Franks	c Rudolph b Rashid	79	114	186	12	-
MA Wagh	c sub b Rashid	90	125	180	14	2
AC Voges	c Brophy b Hannon-Dalby	72	113	139	11	-
SR Patel	c Bairstow b Shahzad	4	17	11	-	-
AD Brown	c Brophy b Shahzad	4	12	13	1	-
*+CMW Read	b Shahzad	47	91	122	8	-
DJ Pattinson	lbw b Patterson	27	32	37	4	-
SJ Mullaney	b Patterson	15	19	29	3	-
AR Adams	not out	0	5	10	-	-
LJ Fletcher	b Shahzad	8	5	3	2	-
Extras	(16 b, 27 lb)	43				
Total	(all out, 102 overs)	413				

Fall of wickets: 1-56 (Hales, 19 ov), 2-187 (Franks, 44.5 ov), 3-278 (Wagh, 64.5 ov), 4-283 (Patel, 68 ov), 5-291 (Brown, 71.5 ov), 6-329 (Voges, 82.2 ov), 7-373 (Pattinson, 92.1 ov), 8-405 (Mullaney, 100.1 ov), 9-405 (Read, 101.1 ov), 10-413 (Fletcher, 102 ov)

Yorkshire bowling	Overs	Mdns	Runs	Wkts	Wides	No-Balls
Shahzad	29	6	100	4	-	-
Patterson	21	2	83	2	-	-
Hannon-Dalby	18	2	71	1	-	-
Ashraf	14	1	50	1	-	-
Rashid	17	4	48	2	-	-
McGrath	3	0	18	0	-	-

Yorkshire second innings		Runs	Balls	Mins	4s	6s
A Lyth	c Hales b Pattinson	45	64	74	4	-
JA Rudolph	c Brown b Pattinson	29	42	58	5	-
A McGrath	c Read b Pattinson	4	7	7	1	-
*AW Gale	b Adams	5	10	12	1	-
JM Bairstow	not out	63	51	83	12	-
+GL Brophy	c Hales b Adams	41	51	57	8	-
AU Rashid	not out	9	31	19	1	-
SA Patterson						
MA Ashraf						
A Shahzad						
OJ Hannon-Dalby						
Extras	(1 b, 10 lb, 2 nb)	13				
Total	(5 wickets, 42.3 overs)	209				

Fall of wickets: 1-70 (Rudolph, 15.2 ov), 2-78 (McGrath, 17.3 ov), 3-91 (Lyth, 19.4 ov), 4-95 (Gale, 20.4 ov), 5-192 (Brophy, 35.3 ov)

Notts bowling	Overs	Mdns	Runs	Wkts	Wides	No-Balls
Fletcher	5	0	23	0	-	-
Pattinson	13	2	67	3	-	1
Adams	16	0	77	2	-	-
Franks	3	0	23	0	-	-
Patel	5.3	2	8	0	-	-

Match 16

LANCASHIRE v NOTTINGHAMSHIRE

September 13th, 14th, 15th, 16th 2010 (4 day match)
Venue: Old Trafford, Manchester
Toss: won by Nottinghamshire who elected to bat
Umpires: NL Bainton & PJ Hartley
Result: Match Drawn
Points: Lancashire 6 (Bowling 3) Nottinghamshire 9 ((Batting 5, Bowling 1)

13th September – Day One

Whether Nottinghamshire liked it or not the country had suddenly become hooked on LV= County Championship fever, with the scenario that any one of three sides could still emerge as the table-toppers as only seven points separated them.

Defeat in their last two matches had seemingly done for Notts. Neutrals and most in the media seemed to be rooting for either Somerset or Yorkshire. The Cidermen had never lifted the title – despite having such luminaries as Botham, Richards and Garner amongst their former players. Additionally, Marcus Trescothick's side had lost in the Final of the twenty20 competition with a dramatic last ball defeat to the Hampshire Royals.

They also had a place in the CB40 competition to look forward to at the end of the week, but it was a maiden County Championship title they had at the top of their wish list.

Yorkshire's credentials had grown significantly having defeated Nottinghamshire a week earlier. Beginning the final round of matches in third place they were, in many ways, the outsiders, but significantly they had a home match (against Kent), whereas Somerset were at Durham and Chris Read's side were in rainy Manchester.

'Rainy Manchester' is often used as a cheap shot at the frequent inclement weather experienced in one of the north west's 'most-happening' cities. On the opening day of this most crucial encounter it would be hard to find an alternative adjective – it rained for most of the day and just one over of play was possible.

Nottinghamshire were boosted by the availability of Ryan Sidebottom. Despite the recent announcement that the 2010 county beneficiary would be leaving the Trent Bridge staff at the end of the season, he had continued to give his all in every match he'd played for the county and to have his services for one last hurrah would surely be a boost. When the line-ups were announced, the understanding player to step aside was Luke Fletcher.

Damp overnight conditions caused a delay, but things had improved sufficiently for the toss to take place at 10.40 am (ten minutes after the scheduled September start-time).

Crucially, the Nottinghamshire skipper called correctly and elected to bat. Significant team news from the home camp was the absence through injury of their captain, Glenn Chapple, with the leadership being handed to Mark Chilton.

— 131 —

Dealings between the two sides had been very amiable in the earlier match at Trent Bridge and it had been 'Chappy' that had offered Nottinghamshire the prospect of making a 'bit of a game of it' on the last day and it resulted in Notts picking up a win which seemed to have taken them to the brink of the First Division title. Through their own misadventures this still hadn't been secured.

Sajid Mahmood bowled the one over that was possible before the showers returned, with both batsmen getting nicely underway. A three clipped through midwicket got Alex Hales off the mark and he followed it up with a boundary after Paul Franks had nudged a single from his first delivery faced. Significantly, fielders seemed to be slipping and sliding everywhere and no-one seemed to mind when the umpires took the players off as the conditions worsened.

The prospect of a resumption rarely materialised during the next few hours and at 3.15pm play was officially abandoned for the day.

Elsewhere on the opening day, neither of the other title contenders had either won the toss or completed a full day's play.

At Headingley Carnegie, Yorkshire, put in by Kent, had reached 205-7, whilst at Chester-le-Street Durham had opted to bat first against Somerset and were 132-2 in another rain-shortened encounter.

Close of Day One – Nottinghamshire 8-0 (Hales 7*, Franks 1*, 1 over)

14th September – Day Two

'Rain, rain go away, come back another day' (or at least leave it a week or so if you can!).

There was a little more play possible on the second day of Nottinghamshire's match against Lancashire at Old Trafford, but it came either side of an utterly bewildering 25 minute stoppage for too much sunlight!

After another filthy wet morning had saturated the whole of Manchester city centre, it took a lengthy drying out period to ensure that any play at all was possible and it wasn't until 4pm that the match was able to resume.

27 overs were eventually contested in which Notts added 81 runs to their overnight score for the loss of both openers. Even by the halfway stage of the match 164 overs had already been lost to the elements and the outlook for the third day was even worse!

Tuesday's early morning updates confirmed that play had started at each of the other grounds that had a bearing on the top of the table, but there was little else that the Nottinghamshire players could do except bide their time in the most productive manner possible.

A lengthy card school kept several of them occupied, whilst one or two others transferred to Old Trafford's Indoor Cricket School to practise their skills.

All in all it made for a very frustrating wait, with the prospect of the title slipping away and the Notts lads being unable to do anything about it.

The attention of one or two was drawn to the fact that another major sporting event was being played close by, later in the day. Manchester United's home Champions League clash against Glasgow Rangers seemed like an attractive proposition, but apart from one or two offers via 'unconventional methods' those interested weren't able to secure any tickets at this late stage.

The inside story of Nottinghamshire's LV= County Championship success

Shortly after the scheduled lunch break the rain began to stop and the ground staff went about their work – with the announcement that it would take 'at least a couple of hours to make conditions fit for play'.

Eventually they began a session that was due to encompass 32 overs, between four and six o'clock, with Alex Hales and Paul Franks resuming their innings.

Franks had taken 'mock' offence earlier at one or two comments made by the Sky Sports commentators (who were in attendance) about him being a 'makeshift opener'. He had reminded them that he had opened the batting when England won the Under 19 World Cup in 1998 and had done it many times since then. He had begun the season with a second innings century at the top of the order against Durham UCCE and had scored 79 there in the previous match against Yorkshire.

Adding even more power to his point the left-hander combined with his younger partner to get the session off to a very brisk start. Fours either side of the wicket brought 31 runs from just the first four overs.

For the second match in succession they raced past 50 and had taken their stand to 75 when Hales fell in the 16th over. He'd made 36 when Gary Keedy spun the ball sharply to find the outside edge and Gareth Cross took a good catch standing up to the wicket.

The dismissal was a blow for Notts and they suffered a further setback when Franks went shortly afterwards to another caught behind, this time from the bowling of Tom Smith. Paul's 40 had been another handy contribution, but the feeling that fate was conspiring against the side was intensified at around 5.25pm.

Facing the bowling of Smith from the Stretford End, Adam Voges drew the attention of the umpires to the fact that he couldn't see the ball due to the setting sun.

Having hoped in vain for a spell of decent weather during their stay in Manchester, it was ironic that the first appearance of the sun came when they least wanted to see it. Shining directly into the eyes of the batsmen from just over the media centre, the bright glare had made cricket impossible and the umpires decided to call a temporary halt and send everyone back to the dressing room.

With the onset of more and more evening cricket – both limited overs and twenty20 – the fact that the square ran east to west was becoming more of a problem and the Old Trafford aficionados had already decided to rotate the square 90 degrees during the forthcoming close season. Indeed, huge polythene bags containing fresh soil were being delivered to the ground throughout this contest.

So Lancashire versus Nottinghamshire in 2010 would be the last occasion in which bowlers would run in from the famed Stretford End, or Warwick Road End, of this famous old Test venue.

At around ten to six the sun had disappeared behind a bank of clouds and a brief passage of play up to the top of the hour saw Voges and Mark Wagh take the total on to 89-2.

Elsewhere Yorkshire had made 261 in their first innings against Kent, with Rob Key's side replying with 216-6, and Somerset had reached 226-4 in response to Durham's 286 all out.

That meant that each of their rivals had so far accumulated four bonus points whilst Nottinghamshire still searched for their first, meaning that the top of the table, hypothetically, read:

What Do Points Make?

Somerset 207 points
Nottinghamshire 205 points
Yorkshire 198 points

Close of Day Two – Nottinghamshire 89-2
(Wagh 3*, Voges 8*, 28 overs)

15th September – Day Three

Not the best photo ever taken by the author – but it was a bit wet!

Rarely has there been so much interest in the actual localisation of the weather forecasts. All three title-deciding matches were scheduled for the 'north' of the country, but whereas the rain seemed to be centred right above Manchester, much brighter, drier conditions prevailed in both Leeds and Chester-le-Street.

Prospects of play sounded bleak even before daybreak, with the rain tap-tap-tapping away on the hotel window through the night. It didn't sound good and it didn't look good at first light either.

Perhaps there is an element of bias in this statement but I genuinely believe that Trent Bridge is easy on the eye, whatever the weather is doing. A bleak, murky day fails to distract from the aesthetic beauty of the ground. Old Trafford – on this particular September Wednesday – didn't hold the same appeal.

Any prospect of play could be eliminated with a cursory step or two onto the squelchy outfield. The grass had taken on the consistency of quicksand and soon disappeared below your feet, engulfed by pools and pools of water.

The umpires did their bit – delaying the inevitable for as long as possible – but the prospects of any play were always less than zero.

Mark Wagh entertained the press with news of his winter plans. A forthcoming charity bike ride from John O'Groats to Land's End was being undertaken with minimum fuss. A bike and a map seemed to be all that he'd need – and the strength of character to complete around one hundred miles a day.

By way of relaxation afterwards he then planned to travel to Rio de Janeiro to spend six weeks doing Capoeira, a type of Brazilian martial arts, before going to south east Asia, where he was planning to spend nine weeks working at an orangutan sanctuary.

Needless to say, on a quiet day for cricket action, the media lapped up the news of Mark and his immediate plans.

Neither Somerset nor Yorkshire had yet put themselves in a definite match-winning situation in their games. Durham were fighting hard in the north east, although Trescothick's side had completed a full collection of eight bonus points, whilst Yorkshire were also a long way from securing a victory and had taken just five bonus points after the first innings had been completed.

With just one day of the season to go, the table didn't look good for Notts:

Somerset 211 points
Nottinghamshire 205 points
Yorkshire 203 points

If Somerset were to go on and win their match now then they would be the LV= County Champions – of that there was no doubt because however you looked at the Old Trafford situation there just wasn't enough time for Notts to get both batting and bowling points and still go on and force a victory.

One factor only lay in favour of Chris Read's side – and that was contained in Para 21.1.7 of the playing regulations for the LV= County Championship season:

'The side which has the highest aggregate of points gained at the end of the season shall be the Champion County of their respective Division. Should any sides in the Championship table be equal on points, the following tie-breakers will be applied in the order stated: most wins, fewest losses, team achieving most points in contests between teams level on points, most wickets taken, most runs scored.'

'Most wins' may yet have some significance because, going into the final round of matches, Nottinghamshire had secured seven victories over the course of the campaign, whereas Somerset had only managed to win six of their games.

Steven Mullaney – as a former resident of the area during his days as a Lancashire player – had organised for his team-mates to visit a local restaurant that evening.

Much as all of the players enjoyed the meal there was only one topic of conversation around the table – how should they approach the final day?

What Do Points Make?

If Somerset (possible) or Yorkshire (less likely) went on to win their matches then Notts would be out of the equation. The general opinion was that both Durham and Kent would do everything in their power to play their matches as hard as they could and try and do what was correct for them.

The reigning champions had fought hard against Notts a couple of weeks earlier and shown that they were playing for as much pride as they could. Under the recently-appointed Phil Mustard they had looked a much more formidable unit and it was felt that they would at least be able to draw their match with Somerset.

Additionally, Kent were still trying to avoid relegation so wouldn't roll over against Yorkshire. The possibility existed that neither rival would win – but Nottinghamshire still had to get at least six points against Lancashire.

Two schools of thought emerged as to how they could go about this. Nottinghamshire could either try and bat as purposefully as possible and get to either 350 or 400 runs – whilst still giving themselves time to pick up the necessary six or three wickets – whichever was needed to ensure the six bonus points.

The alternative was to reflect a little on what had happened at Trent Bridge a month earlier. Then, with his side desperate to try and force a last day result, Lancashire skipper Glen Chapple had engaged in a spot of 'plea-bargaining' with Chris Read and a couple of declarations and a run-chase were agreed.

Notts didn't have to play ball on that occasion, but they did – perhaps Lancashire would do the same this time. The only differences were that it would be the Red Rose side doing the chasing, so all ten wickets would be needed to force a victory on the last day. How viable was that for the Nottinghamshire attack? Also, Mark Chilton was captaining the home side, not Glenn Chapple – although that wasn't seen as being of any great consequence should Chris Read raise the subject.

Apart from the players who were having their say in isolation, similar discussions were taking place all over Manchester. Committee and Board members had travelled up to the north west for the season finale, along with many supporters and members of the media.

Predictably, some felt that a run-chase was the best option – others were swayed towards the bonus point route. Perhaps surprisingly few were concentrating on the weather – it had rained for most of the week – much of the outfield had been under water throughout the third day and the prospects for the Thursday weren't promising.

Close of Day Three – No play possible. Nottinghamshire still 89-2

16th September – Day Four

In the most dramatic of circumstances Nottinghamshire ensured that Thursday 16th September 2010 would be a never-to-be-forgotten day in the history of the County Championship.

At around ten minutes to five Samit Patel hung on to a sharp nick at third slip to ensure a sixth bonus point of the day and, with it, the much-coveted title. It had been an extraordinary day and one which will have thrilled not only those rooting for Chris Read's side but also the sponsors and a huge television audience glued to the most riveting conclusion ever to the four day season.

The inside story of Nottinghamshire's LV= County Championship success

Optimism was in the air, if nothing else, as the players arrived at Old Trafford ahead of their date with destiny, but there soon came a cruel announcement. Although it was a dry, fresh morning, the outfield was still damp and the start of play would be delayed for one hour.

Notts couldn't afford to lose one minute, let alone one hour, but cards were being played very close to the chests of those directly involved as to how the day would pan out. No obvious chat on the outfield between the two captains this time, as there had been at Trent Bridge.

Play began at 11.35am with an allocation of 80 overs available. From the off it was clear that Lancashire were playing hard – there was no hint of any declaration bowling and Chilton was thoughtful and deliberate with his field placings.

Mark Wagh and Adam Voges batted positively and it was soon apparent that the 'bonus point' route was being taken. Could they manufacture the six they needed, whilst still clinging to the hope that neither of their rivals would pull off a victory?

It seemed improbable but the early news from the other grounds looked encouraging for Notts – James Tredwell had taken a hat-trick for Kent against Yorkshire to leave his side on the brink of victory there. Durham continued to bat on and build a substantial lead against Somerset in the north east.

At Old Trafford the total had reached 144 when the first wicket of the day would go down, Saj Mahmood hurrying one through the defences of Wagh to clatter into his off pole.

Voges looked in ominously good touch but soon lost his next partner. Ali Brown also fell to Mahmood, but TV replays gave a variety of reasons for it not being out – predominantly because he hit it and it would also have gone over the top!

Lunch was taken at that point with Nottinghamshire on 172-4, still some way from even their first bonus point.

Two pieces of news surfaced during the luncheon interval. Kent had triumphed at Headingley Carnegie, although events elsewhere had still condemned them to relegation. With Yorkshire now out of the picture Notts were assured of at least finishing in second place – for what would be the third season running.

Also announced 'hot off the press' was the news that Andrew Flintoff had bowed to the inevitable after sustaining a dreadful sequence of injuries and had officially retired from all forms of the game. Whilst Freddie's achievements and contributions will become the stuff of folklore over forthcoming years, the timing of his announcement wasn't great.

On the final day of the County Championship season – with the focus very firmly on the domestic game and all it stands for – there was a sudden attempt to make the chief cricketing story of the day a non-playing one. If that in itself wasn't bad enough then everyone at Old Trafford seemed to have 'sighted' him on the ground.

With the match being televised live it might have been a good opportunity for the Lancashire hero to attend and do an interview there and then, but he wasn't at Old Trafford so the question will remain, why not leave it until the next day to make the announcement?

Nottinghamshire were still looking to make themselves headline news as they began after lunch with Samit Patel joining Voges in the middle. Samit had slipped below Ali Brown in the batting order and there was even a suggestion that maybe Chris Read and Steven Mullaney may both come in ahead of him, but the decision to send him in at six was both insightful and crucial.

Inevitably there had been a number of outstanding partnerships achieved by the Notts batters over the course of the season – but, ultimately, perhaps none as decisive as the stand between the home-town boy and the Western Australian.

— 137 —

What Do Points Make?

They added 153 in 28 overs to pick up the first three batting points required. Quite simply, both players were at the very peak of their game. By his own admission Samit hadn't scored the volume of runs he'd hoped for in the four day format and it was a tough ask to expect an overseas player to fly halfway around the world and be at his best in England in mid-September.

It's worth recording that Lancashire didn't let up their intensity thoughout the entire day. They bowled well, chased everything in the field and seemed determined to end their own season with their heads held high. There were no easy runs on offer.

Adam's 50 had come from 76 balls, whilst his partner raced there from just 60 – but then each kicked on, never losing sight of the bigger picture. Notts really had to make 400 and still have enough time to get three Lancs wickets.

The sun, at last, began to make an appearance at Old Trafford, although things were starting to look a little gloomy for Somerset in their match, with Durham still batting and more than 150 ahead.

A push down the ground off Gary Keedy took 'Vog' to his second ton for Notts, but although he acknowledged the warm applause for his efforts it was apparent he knew his work wasn't done. Congratulations came from Samit, who was in the nineties himself at that point, but he missed out on a century when he hoisted Simon Kerrigan to Kyle Hogg in the deep. As at Leeds earlier in the season, he'd fallen for 96.

Chris Read added a dozen before losing his wicket in almost identical fashion and the players adjourned for tea on 353-6, with the fourth bonus point being snaffled up just moments earlier.

The post-tea session will never be forgotten by those who were there and, as the afternoon wore on, one became more and more aware of 'green and gold' supporters proudly displaying their colours and voicing their encouragement.

If there were two ways of doing things in this match then Notts seemed determined to take the most awkward, as they made hard work of knocking off the remaining 47 runs upon the restart.

Having lost Steven Mullaney almost immediately for nought, they needed Voges to see it through, but with the total on 386 he lofted Kerrigan to long on. Despite a near-faultless 126 he looked distraught at having perished to such a high-risk shot.

Andre Adams made 15, but when he became Kerrigan's fifth victim ten more runs were still needed with only the last pair left to get them.

Was now a good time to mention that Ryan Sidebottom's five previous innings in the County Championship in 2010 had all been 'not outs'?

Over the course of 20 painful minutes, and 5.1 overs, Ryan and Darren Pattinson accumulated ten singles between them. If the Voges/Patel stand earlier had been decisive, this one was as nerve-jangling as it could get until 'Patto' pushed Keedy to mid-wicket to bring up the 400.

There was no need to hang around to look towards the balcony wondering if Ready was about to call them in – the two batsmen just hared off, ready for the next phase of their mission. The declaration was a formality.

It was now all or nothing as news filtered through that Somerset – eventually set 181 in 17 overs – had called off their run chase and settled for a draw.

Nottinghamshire also had around 17 overs in which to pick up the three wickets they needed. Had they given themselves enough time?

Paul Horton and Karl Brown opened the batting for Lancashire, but Nottinghamshire seemed initially to have Ryan bowling from the 'wrong end', the Warwick Road End.

'Patto' bowled the second over and Adams – after the end change – the third. Still no wickets and the clock was ticking. There was also the possibility that a repeat of the 'sunshine escapade' of the second evening might scupper Notts' chances.

Thankfully the champagne corks were being popped long before then as three wickets fell inside the space of eight deliveries.

With the fourth ball of his second over Sidebottom lured Brown into pushing at one just outside his off stump and first slip, Alex Hales, took a fine catch low down to his right.

One down – two to go. Almost before anyone had the chance to start biting fingernails or looking anxiously at the weather, Adams struck a second blow.

His first delivery from the new over was beautifully pitched and it just brushed the bat of Mark Chilton on its way through to Read. The bowler's celebration was spectacular but nothing compared to what was to follow.

Ten seconds from the end..! Shiv pauses to look around at all of the close-catchers

Shiv Chanderpaul had blunted the Nottinghamshire attack for more than three hours on his way to making 92 when the sides had met at Trent Bridge. This time he faced just three balls.

All summer long the sight of a left-handed batsman had prompted Andre Adams to immediately begin his line of attack from around the wicket. On this occasion he stayed over and was rewarded when a low edge flew into the waiting hands of Samit Patel at third slip.

What Do Points Make?

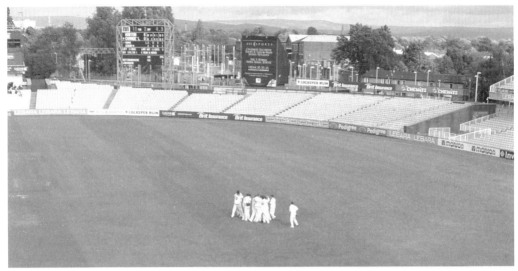

Caught you!
Andre's team-mates eventually catch up with him and the title is won

An instant release of emotion brought joy – laughter – and, yes, tears from all around the ground, but in the middle the players were rapidly chasing a jubilant Andre, who had set off on his own mini-lap of honour. Almost from nowhere Luke Fletcher, Graeme White and Scott Elstone, who had been delivering drinks around the outfield, were caught up in the mass celebrations.

The fall of the wicket had brought Nottinghamshire their sixth bonus point of the day and, although there were still around a dozen overs left, the umpires guided the players off the field. Lancashire, to a man, congratulated their opponents as the victory party began.

In front of the TV cameras Chris Read was presented with the LV= County Championship trophy (or at least a replica – the original was thought to have been despatched earlier towards the Riverside!) and in fading light the players gave their accounts of what had been an extraordinary day – and an extraordinary season.

The traditional 'Champione, Champione' chants gave way to several verses of 'The Grand Old Duke of York' as Paul Franks led the sing-song, pausing to lift the trophy and shouting, "What Do Points Make?"

Two of the quiet men hugged. Mick Newell and Wayne Noon had endured a torrid day in the dressing room, helpless to assist in either the batting or the bowling, but they'd played their part and it was fitting that they had been captured on screen at the critical moment.

Not many though would have observed Mick then momentarily slip away to thank the Old Trafford groundstaff and take them a few beers for their efforts over a particularly difficult few days.

Having had the odds stacked against them at the start of the day, and having defied the rain, the sun, the most worthy of opponents and two very good title contenders, Nottinghamshire had emerged as the LV= County Champions for 2010 and no-one could say it hadn't been deserved.

Nottinghamshire win the title by virtue of having won more matches

The inside story of Nottinghamshire's LV= County Championship success

SCORECARD

Nottinghamshire first innings		Runs	Balls	Mins	4s	6s
AD Hales	c Cross b Keedy	36	41	66	5	-
PJ Franks	c Cross b Smith	40	60	78	6	-
MA Wagh	b Mahmood	32	61	74	4	-
AC Voges	c Croft b Kerrigan	126	183	227	9	-
AD Brown	lbw b Mahmood	10	21	24	1	-
SR Patel	c Hogg b Kerrigan	96	91	100	11	1
*+CMW Read	c Hogg b Kerrigan	12	21	17	-	-
SJ Mullaney	c Cross b Kerrigan	0	5	7	-	-
AR Adams	b Kerrigan	15	21	19	1	-
RJ Sidebottom	not out	7	17	24	-	-
DJ Pattinson	not out	4	19	16	-	-
Extras	(1 b, 13 lb, 4 nb, 4 w)	22				
Total	(9 wickets, declared, 89.4 ovs)	400				

Fall of wickets: 1-75 (Hales, 15.2 ov), 2-79 (Franks, 18.4 ov), 3-144 (Wagh, 36.3 ov), 4-172 (Brown, 42.5 ov), 5-325 (Patel, 70.4 ov), 6-353 (Read, 76.2 ov), 7-365 (Mullaney, 78.3 ov), 8-386 (Voges, 82.3 ov), 9-390 (Adams, 84.3 ov)

Lancashire bowling	Overs	Mdns	Runs	Wkts	Wides	No-Balls
Mahmood	12	0	69	2	-	1
Hogg	10	0	47	0	-	-
Keedy	34.4	3	140	1	1	-
Smith	13	3	50	1	-	1
Kerrigan	20	3	80	5	2	-

Lancashire first innings		Runs	Balls	Mins	4s	6s
PJ Horton	not out	6	14	25	1	-
KR Brown	c Hales b Sidebottom	4	8	15	-	-
*MJ Chilton	c Read b Adams	1	3	1	-	-
S Chanderpaul	c Patel b Adams	0	3	4	-	-
TC Smith						
SJ Croft						
+GD Cross						
SI Mahmood						
KW Hogg						
G Keedy						
SC Kerrigan						
Extras		0				
Total	(3 wickets, 4.4 overs)	11				

Fall of wickets: 1-6 (Brown, 3.3 ov), 2-11 (Chilton, 4.1 ov), 3-11 (Chanderpaul, 4.4 ov)

Notts bowling	Overs	Mdns	Runs	Wkts	Wides	No-Balls
Sidebottom	2	0	6	1	-	-
Pattinson	1	0	2	0	-	-
Adams	1.4	0	3	2	-	-

— 141 —

LV= County Championship Division One
Final Table 2010

	M	W	L	D	Ba	Bo	Pts
Nottinghamshire	16	7	5	4	47	43	214
Somerset	16	6	2	8	53	41	214
Yorkshire	16	6	2	8	41	42	203
Lancashire	16	5	3	8	35	43	182
Durham	16	5	3	8	30	39	173
Warwickshire	16	6	9	1	20	47	166
Hampshire	16	3	6	7	47	41	157
Kent	16	3	7	6	42	44	151
Essex	16	2	6	8	29	43	126

2010 LV= County Championship Averages

BATTING AND FIELDING:

	M	Inns	NO	Runs	HS	Ave	100	50	Ct	St
HM Amla	4	6	1	377	129	75.40	1	4	1	
DJ Hussey	5	7	1	399	251*	66.50	1	1	7	
AC Voges	3	5	0	254	126	50.80	1	1	1	
CMW Read	16	24	4	916	124*	45.80	2	5	59	4
SJ Mullaney	11	17	4	512	100*	39.38	1	3	6	
MA Wagh	15	23	1	853	139	38.77	2	3	8	
AD Hales	12	20	1	677	136	35.63	1	4	12	
AD Brown	16	24	1	805	134	35.00	1	6	11	
PJ Franks	15	21	1	651	79	32.55	0	6	1	
GG White	1	1	0	29	29	29.00	0	0	1	
SR Patel	16	26	2	641	104	26.70	1	3	9	
MJ Wood	4	6	0	148	72	24.66	0	2	1	
NJ Edwards	6	9	0	189	85	21.00	0	1	15	
LJ Fletcher	5	8	3	81	23*	16.20	0	0	2	
AR Adams	14	20	5	240	37	16.00	0	0	13	
BM Shafayat	6	10	0	118	49	11.80	0	0	4	
DJ Pattinson	12	13	4	93	27	10.33	0	0	0	
SCJ Broad	2	3	0	7	6	2.33	0	0	0	
CE Shreck	5	7	1	10	7*	1.66	0	0	4	
GP Swann	1	1	0	1	1	1.00	0	0	0	
RJ Sidebottom	8	6	6	44	18*	-	0	0	3	

BOWLING:

	Balls	Mds	Runs	Wkts	BB	Ave	5wI	10wM
SCJ Broad	396	7	299	19	8-52	15.73	2	1
RJ Sidebottom	1308	58	582	27	5-35	21.55	1	0
AR Adams	2735	101	1508	68	6-79	22.17	4	0
PJ Franks	2318	102	1046	41	3-15	25.51	0	0
CE Shreck	1194	50	577	18	4-81	32.05	0	0
SJ Mullaney	562	19	321	9	4-31	35.66	0	0
DJ Pattinson	1766	49	1128	31	5-95	36.38	1	0
SR Patel	1869	64	954	24	4-55	39.75	0	0
GP Swann	156	5	88	2	2-88	44.00	0	0
LJ Fletcher	866	31	508	9	3-43	56.44	0	0
GG White	138	3	104	1	1-104	104.00	0	0
AD Brown	42	0	53	0				
AD Hales	35	1	26	0				
DJ Hussey	108	1	82	0				
AC Voges	6	0	2	0				
MJ Wood	6	0	11	0				

2010 LV= County Championship Statistics

Centuries (11)

Chris Read (2) 124* v Durham (h), 112* v Kent (a)
Mark Wagh (2) 131* v Hampshire (a), 139 v Warwickshire (a)
Hashim Amla 129 v Kent (h)
Steven Mullaney 100* v Hampshire (a)
Ali Brown 134 v Durham (h)
Alex Hales 136 v Hampshire (h)
Samit Patel 104 v Somerset (a)
David Hussey 251* v Yorkshire (a)
Adam Voges 126 v Lancashire (a)

5 Wickets in an Innings (8)

Andre Adams (4) 5-106 v Kent (a), 6-79 v Lancashire (h), 5-92 v Durham (a),
6-82 v Yorkshire (h)
Stuart Broad (2) 5-89 v Somerset (h), 8-52 v Warwickshire (a)
Darren Pattinson 5-95 v Somerset (a)
Ryan Sidebottom 5-35 v Warwickshire

Century Partnerhips (18)

	Runs	Wkt	Opposition
Brown / Read	237	7th	Durham (h)
Patel / Hussey	184	4th	Yorkshire (a)
Patel / Read	157	6th	Somerset (a)
Wagh / Read	156	6th	Warwickshire (a)
Voges / Patel	153	5th	Lancashire (a)
Franks / Wagh	131	2nd	Yorkshire (h)
Amla / Read	125	6th	Kent (h)
Shafayat / Wagh	125	2nd	Somerset (h)
Wagh / Amla	118	3rd	Hampshire (a)
Hussey / Read	114	5th	Yorkshire (a)
Brown / Mullaney	111	7th	Hampshire (a)
Hales / Wagh	111	2nd	Kent (a)
Hussey / Franks	111	7th	Yorkshire (a)
Patel / Wagh	105	2nd	Kent (a)
Hales / Read	105	5th	Lancashire (h)
Edwards / Amla	103	3rd	Kent (h)
Read / Franks	102	7th	Somerset (h)
Mullaney / Read	101	7th	Essex (h)

REFLECTIONS

In October 2010, after the dust had settled on an emotional end to the season, three eminent figures gave their assessment of a truly amazing campaign: As Director of Cricket, Mick Newell was involved in every moment – every thought – every step of his side's title win. He gives his verdict on the season, as does his able lieutenant, club captain Chris Read. One man who has lived through the drama on previous occasions is author and club historian Peter Wynne-Thomas, who reveals where he heard about the latest chapter in Nottinghamshire's rich history.

Mick Newell

Winning trophies is incredibly difficult and the thin line between success and failure was clearly demonstrated last season.

Everything that we did well in the Friends Provident t20 was undone when Kieron Pollard caught Samit on the boundary, but, fortunately for us, 2010 will be remembered as the year that we came out as champions in the most prestigious domestic competition in world cricket.

Winning the LV= County Championship is always our primary target. I knew that we had a squad that should be finishing in the top three but I was less sure of our capabilities in limited overs cricket. In the end, we exceeded expectations in all three competitions.

We weren't sure what to expect in one day cricket because we'd signed players who were pretty inexperienced and there was a bit of doubt about how it might play out. Not a lot had changed in the four day side so I was hopeful that we'd be competitive if we made a successful start.

The points swing for a win made positive results so much more valuable and that led to much more movement in the table. Where we'd seen docile pitches in 2009, this season they were more conducive to results.

The wickets at Trent Bridge lent themselves to results and having the front end of our season loaded with home fixtures meant that there was an opportunity to make a strong start balanced against a risk that we could make a poor start if we came out on the wrong end of things.

Once we saw the fixture list we thought things would suit us because we had lots of seam bowlers and knew that good performances would give us an advantage over other teams in the competition.

The contribution of our three overseas players was exceptional and to have Hashim Amla in the team in April and May was a major coup and gave us tremendous solidity at the top of the order.

It couldn't have worked out any better in that Hashim helped us to make a winning start in the Championship, David Hussey came in either side of the twenty20 fixtures and Adam Voges helped us to get across the line.

In Hashim, we knew we had a high quality player but we were a little bit edgy after losing the first toss of the season. Any concerns soon subsided when he stepped up and scored a sublime 129, the DVD of which we now use as an educational tool for young batsman at the club.

I look to overseas players to make match-winning contributions and Hashim did that four times with others firing around him. He couldn't have done any more for us and it was pleasing to hear that he enjoyed his time with us and would welcome another spell at Trent Bridge in the future.

Our England players also played their part, and Stuart Broad produced two outstanding spells of bowling against Somerset at home and Warwickshire away that you don't usually see in county cricket.

He knows that he won't play for us very often and he hadn't bowled well in the first innings in either match and felt that he had more to give. What's pleasing is that when he does play he gives us total commitment and he won two games for us by producing fast and aggressive spells that good county players couldn't cope with.

Somerset had riled him a little bit. He wanted to get stuck into Kieswetter and Trego had given him some chat about him not being an international all-rounder, but he made them pay.

As the table began to take shape, Somerset 's challenge didn't surprise me but Yorkshire impressed by maintaining their form after a strong start.

Durham completely outplayed us twice in 2009, so we developed a quiet confidence after beating them at Trent Bridge. Ali Brown and Chris Read batted superbly and we could reflect on an excellent opening run having made the best of the early season conditions.

Home form is always the bedrock of a Championship win and we have a method of playing at Trent Bridge that gives us great confidence. Winning on the road is vital as well and it was very important that we produced the goods at The Rose Bowl where it wasn't swinging or seaming.

Everyone was keen to get into the team and this was the point at which Andre suffered a knock and dropped out, giving Steven Mullaney an opportunity that he grasped with both hands. He was only there because we'd had a one day game prior to the four day game and we'd decided not to send anybody home.

Living with the favourites tag was new to us but we were very careful to remain humble and not to make any bold statements about how things might work out in our favour. The players remained cool-headed but after such a strong start, we almost self-destructed with back to back defeats against Durham and Yorkshire.

Without wanting to disrespect Ben Harmison, I was bitterly disappointed that he was able to rip through our middle order at Chester-le-Street. That defeat put us under a lot of pressure and there was worse was to come.

To summarise the feeling in the dressing room having been dismissed for 59 in the first innings of our game against Yorkshire at Trent Bridge: we felt that we'd blown our Championship chances in one session.

We found ourselves making excuses; we'd prepared the wrong pitch, the ball was swinging more than ever, we lost the game when we lost the toss. The truth was that we played some very poor shots and got what we deserved.

From a position of great strength, we were now in possession of a marginal lead at the top of the table and travelled to Old Trafford with a lot of weight on our shoulders.

We were positive though. There was a belief that we could beat Lancashire and then we heard on the eve of the game that Ryan would be available to us and I felt that things would work out if we had four clear days.

The inside story of Nottinghamshire's LV= County Championship success

The immediate concern was the amount of water on the outfield when we arrived the day before the game and that made us realise that time would be against us if there was rain during the match.

Once we had lost two days of play we knew that there was no way that we would be able to take 20 wickets in the game and we were very frustrated. There was nothing for us to do but follow the other matches.

When the third day was written off our plan became clearer in our minds because the only options available to us were to try and set up a game or to chase the bonus points and rely on favourable results elsewhere.

It was a complete reversal of the circumstances at Trent Bridge in that Lancashire had nothing on the game and were therefore in a position where they didn't have to negotiate beyond stating a run chase they were prepared to offer.

What we thought was realistic and fair was a long way from what they did but the players were very confident about 'Plan B' and doing what they eventually did without the need for a few chuck-ups and a run chase, which is far from an ideal manner in which to win the Championship.

We had a big discussion throughout Wednesday evening and I sat up late in the bar talking to various people about our best way forward. We had very different opinions so we agreed to reconvene at 9 o'clock in the morning and make a definitive plan.

When the start of the fourth day was delayed we were down to 80 overs and I said that I didn't believe we could do it with bonus points and at that point Chris Read went to speak to Glenn Chapple. Their offer wasn't favourable and that made our minds up – we had to chase the bonus points.

Samit wasn't in great form and in ordinary circumstances he would have batted at number eight but we knew he had the ability to score quickly so he was upped to six. We know he likes playing in televised matches, which was great in these circumstances because it gets him going and he responded in the perfect way. I'd like to be able to say that it was a skilful psychological ploy to give him responsibility after taking it away but it was just a needs must situation and he played an innings that only he could have played.

Samit was out twice last year for 96 and I would prefer for him to be more patient in passing a hundred and then kicking on again but then he doesn't think like that when he's in the mood to score freely.

Voges went in at 79-2 and got us to 386, which was remarkable, and although he was hard on himself for falling 14 runs short of our target, he made a major contribution to our success.

I'm so pleased for him because he doesn't get the credit that David and Hashim get and he hasn't won trophies for Western Australia so it's a big deal for him to have been such a big part of a Nottinghamshire Championship win.

We're very lucky now in that Hashim, David and Adam have all got a good relationship with us and won't sign for anyone else until they've spoken to us and that's a great credit to their characters.

Even at 390-9 needing 400, I was backing Darren and Ryan. I didn't have a problem watching but others were hiding in the corridors of the Old Trafford pavilion. Paul Franks didn't see a single ball of it and he watched the footage for the first time in mid-October.

I knew that they would be patient, in contrast to Andre who prefers to score 18 runs in three balls rather than six overs, but they were our final hope and they went about it in a very calm and patient manner.

What Do Points Make?

Having got to 400, Darren and Ryan ran off the field with purpose and confidence and that spurred the dressing room, whereas if we'd have scored 390 and had to have taken six wickets there perhaps wouldn't have been the same spring in our step.

There was an elation in the dressing room that needed to be channelled and the next thing I remember was feeling great frustration looking out on to the pitch and seeing that Ryan had chosen the wrong end to bowl and was trying to swing the ball against the wind. They were quick to rectify this and even on a flat pitch, I knew that Ryan and Andre would make things happen.

My initial reaction to the first wicket falling was to appreciate the quality of Alex Hales' catch because it was a difficult take under pressure.

Andre's delivery to dismiss Chilton was an absolute jaffa and I've seen that replay again and again. He found a great area, it hit the seam and moved away and there was nothing that Chilton could do with it and Ready took a routine catch.

Then there was the small matter of Shiv Chanderpaul, who we've seen dig-in on numerous occasions and sometimes you wonder how you're ever going to get him out. Andre must have had a plan though because he always bowls around the wicket to left-handed batsmen but for some reason he bowled over the wicket to Chanderpaul and it worked.

Andre only bowled ten balls in that match but he found the spot straight away and of all the players, his desire to win the Championship was perhaps higher than anyone else's.

I was half watching the game and half watching the television and only when Samit threw the ball away did I realise what had happened. I heard the screams and saw the lads setting off around the field so I ran out through the balcony door and started jumping around.

A number of people have said how different I look a few weeks on from it all and I'm not sure whether that's a compliment or not but I was certainly affected by the stress of it all and felt tremendous relief rather than elation when we won it. A lot had been written about us 'bottling it' and Ryan's contract negotiations were stalling in the background so it was a difficult time.

Lots of people have congratulated me in coffee shops and at the school gates and that's helped me to realise just how much it means to everyone. I see it as the team's achievement rather than my achievement, but winning it in the way we did with so much drama throughout that final day is something which I will always be immensely proud of.

We had better individual players in 2005 but this team has a great spirit and a fantastic method of playing and some individuals with great skill.

Long-term planning is very difficult because there is always a short-term hunger for success, but we have successfully introduced younger players into the squad and players are emerging in the academy who seem equipped to become professionals.

Alex Hales, Luke Fletcher, Andy Carter, Akhil Patel, Scott Elstone, Jake Ball, Graeme White and Steven Mullaney have all come on to our staff in recent years and used 40-over cricket as a way of establishing their credentials and if they prove that they are ready for it then they can win a regular place in all formats, as Alex and Steven did this season.

It is vitally important to have a strong core of senior players and I will only promote young players to our four day side on merit.

There will be an eye on how we cope following Ryan's departure and we know that Mark Wagh will retire in August, but I'm keen that people are talking about the excellent players we have got rather than those that we haven't at the end of 2011.

Chris Read

I'm always philosophical about the weather. Sometimes it can help you and sometimes it can hinder you.

But when we arrived for the third day of our game against Lancashire at Old Trafford with a fair forecast but never got out of the pavilion I started to lose my marbles because it meant that securing the points that we needed to win the LV= County Championship would be very difficult.

If Lancashire put up decent figures for us to bowl at then I thought that might be the way to go. Trying to get to 400 seemed like a big ask and we ran the risk of putting ourselves out of contention if we didn't make a good start to it. Adam Voges has a lot of captaincy experience and he shared my view that securing a run chase might be the way forward.

Having slept on the options, our opinion changed and we arrived at the ground with a plan to chase the bonus points, but then we were told that the start would be delayed and that almost threw things in the other direction. I went to speak to Mark Chilton and Glenn Chapple but we couldn't agree a satisfactory run chase and we decided that despite having lost an hour, we had time to secure the 311 runs at five an over and take three wickets.

The season had started perfectly well for us. We knew we were contenders when we were leading the way but we don't like to make public statements because it can leave you with egg on your face. We were in a good position from quite a long way out but knew we had to play well to achieve something and avoid coming second or third.

I felt that we were in the hunt from the beginning and winning four from four was an extraordinary start. Prior to the season people were talking up Durham's chances and they were far and away the best side in 2009, but injury hampered them this season.

Beating them so comprehensively at home was a key result and we controlled things from start to finish. It was one of the defining moments of the season and sent a message that we were a force to be reckoned with.

There was never any complacency and we went into the Yorkshire game having prepared exactly the same result pitch that had helped us to make such a strong start to the season. I would do nothing different if I had the chance again because we believed that our form at home was good and we wanted to win the game and make the title secure. Anyone looking on from the outside would see that we were bowled out for 59 and draw their own conclusions and lots of people have said that the total was inexcusable, but I maintain that had we won the toss then we could have run through Yorkshire for less than a hundred.

Durham away was disappointing and I think I was guilty of devaluing the draw. Durham weren't in title contention and it was too easy to write off the draw points on offer as insignificant, and the same could be said of Essex away where we didn't fight hard enough. When we're out of games, we need to fight hard for a draw and we had two sessions to bat at Durham and really should have done enough to come away with a draw, which we threw away with a poor session.

So on to Old Trafford and our quest for bonus points on day four. In this situation I felt that Samit Patel was the right man to give us impetus because his one day form had been excellent and the state of the game meant that he could bring his one day approach to a four day match. I knew he was capable of it and he produced an extraordinary innings.

Adam Voges hasn't played as much international cricket as David Hussey or Hashim Amla but to do what he did under so much pressure at Old Trafford was exceptional. Franksy and I had a word with him afterwards and said 'that must be the best hundred you've ever scored', but he looked at us knowingly and just said 'second best!'

The most nerve wracking time was Darren and Ryan's partnership. I like to get ready to keep wicket towards the end of our innings and I started to put my whites on when we were eight down. When the ninth wicket fell I didn't know what to do. One wicket would throw everything out of the window because getting six wickets in that time would have been unrealistic.

Securing 400 runs when we were nine down heightened the sense of elation and relief and my job in the turnaround was to get the lads together and make it plain that the job was only half done. We needed three wickets and to get them we needed to stay calm. I was very confident in our seam attack to get the ball in the right areas and cause them problems.

Andre Adams has shown superb form throughout both of his spells at Notts and this season he finally got the recognition that he deserved. It was fitting that he took the final two wickets because he'd been my go-to man all year and had got us out of several tricky situations. When he bowled over the wicket to Shiv, which he never does to left-handers, I turned to Adam Voges and said 'what's he doing here?' Left-handers hate facing him because he bowls around the wicket and gets it to go away from them as well as in so it seemed a strange tactic, but he's very strong-minded and I knew better than to question his approach and he got a nick three balls later.

I was elated. We knew that we hadn't played great cricket in the final month of the season but the table showed that over the course of the season, we were the best team in the competition. It was a tough season and I was so proud of the guys for going about that final day in the way that they did.

It was pure ecstasy. I jumped around with the slips and then we chased Andre and I lost my sunglasses somewhere in the crush.

The whole day was unbelievable and it culminated in seeing the boys go berserk on the field because it meant so much to all of us.

The celebrations have been great but almost immediately you put it all to one side and think how are we going to do this again next year? I don't need reminding that we were relegated in 2006 having won it in 2005 and we recognise that areas of our squad need improving because we are nowhere near being a 'complete' side. We're smart in the cricket we play and the tactics that we use and the fact that our players performed to their abilities was one of the main reasons we succeeded this year.

I've certainly found massive positives by handing the Friends Provident t20 captaincy to Huss and it's definitely something that I will consider again. After two years in the job I acknowledged that some of my on-field performances were being compromised and I felt a lot fresher mentally having accepted a break in that particular competition.

We'll miss Ryan Sidebottom in all formats and we're unsure if we'll be allowed to recruit two overseas players for twenty20 next season. There's a little bit of uncertainty about how our team will look and we'll need to make subtle improvements wherever we can.

Mick knows the county game inside out and never misses a stat. We take the heat off each other and I probably frustrate him at times because I'm much more laid back in situations where he's worked up. He's learned to trust me when I want to be positive and push hard for victories with a risk of defeat attached.

We've already sat down and talked about how we can improve and drawn up a shortlist of who we want to bring in. There are still problems at the top of the order and we've lost players in different areas, but we have a number of people here who we want to develop and give opportunities to.

If we go into next season with what would appear on paper to be a slightly weaker side then we will give those that step up our full backing and they'll be keen to prove their worth. The reigning champions tag will make people gun for us and they'll psyche themselves up and try to take us on at Trent Bridge .

Luke Fletcher has a big year ahead of him and needs to come back fit and firing. Alex Hales has shown immense talent and needs to start putting himself in the England frame. Graeme White had a good season in one day cricket and I want to see him push on and try and win a place in the red ball side. Akhil Patel has been here for a couple of years and we're looking for him to push for a slot so we can continue to build.

2010 was a fantastic season for us and I'm looking forward to 2011 with great optimism.

Peter Wynne-Thomas

My wife and I were in holiday in Bolton at the time. For those who take vacations elsewhere, it's not as grim as it sounds. The town hall is palatial and the crescent of offices which curve round its side are impressive. I need hardly tell you, we spent the morning in the library. At one o'clock Edith had the look of lunch about her. A stone's throw away Marks and Spencers beckoned. I grabbed the last empty table. Edith found a tray and a five mile queue. The man at the next table had sent his wife on a similar mission. We asked each other about the weather. I don't recall how cricket nudged its way into the conversation – it just seems to happen like that. He was a Lancashire member; one of the few who bothered to go to Old Trafford yesterday for the final rites.

"Must have been pretty dull – was there any play at all?"

"Haven't you seen a paper? Notts are champions."

I thought this was some sort of hot-pot joke. It wasn't of course. I don't believe they sell champagne in M&S cafes. If I went to find Edith in the queue, I'd lose our table. We'll stay with coffee and hot chocolate.

Short term overseas signings are County cricket's lucky dip. Even more so when some warm-blooded player is invited to leave the sunshine and have a break in an English April. The diehard members, the only cricket watchers who brave such conditions, have probably never seen the new import, possibly never heard of him. Mick Newell however studies form. Hashim Amla had form. In 2009 he had a similar short term contract with Essex (replacing Kaneria) and hit a century on his County Championship debut, finishing his brief stint with an average in three figures. Could he repeat his Essex success?

Dark, dank and chilly describes the opening day of the Championship season at Trent Bridge. Kent looked at the green wicket and had no hesitation in deciding to field. Shafayat was dismissed for four; Wagh failed to score at all. Amla walked to the middle. Did he look a little nervous? The members in front of the pavilion – all scarves and anoraks, some even gloved – were in two minds. Amla took no chances. He played each of the early deliveries on merit. He saw a loose delivery and sent it through a gap in the field for four. The sign of a class player. A second boundary came, a third, a fourth, a fifth. Looking at the scoresheet it reveals that his first nine scoring strokes were all fours. So his innings proceeded. To Lunch. To Tea. By the time he was stumped by Geraint Jones, seventh man out, the score was 367 and Amla had achieved the rare feat of a century on Championship debut for two counties in successive seasons. If I say it's unique, some computer buff will press five buttons and prove me wrong.

Amla's was the highest individual score of the match and Nottinghamshire were on their way with an innings victory. As if to prove it wasn't a fluke, Amla hit the most runs on either side in the next match – a second Nottinghamshire win. His runs in that game proved, in retrospect, absolutely vital – Somerset were beaten by just two wickets.

It was off to The Rose Bowl for match three. Notts required 246 when the final innings started. Edwards was out for 8, Shafayat for 12. Amla joined Wagh, whose early look of anxiety had been replaced by a certain smile. The pair added 118 and Notts were in striking distance of their target – the win was by five wickets.

Amla's fourth game was against distressed Durham. Poor Will Smith, that product of Trent Bridge, now captain of Durham. He had led them to the 2009 Championship, but the team's form in 2010 matched his form with the bat. Two games later he resigned. Amla scored 67 as Nottinghamshire recorded their fourth Championship win. By an innings and 62 runs. Hashim Amla packed his bags.

To the record books. Since a points system has been used for the Championship, Nottinghamshire have in four seasons won their first four matches – 1889, 1892, 1907 and 1922. In two of those seasons they went on to win the title, in the other two Notts were runners-up. Having been to the latter position for the last two summers, we don't wish to create a new record as bridesmaid.

Fast forward to the final four games. The first of these I recall vividly. Rain washed out the third day, Lancashire set us 261. Alex Hales decided to engrave his name on a new page in the Notts Record Book – the first person to be dismissed twice in a match for 90.

By the time I'd dug that fact out, we were approaching the target with overs in hand, but wickets were falling. In strides Andre Adams, the season's bowling hero – Franks had just been out first ball. Adams doesn't do steady. A wild swipe missing his first delivery. The second goes for four; the third goes for four and the match is won.

The team go off to an easy match at Chester-le-Street, but England collar Sidebottom in the middle of the match and Ben Harmison, the batsman and younger brother of Steve, bowls his county to victory. Never mind, we've points in the bank. I'd better gloss over the first morning of the penultimate match. And so to Old Trafford, or in my case Bolton and the man in Marks & Spencer's.

TWENTY20

The England and Wales Cricket Board decreed that due to the growing popularity of Twenty20 cricket that the 2010 fixture scheduling would include 16 round robin group matches for each county – eight at home and eight away.

The 18 counties were split into two groups of nine – North and South, with the top four in each advancing to the quarter finals. Group winners and runners-up would secure home advantage for their last eight clashes.

With each county permitted to field two overseas players Nottinghamshire had recruited the services of Dirk Nannes, an experienced left arm quick bowler who had played for Australia in the ICC World twenty20 Final in May 2010, alongside county regular David Hussey, who had taken over the reins from Chris Read to skipper the side for the duration of the tournament.

As in the LV= County Championship Nottinghamshire made an impressive start, winning their opening four matches. A defeat at Edgbaston against Warwickshire was a temporary blip as away wins over Derbyshire and Durham took Hussey's side clear at the top of the Northern group.

In an astonishing piece of symmetry both home and away matches against Northampton-
-shire were tied but qualification for the quarter final stages was confirmed long before two rain-ruined matches were lost against Lancashire and Leicestershire, enabling Warwickshire to head the group with Notts finishing second.

Match 1
10 June 2010 v Worcestershire,
New Road, Worcester
Nottinghamshire (2 points) won by 6 wickets
Toss – won by Nottinghamshire,
who decided to field
Worcestershire 113-9 (20 overs) Mullaney 3-12
Nottinghamshire 114-4 (14 overs)
Hales 66 not out

Match 2
11 June 2010 v Derbyshire,
Trent Bridge, Nottingham
Nottinghamshire (2 points) won by five wickets
Toss – won by Derbyshire, who decided to bat
Derbyshire 192-6 (20 overs) Durston 111
Nottinghamshire 193-5 (17 overs)
Hales 69, S Patel 62 not out

Match 3
13 June 2010 v Worcestershire,
Trent Bridge, Nottingham
Nottinghamshire (2 points) won by 6 wickets
Toss – won by Worcestershire, who decided to bat
Worcestershire 150-7 (20 overs) Ali 67
Nottinghamshire 155-4 (14.1 overs) S Patel 63

Match 4
15 June 2010 v Lancashire,
Trent Bridge, Nottingham
Nottinghamshire (2 points) won by 26 runs
Toss – won by Lancashire, who decided to field
Nottinghamshire 157-7 (20 overs)
Hussey 44 Mahmood 4-21
Lancashire 131 (18.5 overs) Smith 43, S Patel 3-26

Match 5
16 June 2010 v Warwickshire,
Edgbaston, Birmingham
Warwickshire (2 points) won by 5 wickets
Toss – won by Nottinghamshire,
who decided to bat
Nottinghamshire 176-6 (20 overs)
Hussey 81 not out
Warwickshire 178-5 (18.5 overs) Trott 46

Match 6
17 June 2010 v Derbyshire, County Ground, Derby
Nottinghamshire (2 points) won by 6 wickets
Toss – won by Derbyshire, who decided to bat
Derbyshire 152-7 (20 overs) Park 66
Nottinghamshire 153-4 (18 overs)
Hussey 65, Wood 51 not out

— 153 —

What Do Points Make?

Match 7
20 June 2010 v Durham, Emirates
Durham ICG, Chester-le-Street
Nottinghamshire (2 points) won by 11 runs
Toss – won by Nottinghamshire,
who decided to bat
Nottinghamshire 186-4 (20 overs)
Brown 73, S Patel 51
Durham 175-5 (20 overs) Benkenstein 40

Match 8
22 June 2010 v Northamptonshire,
Trent Bridge, Nottingham
Match Tied – Nottinghamshire (1 point)
Northamptonshire (1 point)
Toss – won by Northamptonshire,
who decided to bat
Northamptonshire 121-7 (20 overs)
Wakeley 43, Hall 40 not out, Pattinson 4-19
Nottinghamshire 121 (20 overs)
Mullaney 53, Wood 41, Vaas 3-16

Match 9
24 June 2010 v Yorkshire,
Headingley Carnegie, Leeds
Yorkshire (2 points) won by 7 wickets
Toss – won by Nottinghamshire,
who decided to bat
Nottinghamshire 158-7 (20 overs)
Hales 62 S Patel 41
Yorkshire 162-3 (18.2 overs) Lyth 43

Match 10
25 June 2010 v Durham, Trent Bridge, Nottingham
Nottinghamshire (2 points) won by 4 wickets
Toss – won by Nottinghamshire,
who decided to field
Durham 155-9 (20 overs) Mustard 35
Nottinghamshire 159-6 (19.3 overs)
Hussey 47 not out

Match 11
27 June 2010 v Warwickshire,
Trent Bridge, Nottingham
Nottinghamshire (2 points) won by 32 runs
Toss – won by Nottinghamshire,
who decided to bat
Nottinghamshire 149-6 (20 overs)
Hussey 56, Carter 3-28
Warwickshire 117 (19.5 overs) White 3-22

Match 12
4 July 2010 v Leicestershire, Grace Road, Leicester
Nottinghamshire (2 points) won by 7 wickets
Toss – won by Leicestershire, who decided to bat
Leicestershire 182-3 (20 overs)
Hodge 103, Taylor 56 not out
Nottinghamshire 185-3 (18.3 overs)
Wood 61, Brown 55

Match 13
11 July 2010 v Northamptonshire,
County Ground, Northampton
Match Tied – Northamptonshire (1 point)
Nottinghamshire (1 point)
Toss – won by Nottinghamshire,
who decided to bat
Nottinghamshire 144-7 (20 overs)
Hussey 41, S Patel 40, Willey 3-33
Northamptonshire 144-8 (20 overs) Vaas 47

Match 14
14 July 2010 v Lancashire, Old Trafford, Manchester
Lancashire (2 points) won by 9 wickets
(Duckworth / Lewis)
Toss – won by Nottinghamshire,
who decided to bat
Nottinghamshire 138-7 (20 overs) Hales 83
Lancashire 83-1 (8.2 overs) Moore 51 not out

Match 15
15 July 2010 v Leicestershire,
Trent Bridge, Nottingham
Leicestershire (2 points) won by 23 runs
(Duckworth / Lewis)
Toss – won by Nottinghamshire,
who decided to field
Leicestershire 145-5 (20 overs)
McDonald 58 not out
Nottinghamshire 107-9 (16.4 overs)
Mullaney 29 not out, McDonald 5-13

Match 16
17 July 2010 v Yorkshire, Trent Bridge, Nottingham
Nottinghamshire (2 points) won by 7 wickets
Toss – won by Yorkshire, who decided to bat
Yorkshire 112-7 (20 overs) Hodgson 39 not out
Nottinghamshire 116-3 (15.4 overs)
S Patel 40, Hussey 37 not out

	P	W	L	T	N/R	Pts	Net R/R
Warwickshire Bears	16	11	4	0	1	23	+0.403
Notts Outlaws	16	10	4	2	0	22	+0.640
Lancashire Lightning	16	9	6	0	1	19	+0.479
Northamptonshire Steelbacks	16	7	6	3	0	17	−0.160
Derbyshire Falcons	16	6	8	0	2	14	−0.151
Yorkshire Carnegie	16	6	9	1	0	13	−0.121
Leicestershire Foxes	16	6	9	0	1	13	−1.234
Durham Dynamos	16	4	8	0	4	12	−1.296
Worcestershire Royals	16	5	10	0	1	11	−0.653

Quarter Final

26 July 2010 v Sussex, Trent Bridge, Nottingham
Nottinghamshire beat Sussex by 13 runs
Toss – won by Sussex, who decided to field
Nottinghamshire 141-9 (20 overs) Wood 36, Brown 31, Arafat 4-34
Sussex 128-7 (20 overs) Goodwin 28, Pattinson 3-17

Notts Outlaws secured their place at the twenty20 Finals Day after edging out Sussex Sharks in front of a very vocal crowd of 8,558.

On a balmy evening the home side were indebted to Ali Brown and Matt Wood for posting a total of 141 from their twenty overs. Two maximums from Brown helped offset the early loss of Alex Hales, but when he fell for 36 it was left to Wood, with 31, and later 20 from Chris Read to set any sort of challenge for the visitors.

When Sussex cruised to 64-1 it seemed inevitable that they would reach their target with overs to spare, but tight bowling from Steven Mullaney and Samit Patel began to apply pressure during the middle overs.

Mullaney's spell yielded only 18 runs and earned him the Man of the Match Award and once Darren Pattison had removed top-scorer Murray Goodwin for 28 Nottinghamshire's jubilant supporters could begin making their coach reservations for a trip to Southampton for Finals Day.

Twenty20 Finals Day - Semi Final

14 Aug 2010 v Somerset , The Rose Bowl, Southampton
Somerset beat Nottinghamshire by 3 runs (Duckworth / Lewis)
Toss – won by Nottinghamshire, who decided to field
Somerset 182-5 (20 overs) Trescothick 60, Buttler 55 not out
Nottinghamshire 117-4 (13 overs) S Patel 39

Nottinghamshire's hopes of lifting the first domestic trophy of the season evaporated in contentious circumstances with rain preventing a finish to their semi final tie against Somerset.

Second on, after Hampshire had defeated Essex in the first match of the day, Notts were denied when the heavens opened with David Hussey's side just behind the run-rate on Duckworth Lewis calculations.

Marcus Trescothick had plundered a rapid 60 at the top of the order for his side before the innings was given late impetus by the impressive Jos Buttler.

Chasing 183 for a place in the Final Nottinghamshire kept up with the run rate until the pivotal dismissal of Samit Patel, caught high above his head at long on by Kieron Pollard. Had the ball been an inch or two higher the maximum – followed by the almost immediate cessation of play – would have resulted in victory going to the Outlaws.

Somerset's day also ended in disappointment when they lost the final to Hampshire from the last ball of the contest.

CLYDESDALE BANK 40 COMPETITION 2010

25 April 2010 v Leicestershire, Grace Road, Leicester
Leicestershire (2 points) won by 47 runs
Toss – Notts, who decided to field
Leicestershire 282-6 (40 overs) du Toit 141, Jefferson 55
Nottinghamshire 235 (37 overs) S Patel 59, Amla 53 White 6-29

An opening stand of 98 in just 15 overs between Jacques du Toit and former Notts batsman Will Jefferson set up this Leicestershire victory. An equally brisk start by the visitors threatened to bring them close before a career-best 6-29 from Wayne White blew away the middle order.

2 May 2010 v Hampshire, The Rose Bowl, Southampton
Nottinghamshire (2 points) won by 35 runs
Toss – Hants, who decided to field
Nottinghamshire 180-7 (24 overs)
Hampshire 145-7 (24 overs)

Damp conditions delayed the start and reduced the match to just 24 overs per side. Alex Hales top scored for Notts with 41 before becoming one of Dominic Cork's three victims. Carberry and Adams scored a brisk 43 at the top of the Hants reply and Liam Dawson ended with an unbeaten 47, but by then they were well behind the rate with Steven Mullaney's 3-24 being the stand-out bowling figures.

8 May 2010 v Kent, Trent Bridge, Nottingham
No Result – Nottinghamshire (1 point), Kent (1 point)
Toss – Notts, who decided to field
Kent 78-2 (6.1 overs)

Once again the rain spoiled things. Eventually the umpires agreed that the conditions would allow a 10 over per side slog but a further downpour meant that the points were shared.

16 May 2010 v Hampshire, Trent Bridge, Nottingham
Nottinghamshire (2 points) won by 12 runs
Toss – Notts, who decided to bat
Nottinghamshire 265-8 (40 overs) S Patel 108
Hampshire 253-7 (40 overs) Ervine 96

A brilliant century from Samit Patel, from just 89 balls with 8 boundaries and 4 sixes, plus 46 from Alex Hales and 43 from Ali Brown, took Notts to 265-8. The Hampshire response fell just short despite the best efforts of Sean Ervine. Andy Carter took 2-42 with the ball for the home side.

23 May 2010 v Scotland, Grange Cricket Club, Edinburgh
Nottinghamshire (2 points) won by 43 runs
Toss – Notts, who decided to bat
Nottinghamshire 256-6 (40 overs) Hales 69, S Patel 61, Wood 60
Scotland 213 (35.3 overs) White 5-35

Consistency from the top order after Chris Read won the toss for Notts and then a career-best 5-35 from slow left arm spinner Graeme White, which included three caught and bowleds, led to a 43-run victory.

25 July 2010 v Durham, Emirates Durham ICG, Chester-le-Street
Nottinghamshire (2 points) won by 5 wickets
Toss – Notts, who decided to field

What Do Points Make?

Durham 181-8 (40 overs) Muchall 77
Nottinghamshire 182-5 (35.5 overs) Hales 96 not out

Alex Hales made short work of chasing down what always looked like a gettable target. The 21-year-old hit nine boundaries and a six from just 113 balls, with Samit Patel's 46 providing the chief support. Earlier, only Gordon Muchall made any sort of contribution for Durham with all six Notts bowlers amongst the wickets.

8 August 2010 v Scotland, Trent Bridge, Nottingham
Nottinghamshire (2 points) won by 75 runs
Toss – Notts, who decided to bat
Nottinghamshire 260-5 (40 overs) Hussey 80, Read 69 not out
Scotland 185 (38.4 overs)

Notts completed the double over Scotland after setting an imposing total. David Hussey's 80 came from 67 balls. Samit Patel added 48 before Chris Read bludgeoned a quickfire 69, ending the innings with Scott Elstone, who made an undefeated 18 on his one day debut for the county. Paul Franks took three of the first four wickets to fall to disrupt the reply.

12 August 2010 v Warwickshire, Trent Bridge, Nottingham
Nottinghamshire (2 points) won by 7 wickets
Toss – Notts, who decided to field
Warwickshire 81-6 (16 overs)
Nottinghamshire 82-3 (8 overs)

On a filthy wet night Notts just got home with David Hussey blasting a maximum into the Radcliffe Road Stand to win the match in driving rain. In a rain-reduced 16 over game Warwickshire failed to exert enough pressure and reached a meagre 81-6. With eight overs needing to be bowled to constitute a game Hussey saw his side home by belting 34 not out from just 12 balls. The win kept Notts within touching distance of Warwickshire at the top of Group C and sent them off to The Rose Bowl for twenty20 Finals day still challenging on all three fronts.

22 August 2010 v Kent, St Lawrence Ground, Canterbury
Kent (2 points) won by 42 runs
Toss – Notts, who decided to field
Kent 135-3 (16 overs) Stevens 49 not out
Nottinghamshire 93-9 (16 overs) Coles 3-7

The long trip to Canterbury resulted in a dismal batting performance after rain had meant a second successive 16-over slog. Darren Stevens, who had taken 197 from the Notts attack in the Championship earlier in the season, made an unbeaten 49 for the hosts, adding 72 in the final six overs with Azhar Mahmood, who made 29. Ali Brown and Matt Wood fell inside the first ten deliveries of the reply and only Alex Hales, with 21, offered any resistance.

29 August 2010 v Leicestershire, Trent Bridge, Nottingham
Leicestershire (2 points) won by 4 runs
Toss – Notts, who decided to field
Leicestershire 219-7 (40 overs) Boyce 60, Taylor 58, Ball 3-32
Nottinghamshire 215-9 (40 overs) Voges 71 not out, Hoggard 3-43

The Foxes completed the double over Chris Read's side by the narrow margin of just four runs. Matthew Boyce and James Taylor combined in a stand of 114 for the 5th wicket as the visitors posted 219-7. Jake Ball, in his first appearance of the season, picked up three wickets but finished on the losing side despite an unbeaten 71 from Adam Voges, batting just 24 hours after getting off a plane from Australia.

— 158 —

The inside story of Nottinghamshire's LV= County Championship success

30 August 2010 v Durham, Trent Bridge, Nottingham
Nottinghamshire (2 points) won by 3 runs
Toss – Notts, who decided to bat
Nottinghamshire 257-7 (40 overs) S Patel 75, Read 66 not out
Durham 254-8 (40 overs) Muchall 47, B Harmison 46, Sidebottom 3-45

Needing ten from the final two deliveries, Durham fell just short despite Chris Rushworth hitting a maximum from the penultimate ball. Notts got off to a dreadful start, having both Alex Hales and Adam Voges run out to leave them 3-2. 38 from Akhil Patel started the revival and another youngster, Scott Elstone, hit 30, but it was seasoned campaigners Samit Patel and Chris Read who gave the innings some gloss. Durham remained in contention throughout but Ryan Sidebottom and Darren Pattinson each claimed three wickets to keep hopes of a semi final place alive.

4 September 2010 v Warwickshire, Edgbaston, Birmingham
Warwickshire (2 points) won by 7 wickets
Toss – Notts, who decided to bat
Nottinghamshire 192 (38.4 overs) Voges 54, Tahir 4-27
Warwickshire 194-3 (36.5 overs) Trott 84 not out, Bell 50

Twenty four hours after losing a Championship match in Durham, a depleted Outlaws side waved goodbye to their hopes of reaching the CB40 semi finals. Bowled out inside their allocation of overs, a total of 192 seemed far from adequate, with only Adam Voges offering staunch resistance. Jonathan Trott, released to play by England, and Ian Bell, returning from a seven week injury lay-off, sped the Bears to victory.

Clydesdale Bank 40 Group C table

	P	W	L	D	T	NR	RR	Pts
Warwickshire	12	9	3	0	0	0	0.31	18.0
Kent	12	7	3	0	0	2	0.77	16.0
Nottinghamshire	12	7	4	0	0	1	0.35	15.0
Hampshire	12	6	6	0	0	0	0.01	12.0
Durham	12	5	6	0	0	1	0.26	11.0
Leicestershire	12	4	8	0	0	0	-0.22	8.0
Scotland	12	2	10	0	0	0	-1.22	4.0

Warwickshire qualified for the semi finals, where they defeated Yorkshire at Scarborough before going on to lift the Trophy with success over Somerset at Lord's.